PHILOSOPHY & THE CHRISTIAN FAITH

COLIN BROWN

A Historical Sketch
from the
Middle Ages
to the
Present Day

InterVarsity Press
Downers Grove
Illinois 60515

InterVarsity Press is the book-publishing division of Inter-Varsity Christian Fellowship,
a student movement active on campus at hundreds of universities, colleges
and schools of nursing. For information about local and regional activities, write
IVCF, 233 Langdon St., Madison, WI 53703.

Distributed in Canada through InterVarsity Press, 1875 Leslie St., Unit 10,
Don Mills, Ontario M3B 2M5, Canada.

Biblical quotations are from the Revised Standard Version of the Bible, copyrighted
in 1946 and 1952 by the Division of Christian Education, National Council of the Churches of
Christ in the USA.

ISBN 0-87784-712-6
Library of Congress Catalog Card Number: 68-58083

Printed in the United States of America

21	20	19	18	17	16	15	14	13	12	11	10	9	8
95	94	93	92	91	90	89	88	87	86	85	84	83	

Contents

INTRODUCTION

By no stretch of the imagination could the relationship between philosophy and the Christian faith be described as an ideal marriage. It is neither ideal, nor, strictly speaking, a marriage. There are many Christians who regard an interest in philosophy as a dubious and dangerous flirtation. And perhaps the majority of professional philosophers today have serious doubts as to the intellectual respectability of courting religious belief. We are left with a tenuous liaison, sustained by sporadic, painful encounters. When the two parties come together, the result seems all too often to be either a string of bitter accusations from the philosophers or a series of lame attempts on the part of the believers to patch things up. And even when the latter succeed in convincing a few of the philosophers, they often seem to do so at the expense of compromising the faith.

As a matter of fact, all down the ages well-meaning friends on both sides have warned against any alliance. In the early church there were those such as Justin Martyr (*c.* 100 – *c.* 165)[1] and Clement of Alexandria (*c.* 150 – *c.* 215)[2] who assured their readers that many a pagan had been led to true religion through philosophy, and that philosophy was to the ancient Greeks what the Old Testament was to the Jews. But such suggestions were swept aside by writers such as Tertullian (*c.* 160 – *c.* 220)[3] who rejected their arguments, pointed out that philosophy was often the root of heresy, and that worldly wisdom without faith could never bring men to a knowledge of Christ.

[1] 1 *Apology*, 5, 46.   [2] *Stromateis*, i. 5, 20.
[3] *On the Proscription of Heretics*, vii.

At first sight, it might seem that Tertullian had the New Testament on his side. The apostle Paul warned his Colossian readers: 'See to it that no one makes a prey of you by philosophy and empty deceit, according to human tradition, according to the elemental spirits of the universe, and not according to Christ.'[4] To the church at Corinth he pointed out that 'since, in the wisdom of God, the world did not know God through wisdom, it pleased God through the folly of what we preach to save those who believe'.[5] It is Christ who is not only our sanctification and redemption, but also our wisdom.[6] If we go back to the Old Testament we fail to find philosophy in the normal sense of the term. It is equally lacking in the teaching of Jesus.

It would also be easy to multiply examples of the recriminations of the philosophers. We shall see enough of them in the course of this book. From all this it would be tempting to draw the conclusion that the history of the philosophy of religion is the story of this repeating pattern of protestations, charges and countercharges. The details of the arguments might vary, but the over-all pattern remains much the same. And if any conclusion is to be drawn, it would be that this sort of discussion leads nowhere.

But to attempt to contract out of the debate is not all that easy. Neither the believer nor the unbelieving philosopher can do so without inviting the charge of intellectual obscurantism. Philosophy is an intellectual discipline which is concerned with the nature of reality and the investigation of the general principles of knowledge and existence. While the apostle Paul rejects alien philosophies, it must be admitted that the Christian faith inevitably raises philosophical questions which probe the grounds on which it makes its claims. Why do we believe in God? How do we know? What are the nature and logical status of religious utterances? How does Christianity compare with other forms of belief and theories about the world? On the other hand, if philosophy is concerned with reality and truth, it cannot turn its back upon religious issues. No genuine seeker after truth will be put off by the sound and fury of the opposition. In the long run what counts is not the

[4] Colossians 2:8.   [5] 1 Corinthians 1:21.   [6] 1 Corinthians 1:30.

volume of noise made by the different parties, but whether ideas and arguments correspond with reality.

The aim of this book is to make a survey of the main thinkers and intellectual movements of western thought of the past thousand years, with a view to showing how they affect Christian belief. It is written from the standpoint of one who is deeply committed to the Christian faith. But in the first instance it has not been my intention to indulge in polemics and apologetics. I have not attempted to construct a blunderbuss which would shoot down all the opposition at one go. Blunderbusses are notoriously ineffective instruments, especially when the target calls for precise marksmanship. Instead, I have tried to analyse for the student and general reader the principal factors which have made the present intellectual climate what it is. Inevitably, such an undertaking will partake of something of the character of a *Who's Who*. This is intentional. But unlike the latter work I have not refrained from commenting on what seem to me to be the strengths and weaknesses of the person or movement concerned.

While there are available numerous histories of secular philosophy, detailed studies of this or that personality or movement, and some valuable introductions to the problems of philosophical theology, there is an acute shortage of books which attempt a bird's-eye view of the history of philosophy down to the present day and of its relationship with Christianity. And even those that do cover part of this field seem peculiarly unaware of the Reformation and of biblical theology and their relevance to the philosophy of religion. The present work is an attempt to help fill this gap.

The drawbacks of such an undertaking are all too obvious. It has to avoid being too technical for the general reader who is just launching out upon the subject. But it has to be sufficiently detailed to be of use to the student who is faced with genuine difficulties and who wants a positive lead. All academic disciplines have their own jargon, and philosophy is worse than most. Moreover, in a general survey like this the treatment has to be highly selective and brief. If the general reader is to find his way about at all, it has inevitably to follow what has been dubbed as the next-philosopher-please pattern.

Yet for most of us such a pattern is not without some value. Whether we like it or not, we cannot help forming over-all impressions, and some information and guidance is better than none at all. Not everyone has access to large libraries, the leisure to browse through the whole history of western philosophy, or at first even the know-how to decide what he is looking for and to know where to find it. There are many people who have heard of such names as Kant, Hume, Aquinas and Kierkegaard and keep coming across terms like empiricism, rationalism, Existentialism and Logical Positivism, and who want to know what they mean and how they affect Christianity. It is for such people that this book is written. It is hoped that it will serve like scaffolding – that it will give the reader access to an area of work which might otherwise be inaccessible to him. Once he is there and able to work on his own, he can throw the scaffolding away.

What I have tried to do is to pick out a selection of those thinkers and movements that *either* have had something important to say, *or*, for good or ill, have exerted an influence that is still felt today. (Sometimes the two coincide, and sometimes they do not.) In each case I have based my account upon my own reading and research. This has often compelled me to leave the beaten paths of the older textbooks and include material which is sometimes neglected, and offer interpretations which differ from the familiar ones. For the sake of the general reader wanting to find his way about and the student who may be concerned only with certain sections of this account, I have not hesitated to pin labels on all the main sections and sub-sections of this account.

In my use of sources the following plan seemed best. Where possible, the reader is referred to primary sources of the author under consideration. These are not necessarily the best critical editions or translations. It seemed more important to refer the reader to the handiest readable edition, so that he could follow up the thought for himself, than to direct him to a work which might be accessible only in the depths of a university library. On the whole, cross references to learned discussions in secondary sources have been kept to a minimum. Like every other writer I owe an enormous debt to such sources. But this has been done so as to avoid making more difficult a subject which already presents enough difficulties to the non-specialist. However, I have tried to make good this deficiency in the *Note on Books* at the end of this survey.

Histories of philosophy are not normally designed to be read through in bed, and the present one is not necessarily intended to be read through consecutively. Attention is concentrated on four main phases. A glance at the contents pages will tell the reader what has been included in each. The main emphasis falls on different interpretations of philosophy and the Christian faith from the Reformation to the present day. But chapter 1 contains a brief sketch of medieval philosophy. This has been deliberately kept down to the barest outlines for reasons of space and because most readers are naturally interested in more recent thought. Nevertheless, it has been included partly because medieval philosophy is important in its own right, partly because it sets the pattern for so much subsequent thought, and partly because medieval thought is still of some account today. Whether we like it or not, each generation is affected by what has gone before. One of the most interesting things about studying the history of philosophy is the discovery of how many ideas which are dressed up as modern have been tried out (and answered) generations ago.

It remains for me to thank many friends who have commented on this manuscript and given their precious time in discussing different points, especially the readers and staff of the Tyndale Press and my colleague at Tyndale Hall, the Rev. A. C. Thiselton. I would like to thank the Editor of the *Church of England Newspaper* for permission to make use of material I originally wrote in a review of *Objections to Humanism* which first appeared in his columns; also the Editor of the *Theological Students' Fellowship Bulletin* for permission to make use of material which first appeared there on Paul Tillich and trends in nineteenth-century theology. Some of the points raised in discussing Karl Barth also appear in my more detailed study *Karl Barth and the Christian Message*.

1 MEDIEVAL PHILOSOPHY

Philosophy did not begin with the Middle Ages, but the Middle Ages are a good point to begin an account of philosophy and the Christian faith. For one thing, they began to take each other seriously as never before! In the early centuries of the church individual thinkers had alternately flirted with and denounced philosophy.[1] In the Middle Ages there was scarcely any important thinker who did not take philosophy seriously. For good or ill (and all too often it was the latter) philosophical ideas entered the blood-stream of medieval theology, and this in turn affected the life and thought of Christianity in later ages.

It is no exaggeration to say that a thinker such as Thomas Aquinas is more influential now through his writings and his impact upon Catholicism generally than he was in his lifetime. The difference between Reformed theology and Catholic theology is due in no small measure to the different attitude each takes to philosophy.[2]

Many of the questions asked and answered by medieval thinkers were to shape the course of European thought for centuries to come. Some of them are still with us today. Does God exist? How do we know? What proof have we? In this chapter we shall look at some of the different answers that were given to these questions in the Middle Ages. But first we shall try to get a bird's-eye view of the period as a whole and look at some of its outstanding personalities.

[1] See above, pp. 7f. and below, pp. 13f.
[2] On this see below, pp. 32–36, 37ff., 43–48.

I THE ROOTS OF MEDIEVAL THOUGHT
Augustine and the early church

On some estimates the Middle Ages begin around the tenth century AD. But in a broader sense the Middle Ages span the thousand years from the fifth to the fifteenth centuries. They have roots in the early church and stretch out as far as the age of the Renaissance and the Reformation.

In the early church there was a kind of love-hate relationship with secular philosophy. The Greek-speaking father Justin Martyr (died *c.* 165) had long been a student of philosophy before he became a Christian. Even then he still wore the pallium, the philosopher's cloak, proclaiming that the Christian faith was the 'only reliable and profitable philosophy'.[3] He argued that the divine Logos (Word or Reason) had enlightened thinkers like Socrates to see the errors of paganism.[4] The logical conclusion of such enlightenment was Christianity. The Latin writer Tertullian (*c.* 160 – *c.* 220), on the other hand, denounced philosophy as the root of all heresy,[5] and insisted that worldly wisdom without faith was vain. The Alexandrian fathers Clement (*c.* 150 – *c.* 215)[6] and Origen (*c.* 185–254) went even beyond Justin in their respect for classical philosophy. Origen used Platonic ideas to reinterpret the whole range of Christian teaching on God, Christ and salvation.[7]

While these debates were going on at a fairly intellectual level, battles were being fought more on the level of the man in the street, first with Gnosticism and then with Manichaeism. It used to be said that Gnosticism was the acute Hellenization of Christianity, *i.e.* that it was a form of Christianity perverted by alien Greek philosophical ideas.[8] But more recent scholarship is inclined to see it as a hotchpotch of religious ideas, drawn generally from Judaism, Near Eastern religions, semi-

[3] *Dialogue*, viii.　　　　　　　[4] 1 *Apology*, 5, 46.
[5] *On the Proscription of Heretics*, vii.　　[6] *Cf. Stromateis*, i. 5, 20.
[7] *Cf.* Charles Bigg, *The Christian Platonists of Alexandria* (OUP, 1886); and J. Daniélou, *Origen* (Sheed and Ward, 1955).
[8] The name derives from the Greek word *gnōsis* ('knowledge') and applies to a variety of religious sects which claimed to give a higher knowledge of reality.

popular philosophy and Christianity.[9] It was the early church equivalent of sects like Jehovah's Witnesses and Theosophy. Gnosticism began to be superseded by Manichaeism in the third century. Its founder was Mani (c. 215–275), and its teaching was based upon a supposed primeval conflict between light and darkness. The cures proffered by such sects for the world's ills and the soul's salvation lay chiefly in the latter's escape from the prison-house of the body. Everything material was bad; only the spiritual was good. The remedy was to be found in a variety of solutions ranging from the possession of passwords and secret knowledge to asceticism and vegetarianism.

The most outstanding thinker of this early period was Augustine (354–430), the saintly Bishop of Hippo in North Africa. Augustine had not always been a Christian. In his earlier years he had committed more sins that most men. He had also dabbled in more philosophies than most. But it was not philosophy that brought him peace with God or gave meaning to life for him. It was encounter with Christ.[1] His conversion – which he himself recounts in his autobiographical *Confessions*, one of the great spiritual classics of all time – not only changed his life, but re-energized his thinking.

How far Augustine's later thought was coloured by the philosophical ideas of his time is still a matter of debate amongst scholars. But it was the Word of God in Scripture that was the chief influence on him. From his conversion onwards Augustine devoted himself to bringing this to bear on the current questions of the day.[2]

With the Manichaeans (to whom he had once belonged) Augustine debated the problem of evil. Against their view that

---

[9] *Cf.* R. McL. Wilson, *The Gnostic Problem: A Study of the Relations between Hellenistic Judaism and the Gnostic Heresy* (Mowbray, 1958) and *Gnosis and the New Testament* (Blackwell, 1968); F. L. Cross (ed.), *The Jung Codex* (Mowbray, 1955); R. M. Grant and D. N. Freedman, *The Secret Sayings of Jesus* (Fontana, 1960); R. M. Grant, *Gnosticism: An Anthology* (Collins, 1961); and Ugo Bianchi (ed.), *Origins of Gnosticism* (Brill, Leiden, 1967).
[1] *Confessions*, vii. 9. 21; viii. 12.
[2] An important recent study is that of Gerald Bonner, *St Augustine of Hippo: Life and Controversies* (SCM Press, 1963). Peter Brown's *Augustine of Hippo: A Biography* (Faber, 1967) is now the definitive life.

there was an eternal evil principle opposed to God, Augustine argued that God was the sole creator and sustainer of all things. Evil was a deprivation of good. In the case of man, evil arose out of man's misuse of his God-given freedom. With the Pelagians (who argued that man could and should put himself right with God by doing good) Augustine debated the freedom of the will. Experience and the Christian revelation showed that man was too far gone in sin to be able to help himself. God alone could put a man right with himself and free him from the consequences of his own sins. Against the pagans who blamed the fall of Rome to invading hordes from the north on the corrupting, enervating influence of Christianity, Augustine wrote *The City of God*. It was the first attempt at a Christian philosophy of history. In it Augustine tried to analyse the trends at work in human affairs. He saw the kingdom of God as the goal of all history.

It has often been said that both Catholicism and Protestantism stem from Augustine. The former takes from him (though not exclusively from him) its high view of the church and the sacraments. The latter follows Augustine in his vision of the sovereignty of God, man's lostness in sin and the grace of God which alone can bring salvation to man. As with all slick dicta, this saying about Augustine oversimplifies. There are certainly Catholics today who share Augustine's view of salvation and Protestants who do not. But be that as it may, it was from Augustine more than any other single theologian that medieval thought took its theological framework of ideas. Even when later thinkers substantially altered the picture within it, the framework with which they started out was the theology of the early church in general and of Augustine in particular.

Greek philosophy

A root of medieval thinking which stretched even further back in time was Greek philosophy. Nearly four centuries before Christ the Athenian philosopher Plato (427–347 BC) had taught that the world which we see with our eyes and touch with our bodies was in reality only a world of shadows. It was a copy of the eternal world of spiritual Forms to which the pure soul could attain by philosophic contemplation.[3] Succeeding Greek thinkers might attack, modify or popularize Plato's teaching, but the latter's influence continued scarcely unabated down the centuries. Philo (c. 20 BC – c. AD 50), the Jewish thinker of Alexandria, adapted it to Judaism. Platonism permeated the teaching of the Christian theologians of Alexandria, Clement (c. 150 – c. 215) and Origen (c. 185 – 254).

In the third century AD Plotinus (c. 205–269) developed what came to be known as Neo-Platonism. It was a belief in an ultimate One which lies behind all experience. In the One all distinction between thought and reality is overcome. The One is known by a method of abstraction – by saying what it is *not* like. By this Way of Negation all the non-essentials are removed. The One is known by profound, inner, mystical experience.

Besides the various forms of Platonism, medieval thought was also deeply influenced by Aristotle (384–322 BC), many of whose works were translated into Latin in the twelfth century. Plato believed in a world of spiritual Ideas or Forms which were interrelated, and at the head of which stood the Form of the Good. This was the real world. By contrast, Aristotle believed that ideas existed only as they were expressed in individual objects. He was also interested in the different kinds of *causes* which produced things.[4] For the world as a whole, Aristotle believed that there was a First Cause who is the Unmoved Mover of all things.[5] Aristotle was also deeply interested in ethics and logic, and his writings on both subjects deeply influenced posterity.

Platonism percolated through to the medieval church by its influence upon individual theologians and through Neo-Platonists such as the Pseudo-Dionysius.[6] The main body of

---

[3] This is set out in Plato's best-known work, *The Republic*, vi and vii, where he outlines his conception of the ideal state (*cf.* the translation of H. D. P. Lee, Penguin, 1955, pp. 265–286).

[4] *Cf.* Aristotle, *Metaphysics*, Eng. tr. by John Warrington with introduction by Sir David Ross (Everyman, 1956), pp. 4ff.

[5] *Ibid.*, pp. 333–347.

[6] His writings probably date from the sixth century. In the Middle Ages they were taken at face value as the work of Dionysius, the convert of Paul (*cf.* Acts 17:34).

Aristotle's writings did not become generally available to scholars until the close of the twelfth century. But in the meantime some of Aristotle's ideas were absorbed and transmitted by the sixth-century philosopher-statesman Boethius (c. 480 – c. 524). At the height of his power Boethius was accused of treason and executed. While in prison he wrote his most famous work, *On the Consolation of Philosophy*, which describes how the soul is able to rise above adversity and attain a vision of God through philosophic contemplation. In later centuries it became a classic philosophical manual. But perhaps even more significant was his plan (only partially fulfilled) to translate into Latin the works of Plato and Aristotle, his philosophical commentaries and original works on logic. These not only helped to preserve the culture of classical antiquity; they helped to shape the philosophical vocabulary and questions of the later Middle Ages.

One of the minor facts of history, still kept alive by historians and the curious, is the fact that *On the Consolation of Philosophy* was translated into Anglo-Saxon by King Alfred. At least it goes to show that the Dark Ages were not the complete intellectual blackout that they are sometimes popularly imagined to be. But the fact remains that the collapse of the old Roman Empire was accompanied by a decline in intellectual activity. When the latter revived in the eleventh century, it followed the paths marked out by such men as Augustine and Boethius. Its goal was the quest of ultimate truth. The maps it used on the way were conflations of those drawn earlier by the theologians of the church and the philosophers of the ancient world.

II METAPHYSICS

Generalizations are notoriously deceptive. But if one may be permitted at this point, it is that the thought of the later Middle Ages was characterized by an interest in metaphysics rather than physics. By and large, the great minds of the Middle Ages were not interested in the physical universe for its own sake: they were interested in the reality which they believed lay behind it. They were not so much concerned with scientific questions about natural phenomena. What interested them was the relationship between the natural and the supernatural.

This showed itself in many ways. One was the Scholastic interest in theological questions with a philosophical slant. Scholasticism – the term refers to those medieval schools of thought which were concerned with defining and systematizing the Christian understanding of reality – was above all concerned with the relations of God and the world. Different Schoolmen had different approaches. There was no one generally-accepted system. But whether we look at Anselm or Aquinas (as we shall do shortly), they share the same interest in asking ultimate questions and in relating Christian belief to rational thought.

Another way in which the medieval interest in metaphysics showed itself was the interminable debates about the nature of things and the way that they were related to each other. When we talk about *goodness*, or even perhaps the colour *green*, is there such a thing as *goodness* or *greenness* (a *universal*, to use the technical jargon) which exists over and above particular things? Or do *goodness* and *greenness* exist only in particular objects? If so, does this mean that, when we use such terms, it is only just a fashion of speaking? Might this not even mean that so much of our everyday language is a matter of convenience, and that in fact there are no real entities which correspond to many of our words which look so solid, respectable and meaningful?

Medieval thinkers differed a lot in the answers that they gave. The *Realists*[7] followed Plato in holding that *universals* were real. The things that we see and touch are really copies of an eternal archetype which in some way has brought them into being. The *Nominalists*[8] took the opposite view. They

[7] Among the medieval Realists were John Scotus Erigena (*c.* 810 – *c.* 877), Remigius of Auxerre (*c.* 841 – *c.* 908) and William of Champeaux (*c.* 1070–1121).

[8] The term derives from the Latin *nomen*, a name. Universals were merely names, not things. Roscellinus (died *c.* 1125), the possible founder of the movement, pushed his Nominalism to the point of denying the doctrine of the Trinity. The later Nominalist, William of Occam (*c.* 1300 – *c.* 1349), believed that since only individual things existed, intuition was the only

rejected the idea of *universals* altogether. They believed that there was no such thing as *goodness* or *greenness* apart from particular good or green things, and that all such general, abstract words were merely a manner of speaking. The *Conceptualists*[9] steered a middle course. They took the view of Aristotle that *universals* do, in fact, belong to the realm of thought; but they also stand for something which is actually there which gives unity to the diversity of the world of our experience. It was a view which was neither so far-fetched nor so sceptical as its rivals, and coincided more with common sense.

Debates on such questions dragged on over the centuries. They did much to earn for medieval philosophy its not entirely deserved reputation for obscure hair-splitting. As a matter of fact, they are not altogether removed from the concerns of linguistic philosophy in our own day. The relation of thought and language to their objects was and still is an important and worth-while study. Nevertheless, it is a just complaint against much medieval philosophy that, despite its alleged concern with eternal truth, it neglected the central truths of the Christian revelation. This charge does not altogether stick, as a first-hand reading of Anselm and parts of Aquinas readily shows. But there is a good deal in it that is uncomfortably true.

Medieval thought was a curious mixture of Christian faith and pagan philosophy. The church had a monopoly of learning and most medieval philosophers were clerics. They were amateurs in the sense that they were non-professionals, and in the sense that they did it because they loved it. The church had inherited from the past its Scriptures and writers like Augustine. From them it learnt and taught doctrines of God, creation and salvation. But it also inherited a good deal of Greek philosophy. And many of its best minds were concerned to bring the church up to date and produce a synthesis of the two. Greek arguments and concepts were used to defend Christian ideas and *vice versa*. Not unnaturally the result was often a hotchpotch. It is

---

way of acquiring knowledge. He entirely rejected the possibility of acquiring a rational knowledge of God apart from faith.

[9] Peter Abelard (1079–1142) and Thomas Aquinas (1225–74) have been variously described as Moderate Realists and Conceptualists.

difficult to tell which was the more disastrous consequence: the distortion of Christian teaching by foisting upon it non-Christian ideas, or the fact that, when such ideas were attacked by later critics, the critics believed that they had disposed of Christianity itself.

Greek thought left its mark not only upon the content but also upon the form of much medieval Christian writing. Whereas Augustine was direct, personal and biblical, later medieval writing was often logical but formal, thorough but thoroughly dry. This is true in varying degrees of the two medieval thinkers who count for most in philosophical theology today, Anselm of Canterbury and Thomas Aquinas.

III ANSELM AND THE ONTOLOGICAL ARGUMENT

In some ways Anselm (c. 1033–1109) may be regarded as part of the Norman conquest. An Italian by birth, he eventually became Abbot of Bec in Normandy and Archbishop of Canterbury. But in the history of thought Anselm is largely remembered for two things. One is his important work on the atonement, *Why God Became Man*, in which he tried to set out the logic of the atonement. On the basis of what we know from Scripture of the character of God and the sin of man he set out to demonstrate the inner necessity of why Christ came and died.

The other thing for which Anselm is remembered is his ontological argument.[1] Here he tried to work out a logical demonstration of the existence of God. He describes God as *That than which no greater can be thought*. His argument is usually thought of as an attempt to deduce the existence of God from this *idea* of the most perfect being. It cannot be denied that people do have such ideas of a perfect being in their minds. How then could such an idea get there if there was no such being? If it were merely an idea of the mind and did not actually exist, it would not be the most perfect being. For to

---

[1] The term *ontology* denotes that branch of philosophy which is concerned with *being*. But the term *ontological argument* is usually used of this argument for the necessity of God's being, which depends not upon observable facts but upon the implications of certain ideas. Anselm's statement of it appears in his *Proslogion*, ii–iv.

lack the quality of existence would mean that the being was not perfect.

To put the argument in this way is doubtless to oversimplify it. But most ways of stating it give the impression of a conjuring trick. Somewhere or other the hearer feels that he is being treated to more than a little sleight of hand. Nevertheless, the argument has fascinated some of the greatest intellects in history. Some, like Descartes[2] and Leibniz,[3] have restated it and adapted it to suit their own philosophies. Others, like Aquinas and Kant,[4] have been bent on refuting it. In his own day another monk, Gaunilo of Marmoutiers in France, wrote a reply entitled *On Behalf of the Fool*. In it he argued that he could imagine the most perfect islands, but that did not mean to say that they existed. This prompted Anselm to further elaboration of his argument.

The debate is by no means dead even today. But most modern British philosophers are inclined (in my opinion rightly) to discount the argument, as stated above, on two counts. On the one hand, merely to define a thing does not mean to say that it exists. Definitions do not tell us anything about reality, unless they are confirmed by observation. The argument, therefore, falls on this count, if *That than which no greater can be thought* is merely the definition of an idea. On the other hand, to make the argument work, existence has to be treated as a quality. But existence is not one quality which an object may or may not have alongside others, and yet still continue to be there. An object either exists or it is not there at all. The point is well brought out by G. E. Moore's celebrated comparison of the two sentences: 'Some tame tigers do not growl' and 'Some tame tigers do not exist'. The latter is nonsense. But in order to make its point the ontological argument has to treat existence as the quality which transforms the *idea* of the most perfect being into reality.[5]

---

[2] Descartes, *Meditations*, iii, iv; *Discourse on Method*, iv. See below, p. 51.

[3] Leibniz, *Monadology*, xlv. See below, p. 56.

[4] Aquinas, *Summa Theologiae*, I, Q. 2, art. 1. See below, p. 26. Kant, *Critique of Pure Reason*, Transcendental Dialectic, Book II, ch. iii. See below, pp. 97ff.

[5] In recent years J. N. Findlay has tried to invert the argument and show

But if these objections sink the argument as it is commonly understood, it is still possible that they leave Anselm's actual argument unscathed. For Karl Barth has argued in a brilliant line-by-line commentary on Anselm's work that Anselm's point was not to prove the existence of God by reason alone without any appeal to experience and the Christian revelation. His argument was intended to show that we cannot rationally deny the living God once we know who he is – the most perfect being.[6]

---

that, since God is not the necessary being that this and the other traditional proofs make him out to be, he *cannot* exist (*cf.* 'Can God's Existence be Disproved' and the following essays in *New Essays in Philosophical Theology*, edited by A. Flew and A. MacIntyre, SCM Press, 1955, pp. 47–75). But this too has the air of a conjuring trick. It all depends upon what we mean by *necessary*. On this see the reply by G. E. Hughes (*ibid.*, pp. 56–67); the important restatement by Norman Malcolm, 'Anselm's Ontological Arguments' (reprinted in *The Existence of God*, edited by John Hick, Macmillan, 1964, pp. 47–70); and Anthony Kenny's survey and critique of this and other debates, 'God and Necessity' in *British Analytical Philosophy*, edited by B. Williams and A. Montefiore (Routledge, 1966, pp. 131–151).

[6] Karl Barth, *Anselm: Fides Quaerens Intellectum. Anselm's Proof of the Existence of God in the Content of his Theological Scheme*, Eng. tr. by Ian W. Robertson (SCM Press, 1960). Barth rightly points out that traditional ways of stating the argument tend to ignore both its context and Anselm's approach generally to theological questions. With Anselm it is not a case of proving first and then believing. It is only when we believe that we are in a position to understand its grounds and significance. In its context the ontological argument seeks to answer the question raised by the Psalms, how it is that the fool can say in his heart that there is no God (Psalms 14:1; 53:1). According to Barth, Anselm is drawing a distinction between an idea and that which the idea represents. What the fool denies is the former. We cannot rationally deny the latter, once we grasp what God is.

On Barth and Anselm see further the study by the present writer, *Karl Barth and the Christian Message* (Tyndale Press, 1967), pp. 21f., 29, 90ff. It should be added that the latest critical edition of Anselm disagrees with Barth, though largely on circumstantial grounds rather than on the interpretation of Anselm's actual words. *Cf.* M. J. Charlesworth, *St Anselm's Proslogion; with A Reply on Behalf of the Fool, by Gaunilo, and The Author's Reply to Gaunilo* (OUP, 1965), pp. 40–46.

Another recent study is Charles Hartshorne, *Anselm's Discovery: A Re-examination of the Ontological Proof for God's Existence* (Open Court, Lasalle, Illinois, 1965). Hartshorne contends that the argument is intended to show that God's existence is logically necessary. But apparently even Anselm did not fully appreciate his own argument, still less the great array of thinkers down to Hartshorne whom the latter reviews at length. Hartshorne

According to the usual interpretations, Anselm was indulging in a piece of natural theology. He was trying to prove the existence of God without appealing to Christian faith and teaching. He was trying to find some common ground on which both the believer and the unbeliever could stand in the hope of winning over the latter, and convincing himself that belief in God was not a delusion. It was a line of approach pursued in their different ways by many of Anselm's contemporaries and many others down the centuries. Its attitude is: Prove first and then you may believe. It adopts a kind of two-step process in apologetics. Step one is to use philosophy to lay the foundations; step two is to introduce the Christian faith on the strength of the philosophical arguments. The difficulty is that if step one fails, step two is left hanging in the air, and we are left wondering whether there are any good grounds for taking it.

In this study we shall have cause to look at this general view of philosophy and faith time and time again. We have suggested that, in the case of the usual interpretations of the ontological argument, it is not really convincing. We shall also have cause to ask whether such a line of approach is ever really convincing or right, and whether there might not be other and more valid ways of looking at philosophy and the Christian faith.

If Barth's interpretation of Anselm is correct, then Anselm was trying to do just this. His work was not a piece of natural theology at all. The object of the exercise was not to discover rational, objective proofs for the things we believe in by faith. God is known in experience through personal encounter. The aim of philosophy is to understand the nature of this experience in depth.

---

believes that whilst Anselm's God is greater than anything outside himself, he can surpass himself. And in fact he does so, for God is in continual process of development in and through the universe. Anselm was a process philosopher without knowing it!

The more important discussions from Anselm onwards have been reprinted in Alvin Plantinga (ed.), *The Ontological Argument from St. Anselm to Contemporary Philosophers* and John Hick and Arthur C. McGill (eds.), *The Many-Faced Argument: Recent Studies on the Ontological Argument for the Existence of God* (both Papermacs, 1968).

Anselm's general approach is summed up in a celebrated
phrase which immediately precedes his ontological argument:
Credo ut intelligam ('I believe so that I may understand').[7] It is
not a case of proving first and then believing. We cannot
believe theological truths for non-theological reasons. Rather,
it is only when we encounter the living God in faith that we
are in a position to grasp the truth of Christian faith. The task
of philosophical theology is to examine the implications of this.
It does so for the benefit of both the believer and the unbeliever,
to enable them to see where matters stand. It is neither an
alternative nor a short cut to faith. It is more like an attempt
to let faith take stock of its position.

Clearly, the last word has not been said about Anselm. It
may be that Barth's interpretation of the ontological argument
may require modification or even complete rejection. But this
of itself would not rule out the view of philosophy and faith
that has just been sketched. For this basic approach to truth
in religion was shared by the Reformers, the Puritans and
Evangelicals generally down to the present day. In the course
of this study we shall argue that this approach was adopted
in the Bible. But it was not shared by Thomas Aquinas and
the great host of Catholic thinkers who followed him.

IV THOMAS AQUINAS

The works of Anselm were relatively few in number and slim
in size. It was otherwise with Thomas Aquinas. Everything
about him was big. In his student days his ponderous bulk
earned him the nickname 'the dumb ox'. In later years his
voluminous writings, massive in scope as well as in bulk, won
for him the title of the *Angelic Doctor*. So profound has been his
influence that in more recent times he has been called the
Common Doctor of the Catholic Church.

Like Anselm, Aquinas was an Italian. But he lived a good
hundred years later. He was born in 1225, and died in 1274.
Despite family efforts to dissuade him – efforts which went to
the length of imprisoning him in the family castle – Thomas
entered the Dominican order. He studied theology and
philosophy under Albertus Magnus and taught with him for

[7] *Proslogion*, i.

a time at Cologne. His later life was spent studying, writing and teaching in different centres of learning in Europe. It was a life dedicated to the intellectual defence and propagation of the faith, as he understood it.

His two main works are two massive *Summae* or compends of theology and philosophy. The *Summa contra Gentiles* was designed as a textbook for missionaries. The *Summa Theologiae* (the latest critical edition of which runs into sixty volumes[8]) has been described as 'the highest achievement of medieval theological systematization and the accepted basis of modern RC theology'.[9] Another writer has called it a lake into which many streams have flowed and from which many have drawn, but it is not a spring.[1]

These verdicts are just. The *Summa Theologiae* has scarcely a rival for size, thoroughness and systematic presentation. The whole work is divided up into questions which in turn are subdivided into articles. Each of these begins with a statement of possible objections to the point Aquinas is going to make. Then comes a statement of the authority or evidence on which Aquinas is going to base his case. It is only at this point that he leads into his reply. Finally, he makes a number of smaller points designed to mop up the objections.

But the originality of Aquinas lies less in any new insights of his own than in his capacity to produce a brilliant synthesis of previous thinking. His thought is an alloy of the teaching of the Bible, the traditions of the church, and philosophy, especially that of the recently rediscovered Aristotle (whom he obliquely but regularly refers to as *the philosopher*). As such it has much strength. But it also has the weaknesses of an alloy. For there are times when the constituent elements do not really mix, and when one or other of them proves to be insufficiently durable.

[8] This is the Latin-English edition published under the general editorship of Thomas Gilby and T. C. O'Brien (Eyre and Spottiswoode, 1964–). The work is often referred to as the *Summa Theologica* and various other names. But this title lacks thirteenth-century warrant.
[9] *The Oxford Dictionary of the Christian Church*, ed. F. L. Cross (OUP, 1957), p. 1352.
[1] James Denney, *The Christian Doctrine of Reconciliation* (James Clarke, (1917) 1959), p. 84.

As with most of the thinkers we shall be looking at, many volumes have been written on the man and different aspects of his thought. But for present purposes we shall have to be content with singling out two items of his teaching which have bearing on present-day discussions. The one is his proofs of the existence of God. The other is his doctrine of analogy. The former is of interest not only for its own sake, but also because it typifies a basic approach of Catholic philosophy. The latter is of interest because of its relevance to the contemporary debates on the status and meaning of religious language. Whereas the former seems (to the present writer at least) to be a false step, the latter is suggestive and important.

The Five Ways

Aquinas's proofs of the existence of God are known as the Five Ways.[2] They include what later came to be known as the Cosmological and Teleological Arguments (the former looking for an ultimate cause of the cosmos, and the latter for an ultimate designer). It has often been debated whether these five different ways of trying to prove the existence of God are really five different proofs, or whether they are not variations of one (or more) basic argument. We cannot enter into a full discussion now. All we can do is to try to give some idea of the way Thomas's mind was working.

His starting-point was the conviction that the existence of God was not evident of itself to men. It required proof.[3] Proof was possible because God was the creator of the world. And just as a cause can be known at least partially by its effects, so the First Cause of the universe could be known from the created order.[4] Taking his cue from Aristotle's pre-Christian idea of an Unmoved Mover and what he understood the apostle Paul to have meant in Romans 1:20,[5] Aquinas believed that one could argue back from the things that we observe in the world to a prime mover, a first cause or a great designer behind it. In each case the drift of the argument follows the same basic pattern. Every event must have a cause. Nothing causes (or, for that matter, moves or designs) itself. If we press

---

[2] *Summa Theologiae*, I, Q. 2, art. 3.   [3] *Ibid.*, I, Q. 2, art. 1.
[4] *Ibid.*, I, Q. 2, art. 2.   [5] *Ibid.*

far enough back, we must acknowledge some first cause, prime mover or great designer of all things. Otherwise they would not have come into existence at all. And this is what we mean when we speak about God.

Such arguments are attractive and plausible. They seem to offer objective proof of the existence of God without having to fall back upon mere faith and Christian testimony. But on closer inspection certain gaps and flaws become visible. The very least of these is the objection that, in the case of the Unmoved Mover, the argument leans heavily upon an outdated, Aristotelian pre-scientific view of the world.[6] Quite apart from Kant's objection, that they contain implicitly the untenable ontological argument,[7] there is the problem of demonstrating that the first cause is the same as the prime mover and the great designer, and that both are the same as the Christian God.

Logically, we are not entitled to attribute to a cause any capacities other than those necessary to produce the effect in question.[8] That is, when we try, as the arguments do, to get at the causes simply by looking at the effects, we cannot say that the different effects must have been produced by the same cause. If (for the purposes of argument) we grant that there is a first cause, the proof of itself does not entitle us to say that he (or it) is the same as the designer. The maker and the designer are not necessarily identical. Nor do the arguments themselves furnish this missing link of proof, unless (as some people suspect) they are really disguised forms of the same argument. But in that case we have not four or five different proofs, but only one.

[6] E.g. by the way it speaks of everything being in motion and in a state of transition between potentiality and actuality. Thus wood, when it burns, is said to be actually hot. Before it burns, it is said to be potentially hot. It may be that the point could be restated in a way which harmonizes with modern scientific views. Nevertheless, it is put in a form which is borrowed from the Aristotelian view of the world.

[7] Kant argued (*Critique of Pure Reason*, Transcendental Dialectic, Book II, ch. iii) that to convert the *idea* of an ultimate cause into actual *fact*, the ontological argument had to be invoked, whether consciously or unconsciously. See below, p. 98.

[8] This point was well made by the sceptic David Hume in his *Enquiry Concerning Human Understanding* (1777), xi. 110.

The irony is that the more 'proofs' we have of this kind, the more the difficulty is intensified. It reaches its climax when we try to identify the different 'gods' of the different arguments allegedly arrived at by reason with the God that Christians believe in by faith. It is true that the Christian belief in God as the Creator means that he is the ultimate cause and designer of the universe. But this is an article of faith based on an awareness of God over against ourselves – not a rational deduction to be drawn by those capable of following certain arguments. In other words, to claim that we have proved the God of Christian faith by using these arguments is a deceptive piece of conjuring. For its effect it depends upon the ambiguity of the word *God*. Mere use of the word does not mean that we have proved the God of the Christian faith. The argument uses the word in two senses which are not necessarily the same. In short, there is a gap between the 'gods' of the different arguments and the God of the Christian faith. Some bridge it by a leap of faith. Others stagger across carried on by the momentum of their own enthusiasm. But so far as offering *rational proof* for the Triune God of Christian faith is concerned, we are back to square one.

But this is by no means the only difficulty. The conclusion of the argument (that there must be an uncaused cause or an undesigned designer, *etc.*) denies one of the argument's initial premises (that nothing can cause or design itself). Even if we accept Thomas's point that the whole process would never have started without some first cause, the conclusion is unavoidable that this cause is hypothetical. It is lost far beyond the grasp of the human mind in the mists of infinity. We cannot know what it is really like. It is hidden from view behind the myriads of secondary causes between itself and our experience of the actual world. It is a hypothesis in the strictest sense of the term. In itself it is unknown. It is posited to explain certain situations. It is very far removed from the God that Christians claim to know and worship as their heavenly Father.

In making these points, I have tried to assess the value of such arguments for us today. The subsequent history of philosophy shows that such proofs have been alternately welcomed and neglected, advocated and refuted right down to the present day. In later chapters we shall note some of the more outstanding debates. But before we leave them for the time being it should be noted that there is a world of difference between the value of a point and the validity of any particular formulation of it. A point may be valid, but the argument putting it may be hopeless. It is one of the occupational hazards of the philosopher that he may do an impressive job shooting something down, only to find that he has shot down an Aunt Sally.

The traditional arguments for the existence of God seem to me to be just such an Aunt Sally. Philosophers have shot them down and gone home thinking that they have disposed of the Christian religion once and for all. The truth of the Christian faith does not depend upon them. Nevertheless, they are trying to make an important point.

We cannot get away from the fact that we are in the world, and that the world is a highly complex machine, organism or call it what we will. These facts do raise questions, and the medieval thinkers were right to ask them. For modern man to get lost in technology and become so preoccupied with aspects of the physical world that he sees nothing else is a form of intellectual obscurantism and escapism. To use an old biblical simile, it is like straining out a gnat and swallowing a camel.

Whatever may be said about evolution, or the difficulties of detecting a loving purpose in a good deal of human experience, it remains an impressive fact that we live in this complex world which is not of our own making. In the last analysis, we are faced with the choice as to what to make of it. Are we to regard it as the product of pure chance, and believe that everything happens at random without rhyme or reason?[9] In

[9] A classic critique of the design argument occurs in David Hume's *Dialogues Concerning Natural Religion* (1779). He claimed that any universe was bound to have the appearance of being designed (Part viii). There could be no universe at all if the parts of it were not mutually adapted to a considerable degree. But this, like so many of the things that Hume said, begs the question. We are not talking about *any* hypothetical universe which does not exist, and which in any case requires an independent intelligent mind to conceive it. We are talking about one which actually does exist. The question remains whether this universe with its tremendously

which case we must say that the rational observations of the natural scientist are really about things which are ultimately irrational. Or might there not be some rational, creative force or forces working in and through natural phenomena, but not dependent upon them for its own existence? Does it not make better sense of the world – and of our thought about it and behaviour in it – if we presuppose the biblical view of God as its author and sustainer? We may want more time and evidence before making up our minds. But we cannot continue putting off the question without incurring the charge of intellectual escapism. And more important, to go through life putting off thought about ultimate questions is to miss the whole point of human life.

The doctrine of analogy

Aquinas's teaching on analogy[1] is especially relevant in the light of the fierce debates on the meaning and nature of language – especially religious, metaphysical and moral language – which have raged in British philosophy over the past quarter of a century. It has been a common complaint of agnostic philosophers that, because they could not read into religious statements the same meanings that they found in secular language, religious utterances were either meaningless or disguised pieces of wishful thinking.

We shall look more closely into this question in chapter 4. In the meantime it is worth noting that already in the thirteenth century Thomas Aquinas was well aware of the problem. He pointed out that when we make statements about God, we are using language in rather a special way. Our words have neither a *univocal* nor an *equivocal* sense. In the former case our words

---

complex, mutually independent structures could have fortuitously come into being.

We are all familiar with the question whether a group of monkeys, given typewriters, the requisite materials and an infinity of time, could have written the works of Shakespeare. The question here is infinitely magnified. Monkeys have a relative intelligence; typewriters, *etc.* are highly sophisticated tools; and the universe is infinitely more complex than the works of Shakespeare.

[1] *Summa Theologiae*, I, Q. 13. On analogy and further literature see also the present writer's *Karl Barth and the Christian Message*, pp. 47–54.

would mean exactly the same thing whenever we used them. But when Christians speak of Christ as the Lamb of God, they are not thinking of a four-legged, woolly animal. When they call God their Father, they do not mean to say that he is a human being, existing in time and space, who has brought children into the world by natural procreation. On the other hand, Christians believe that they are not using language in an *equivocal* manner, so that their words mean something on a human level, but that they mean something entirely different on the religious level.

If religious statements belonged to the former category, we should be reducing God to the level of being an object or being, existing in time and space. If they belong to the latter, religious language would be meaningless. For whatever we said, our meaning would be quite different from our words. Aquinas pointed out that valid statements about God were *analogical*. In other words, when we call God our Father, he is neither wholly like nor wholly unlike what is best in human fathers, but there are genuine points of similarity.

We cannot here go into the ways in which Aquinas developed and defended his teaching. Merely to claim that religious language is the language of analogy is not enough. It has to be shown that there is a genuine correspondence between language and its object. The problem is apparently made more acute by the fact that we cannot step outside our language and thought forms and see God directly, as he is in himself, so that we could test them. Having said what we have said about the inadequacies of the old proofs of the existence of God, we cannot fall back on them to establish an analogical relationship between God and the world.

The vindication of the doctrine of analogy lies elsewhere. As a matter of fact, the biblical writers themselves give us more than a clue. They draw attention to the fact that God has revealed himself in action, thought and word. In proclaiming Jesus as (for example) the Lamb of God, the Light of the World, or the Good Shepherd, they were doing so on the basis of their experience. In view of their encounter with him, such expressions were entirely appropriate. The same could be said of the Old Testament prophets and writers, and even of Jesus himself. They could say what God was like because of their encounter with him. Because of Jesus' unique relationship with the Father he could say what God was like.

But it is not just a case of having the word of the biblical writers, and then being told to take it or leave it. The biblical writers believed that what they proclaimed brought light and meaning to human experience. Their message was the vehicle of encounter with God. Those who received it would prove its truth for themselves. The words of John 8:12 might be taken as a specimen test case of the biblical idea of truth: 'I am the light of the world; he who follows me will not walk in darkness, but will have the light of life.' On the one hand, a proclamation is made – not a literal one, but one using the language of analogy. On the other hand, the truth of it can be fully proved only by experimental verification in life.

All this has taken us some way from Aquinas's original exposition of analogy. But his main point is fundamental. When we speak about God, we are not speaking the literal truth. Our language cannot be other than figurative and analogical. For God is no mere object in time and space. He breaks into our world: but he is above it. Nevertheless, Christian experience testifies to the fact that God reveals himself in a way that is comprehensible to men. Even though, in the nature of the case, divine truth has to be refracted and expressed in terms of human words and finite images, nevertheless it can be expressed in meaningful terms.

V THE SIGNIFICANCE OF MEDIEVAL PHILOSOPHY
Two approaches to truth in religion
In a brief study one has to be selective, and the present one has opted to concentrate largely on Anselm and Aquinas in view of their crucial position and ideas. But it should not be imagined that Anselm and Aquinas were the only two important thinkers, or that everyone agreed with them. Indeed, as we saw, they differed between themselves not only in style, presentation and emphasis but on basic teaching. Aquinas believed that God's existence could be proved to any rational man who would face the facts of nature and be willing to draw the right conclusions. With his watchword, 'I believe so that

I may understand', Anselm stressed the importance of commitment and faith as a prior condition to understanding the central truths of the Christian faith.

It was not that Aquinas wanted to eliminate faith and minimize the importance of revelation. In the course of the *Summa* he has a good deal to say about both. Rather, he was adopting what we earlier called a two-step process in presenting the case for Christianity.[2] The first step is to use philosophical arguments to lay the foundations; the second is to try to complete the job by appealing to Christian teaching. We might also call it the two-storey view of philosophy and faith. The ground floor is built by reason, and the top floor by faith. It recognizes that rational argument can take you only so far, but it wants to assert such things as the doctrines of the Trinity, atonement and salvation, which it accepts on the basis of faith.

Anselm's basic position was very different. It was not a case of faith taking over where reason left off. In apprehending religious truth, faith and reason must go hand in hand. Faith is the act of self-commitment which puts a man into a right relationship with God which in turn enables him to reflect upon it. Reason plays its part in grasping and reflecting upon that relationship.

Thus in the Middle Ages two basic types of theology began to crystallize. On the one hand, there was *natural theology* according to which a genuine knowledge of God and of his relationships with the world could be attained by rational reflection on the nature of things without having to appeal to Christian teaching. And on the other hand, there was *revealed theology* which was concerned with what was disclosed to man by God through the revelation recorded in the Scriptures. Within these broad divisions there were various sub-divisions. There were men like Anselm (if our interpretation of him is correct) who accepted the latter but not the former. And there were men like Aquinas who accepted both. These two trends were already in process of formation in Augustine and Boethius. And in fact they are much older still. *Revealed theology* goes back to the biblical revelation, and *natural theology* back to the classical Greek philosophy of Plato and Aristotle. The really

[2] See p. 23.

B

significant fact is that not only in the Middle Ages there were thinkers who were conscious of the two different approaches, but that from Aquinas onwards it became accepted in large sections of the church that *natural theology* with its secular philosophical arguments provided the intellectual basis of Christian faith. This was challenged at the Reformation. And even today when *natural theology* has become very threadbare, it is still looked upon by some as the only intellectually respectable defence of Christianity.

The historical significance of Aquinas

In his own day Aquinas's synthesis of philosophy and faith caused him to be regarded as something of an innovator. But the innovations of one generation have a habit of becoming the orthodoxy of the next. Today his influence is greater than ever. What we have called the two-storey approach to philosophy and faith was officially endorsed by the Roman Catholic Church at the First Vatican Council (1870).[3] It has become a familiar feature of much Catholic apologetic. Aquinas himself has come to occupy a unique place in Roman Catholic thinking. In 1879 Pope Leo XIII published an encyclical letter asserting the permanent value of his teaching, and urging Catholic philosophers to draw their inspiration from it.[4] Not all have done so. But as recently as 1963, at an audience commending the new edition of the *Summa*, Pope Paul VI said that his teaching was 'a treasure belonging not only to the Dominican Order but to the whole Church, and indeed to the whole world; it is not merely medieval but valid for all times, not least for our own'.[5]

Outside the Roman Catholic Church the two-storey approach has continued to make headway even among those who have never read a word of Aquinas. We shall trace some of its fortunes in the next chapter, and we have already seen

---

[3] Cf. *The Dogmatic Constitution on the Catholic Faith*, produced at its Third Session.
[4] *Aeterni Patris*.
[5] The full text is reprinted at the front of each volume of the new edition (see above, p. 25, n. 8).

something of its vulnerability. In the meantime it is important
to notice two significant side-effects.

The first is that, where a theology is based partly upon the
Christian revelation and partly upon alien philosophical ideas,
the result is often a misguided hotchpotch. At best the end-
product is a mixture containing ideas which cancel each other
out. At worst the alien philosophy has been so allowed to
crowd out and transform that the result is scarcely recognizable
as Christianity at all. The early phases of this process can be
seen already in Aquinas. There is much that is valuable in his
writings and that well repays careful study, whether we are
Protestant or Catholic. On the other hand, the non-Christian
element in his teaching tends to neutralize so much of what is
good. This comes out, for example, in his teaching on salvation.
His exposition of the cross reveals penetrating insights into the
New Testament message.[6] But his non-Christian ideas cause
him to read into biblical teaching such contradictory ideas as
that man can accrue merit with God and so contribute to his
salvation.[7] Admittedly, Aquinas is at pains to qualify carefully
what he says on this subject. Nevertheless, it is there. And it
would not have been if he had subjected these ideas to the
criterion of the New Testament.

Perhaps an even more conspicuous example of the direct
influence of Aristotelian thinking was the part it played in the
formulation of the doctrine of transubstantiation which in turn
influenced the whole of Catholic thinking on the Lord's
Supper.[8] It was used to explain how in the alleged conversion
of bread and wine into the actual body and blood of Christ as
an offering to God for sin, the bread and wine still retained
their natural appearances.[9] It thus helped to foist upon

[6] *Summa Theologiae*, III, QQ. 46–52. To say this is, of course, not to endorse
everything that Aquinas says in these pages.
[7] *Ibid.*, I-II, Q. 114 on Merit; *cf.* also III, Supp. Q. 25 on Indulgences.
[8] The word transubstantiation was already widespread in the latter half
of the twelfth century, and the doctrine was officially adopted as an essential
part of Catholic teaching by the Lateran Council (1215). Aquinas gave it
classical formulation in the *Summa*, III, QQ. 73–78. It was further endorsed
by the Council of Trent, Session 13, ch. 4 (1551).
[9] It drew upon the Aristotelian distinction between *substance* (the essential
matter of a thing) and *accidents* (its outer, non-essential qualities). In

Christendom teaching which was not only wrong in itself, but, in view of the importance it was given, teaching which diverted attention away from the central issues of the Christian message.

With Aquinas the elements of Christianity are still plainly recognizable. With other philosophers the philosophical element has been so allowed to predominate that the result, though allegedly a restatement of the Christian faith, bears scant resemblance to New Testament Christianity.

This brings us finally to the second unfortunate side-effect of adopting the two-storey type of approach to philosophy and faith. It is that when Christianity is so wedded to a particular philosophy, and when that philosophy passes out of fashion or is shown to be inadequate, then there are those who fall into the mistake of concluding that Christianity itself has been disposed of. This way of thinking affects both sides. The history of thought is littered with the memories of able men who have spent their days shooting at Aunt Sallies. It is also evidenced in a high toll of half-hearted, would-be defenders of the faith who failed to call their critics' bluff. Perhaps there is a lesson in this somewhere for us in the twentieth century.

---

transubstantiation the *substance* of the bread and wine are changed into the whole *substance* of the body and blood of Christ, but the *accidents* remain those of bread and wine. The distinction is thoroughly artificial and unscientific, as well as being theologically misleading.

FROM THE REFORMATION TO
THE AGE OF ENLIGHTENMENT

The period from the Reformation to the Age of Enlightenment
spans three hundred years. Looking back on these years, it is
now clear that the sixteenth, seventeenth and eighteenth centuries were the cradle of modern thought. In the last chapter
we saw that modern Catholicism took its decisive shape from
the Middle Ages. Protestant theology took its form from the
Reformation in the sixteenth century, and the modern secular
outlook from the rational, enlightened philosophies of the
seventeenth and eighteenth centuries.

This is not to say that the eighteenth century contributed
nothing to Christian theology, or that later secular thought
appeared like a bolt from the blue. The Evangelical Revival,
led by men like John Wesley (1703–91) and George Whitefield
(1714–70), brought new life to the churches and gave to thou-
sands a knowledge of God in their personal experience. But
like the Puritan movement a century earlier, the Revival
was essentially a continuation of the Reformation. On the
other hand, there were active rationalists in the Reformation
era, men like Faustus Socinus (1539–1604) who rejected the
doctrine of the Trinity in favour of Unitarianism and condemned the doctrine of atonement as immoral and irrational.
The Reformation itself owed not a little to that rebirth of
secular learning and quest for knowledge which blossomed
in the fourteenth century and which is known as the Renaissance.

All the same, these three hundred years are dominated by
certain tides of thought, which have made the present intellec-

tual situation what it is. Like all tides, they ebbed and flowed. But, taking the period as a whole, certain broad movements are discernible.

The first is a rediscovery of God, at the time of the Reformation. He was neither the object of abstruse speculation nor a mere article of the church's creed, but the one with whom all men have to do, one who had stepped into human affairs, who had spoken through the Scriptures, who continued to speak through them and who deals with all men personally. This was the basic discovery of the Reformers which brought the Reformed churches into being, and which was the foundation of the Puritan movement and the Evangelical Revival in the seventeenth and eighteenth centuries.

Close behind this first wave came a second. It was an interest in the world in general and man in particular for their own sakes. In one sense, it had begun already with the Renaissance in the middle of the fourteenth century. It found expression not only in literature, architecture and art,[1] but also in the rise of modern science and technology. But in another sense, it was partly a by-product of the Reformation. Having found God in Christ through Scripture, the Reformers had no interest in medieval natural theology. To many this meant that they could stop looking at nature for proofs of a reality beyond it; they could study it and appreciate it for its own sake as the creation of God.[2] But sooner or later this was bound to give rise to a fresh round of philosophical questions. As time went on, some people came to think that science could explain everything in terms of natural causes. Was there any room left for God? If so, how does God fit into the natural scheme of things? In the seventeenth and eighteenth centuries different and contradictory answers were given to these questions. Some philosophers believed in God and some did not. Some revived the medieval proofs of the existence of God, and others

[1] On the outlook of Renaissance thinkers see *The Renaissance Philosophy of Man*, edited by Ernst Cassirer, Paul Oskar Kristeller and John Herman Randall, Jr., which contains selections from the writings of Petrarca, Valla, Ficino, Pico, Pomponazzi and Vives (University of Chicago Press, 1948, reprinted as a Phoenix paperback).

[2] *Cf.* R. Hooykaas, *Philosophia Libera: Christian Faith and the Freedom of Science* (Tyndale Press, 1957), pp. 16ff.

attacked them. Descartes turned upside down the whole approach of Aquinas. Whereas the latter had used the world to prove God, Descartes used God to prove the existence of the world. This change was something more than a change of methods. It was a symptom of the greater change that was coming over European thought in which God was pushed more and more to the perimeter and sometimes outside altogether.

Karl Barth has drawn attention to the way this process has worked out in the two classic revolutionary documents of the eighteenth century, the Declaration of Independence of the United States of America of July 1776 and the Statement of Human and Civil Rights ratified by the French National Assembly in August 1789.[3] Both retain a veneer of religion, but in many places it is worn so thin as to be almost non-existent. The French one speaks of the *Supreme Being* in its preamble, and the American one makes passing acknowledgment of the *Creator*. But neither have much time for him. Both are concerned with man and with what seems to be so obviously right in itself. The rights they assert are believed to be natural. (The French were concerned with freedom, property, security and the right to protect oneself from violence; the Americans with life, liberty and the pursuit of happiness.) There is no question of obligations towards God except in the most general terms. Law is the expression not of the mind of God but of the will of the people. Governments derive their authority not from the Almighty but from the consent of the governed.

In so far as there is religion at all here, it is Calvinism and Catholicism respectively gone to seed. But in the eyes of modern man this is not a bad thing. What has happened is that man has become more rational. He has thrown off outmoded beliefs. He has rejected, if not God, then at least the ritual and paraphernalia of the churches. It is all part and parcel of man coming of age and living a life of his own.

Since then man has come quite a long way. His ideas and questions have taken new twists and turnings. Some of them have taken very hard knocks. All too often secular man has

[3] *From Rousseau to Ritschl*, Eng. tr. by B. Cozens, H. Hartwell and others (SCM Press, 1959), pp. 27ff.

turned a blind eye to the real grounds of the Christian faith as set out in Scripture, and then complained at the lack of evidence. But the fact remains that, just as the adult person grows out of the child, so contemporary thought has grown out of that of earlier centuries. In later chapters we shall ask how it did so. In the meantime, to appreciate the process, it is necessary to turn in more detail to the centuries which link the Reformation to the Age of Enlightenment, the centuries which were the cradle of modern thought.

II THE REFORMERS AND THEIR SUCCESSORS
Luther
The first major figure of the continental Reformation was Martin Luther (1483–1546). For most of his life he was a professor of theology at Wittenberg, a university which by sixteenth-century standards ranked as rather upstart and definitely 'redbrick'. In his student days Luther had abandoned the study of law to seek peace with God by entering an Augustinian order of monks. He found it, but not in the way he had expected. The traditional ways of the church – the sacramental system, the penitential discipline, the study of medieval Scholasticism – only made God seem more remote. The turning-point came through the advice of his superior to study and teach the Scriptures. Through them Luther encountered God not as an alien but as a friend, not as judge but as a saviour who forgave those who turned to him in simple faith.

This new insight found expression in the doctrine of justification by faith which became the keystone of the Reformation. It featured prominently in the Confession of Augsburg (Art. IV, 1530) which became the classic statement of the Lutheran position: 'Men cannot be justified in God's sight by their own strength, merits or works; on the contrary, they are justified freely on account of Christ through faith, when they believe that they are received into grace and that their sins are remitted on account of Christ who by his own death made satisfaction for our sins. This faith God imputes for righteousness in his own sight. Rom. iii and iv.'

This discovery, made by Luther between 1513 and 1516,

marked the beginning of the continental Reformation. For Luther it meant that everything must be looked at afresh in the light of the Word of God in Scripture. It meant not only changes in his private life and devotions; it meant the reformation of the life, thought and worship of the whole church. At first Luther cherished the fond hope that the authorities would prove sympathetic. But his appeals for reform and protests against indulgences[4] and other abuses in his *Ninety-Five Theses* of 1517 and other works only served to entrench them in their positions. His writings were condemned, and he himself was excommunicated and even placed under the imperial ban. Yet despite enormous opposition the Reformation cause went from strength to strength.

The Reformation outside Germany

Without Luther the Reformation would have taken a different course, but it would have happened all the same. Elsewhere men of independent minds and working independently of Luther felt the same call from God to seek reformation in the light of the Word of God. Like Luther, they were often accused of being upstarts and innovators. But also like him, their consciences were captive to the Word of God.

In Switzerland the Reformation was led by Zwingli (1484–1531) at Zürich and Calvin (1509–64) at Geneva. Both had come from backgrounds coloured by Renaissance Humanism, but both became convinced that Humanism alone was not enough. Like Luther, they were scholars. But again like him, they found themselves compelled by events to be practical men. One of the most striking things about the teaching of all the leading Reformers was its unanimity. There were differences of emphasis, especially on the Lord's Supper, but they were united in taking the Word of God in Scripture as their primary datum for thinking about God. There was, however, one way in which Calvin differed from Luther and Zwingli. The writings of the latter were largely occasional, dashed off to meet the needs of the moment. Calvin also turned his hand to this important but ephemeral kind

[4] On indulgences see above, p. 35. See also James Atkinson, *Martin Luther and the Birth of Protestantism* (Pelican, 1968).

of work. But he also tried to summarize Reformed teaching in his *Institutes of the Christian Religion*. It began life as a small handbook, then over the years successive editions added to its size. The final edition of 1559 was still no rival in bulk to the *Summa Theologiae* of Aquinas. But its influence over succeeding generations was scarcely less; and, like the *Summa*, it continues to be translated and reprinted today.[5]

Whereas on the Continent the Reformation was first doctrinal and then political, in England it was the reverse. The occasion was Henry VIII's desire to divorce Catherine of Aragon which finally drove him to take the affair out of the hands of the pope and into his own. But the cause of the religious reformation was the same as on the Continent. So long as Henry VIII remained on the throne, the official religion of England was virtually Catholicism without the pope. But all the time such men as Cranmer, Ridley and Latimer felt the call to reform life and thought in the light of the Word of God. For each of these three their faith brought them martyrdom. It fell to their successors to establish the Protestant faith in this country. The approach of the Reformers can be studied in summary form in the Thirty-Nine Articles of the Church of England (1571)[6] which may readily be compared with other sixteenth-century confessions of faith.[7] In the next century the classic statement of Protestant faith was the Westminster Confession (1646), produced by the Presbyterians. Whereas the latter differed from the Anglicans on matters of church government, their approach to truth was basically the same.[8]

[5] The latest English translation is the definitive critical edition edited by John T. McNeill and translated by Ford Lewis Battles, 2 vols. (SCM Press, 1961).
[6] The Articles are to be found at the back of the Book of Common Prayer. The date given above is that of their final Elizabethan form. They were first published in 1563, but their substance goes back considerably earlier. On the teaching of the English Reformers generally see P. E. Hughes, *Theology of the English Reformers* (Hodder and Stoughton, 1965).
[7] *Cf.* Arthur C. Cochrane, *Reformed Confessions of the 16th Century, Edited with Historical Introductions* (SCM Press, 1966); Wilhelm Niesel, *Reformed Symbolics: A Comparison of Catholicism, Orthodoxy and Protestantism*, Eng. tr. by D. Lewis (Oliver and Boyd, 1962); Erik Routley, *Creeds and Confessions: The Reformation and its Modern Implications* (Duckworth, 1962).
[8] For the approach of post-Reformation thinkers *cf.* H. Heppe (ed.),

This also applies to the Evangelicals of the eighteenth century, many of whom (including the original Methodists) were Anglicans. What they sought was not a new approach to truth, but a fresh application of the truth they already had in Scripture to contemporary life.

All this may seem to be a far cry from contemporary, or for that matter from classical, philosophy. Is there any connection at all? And if so, what?

Philosophy and the Reformers

Luther's last sermon at Wittenberg has gone down in history as a classic invective against reason, 'the Devil's Whore'. But it is by no means an isolated attack on philosophy. Those who have taken the trouble to comb through the indices of Luther's collected works have experienced little difficulty in finding references to Aristotle as a 'destroyer of pious doctrine', a 'mere Sophist and quibbler', an 'inventor of fables', 'the stinking philosopher', a 'billy-goat' and a 'blind pagan'.[9] The list could easily be extended. This sort of thing has earned for Luther the reputation of being an irresponsible irrationalist. It has also contributed to the widespread impression that philosophy and biblical theology have nothing to do with each other.

But this is only half the picture. In a less heated moment Luther reflected: 'When I was a monk they used to despise the Bible. Nobody understood the Psalter. They used to believe that the Epistle to the Romans contained some controversies about matters of Paul's day and was of no use for our age. Scotus, Thomas, Aristotle were the ones to read.'[1] Circumstances change, and the academic world has its fashions like anyone else. We might substitute for the names of Scotus,

---

Reformed Dogmatics, Set out and Illustrated from the Sources, Eng. tr. by G. T. Thomson (Allen and Unwin, 1950) and compare J. K. S. Reid, The Authority of Scripture: A Study of the Reformation and Post-Reformation Understanding of the Bible (Methuen, 1957).

[9] Cf. B. A. Gerrish, Grace and Reason: A Study in the Theology of Luther (OUP, 1962), pp. 1f. This work is a definitive study of Luther's approach to philosophy and theology.

[1] Cf. Gerrish, op. cit., p. 36.

etc., those of Sartre, Ayer and Wittgenstein. But the situation Luther is describing is not all that far removed from that in the western universities today. Philosophy has made the Bible irrelevant, and reason has taken over the place of revelation.

For a man of Luther's temperament, living in that age and under such pressures, it is not surprising that he expressed himself in the way he did. But as modern research has shown, Luther was not condemning reason as such. He himself employed it with great effect. The real target of his attacks was the abuse of reason, situations where philosophy had crowded out the truth of the Christian faith. Reason had its legitimate place in science and everyday affairs. It had its true function in grasping and evaluating what was set before it. But it was not the sole criterion of truth.

For Luther there were three lights which illuminated human existence.[2] There was the light of nature where reason and common sense sufficed to solve many of the questions of everyday life. There was the light of grace by which the revelation in Scripture gave man a knowledge of God which was otherwise unattainable. And there was the light of glory which belonged to the future. For there were many questions which Scripture left unresolved. There were apparent contradictions, like the sovereignty of God and the responsibility of man for his actions, to which both Scripture and Christian experience testified but which neither Scripture nor reason resolved. Luther believed that the right approach was not to let these antinomies cancel each other out, but to hold both in tension and leave it to the light of glory to resolve them.

In the meantime God had revealed all that man needed – or could bear – to know of himself in Christ. 'It is perilous', he said, 'to wish to investigate and apprehend the naked divinity by human reason without Christ the mediator, as the sophists and monks have done and taught others to do . . . There has been given to us the Word incarnate, that is placed in the manger and hung on the wood of the Cross. This Word is the Wisdom and Son of the Father, and He has declared unto us

[2] *The Bondage of the Will* (1525), Eng. tr. by J. I. Packer and O. R. Johnston (James Clarke, 1957), p. 317; *cf.* Gerrish, *op. cit.*, p. 171. For a general survey of Luther's teaching see P. S. Watson, *Let God Be God* (Epworth Press, 1947).

what is the will of the Father toward us. He that leaves this Son, to follow his own thoughts and speculations, is overwhelmed by the majesty of God.'[3]

Calvin's approach was set out less colourfully but more systematically than Luther's. But in essentials it was the same. Both could speak of a *twofold knowledge* of God.[4] On the one hand, there is a general awareness of God that all men have. It is not a matter of the Scholastic proofs. It is a profound inner awareness of God over against us.[5] It may not be well defined or easy to pin down. Nevertheless, it is there. Furthermore, the glory of the created order reflects God's own glory.[6] But despite this, man is so far gone in sin that his spiritual sensitivity has become blunted.[7]

On the other hand, God has revealed himself through Scripture not only as the creator but as the redeemer in Christ.[8] In Scripture God had spoken to man and revealed himself in a special way, a way which was significant for all ages.

Now this raises a whole host of important questions. What is the relationship between history and faith? What is the connection between events in the past and religious experience today? What is the precise part or parts played by the Scriptures in this encounter of God and man? What is meant when Scripture is said to be the Word of God? What are the connections between the written word and the Word made flesh? On what grounds are we entitled to say that Scripture is the Word of God? On what grounds is it given a normative place in interpreting religious experience and ideas? What is the status, nature and function of religious language? What is the connection between this type of revelation and revelation

[3] *Cf.* Watson, *op. cit.*, p. 95.
[4] *Cf.* Watson, *op. cit.*, pp. 73ff. with Calvin, *Institutes*, I. ii. 1. On Calvin's approach see Edward A. Dowey, Jr., *The Knowledge of God in Calvin's Theology* (Columbia University Press, New York, 1952); T. H. L. Parker, *The Doctrine of the Knowledge of God: A Study in the Theology of John Calvin* (Oliver and Boyd, 1952); and B. B. Warfield, 'Calvin's Doctrine of the Knowledge of God' in his *Calvin and Augustine*, edited by S. G. Craig (Presbyterian and Reformed Publishing Company, Philadelphia, 1956), pp. 29–130.
[5] Calvin, *Institutes*, I. iii.   [6] *Ibid.*, I. v.   [7] *Ibid.*, I. iv.
[8] *Ibid.*, I. ii. 1. For Calvin's further discussion of Scripture see *Institutes*, I. vi–xiv.

in nature? What are the nature and scope of that revelation? Does it entitle us to embark upon a natural theology? In what ways does the Reformers' view of revelation in nature differ from that of Catholic thinkers such as Aquinas?

In a general sketch of trends in philosophy and faith spanning a thousand and more years it is impossible to stop and deal satisfactorily with all these questions. I have attempted to look at some of them in more detail in a study of a modern restatement of the Reformed approach, *Karl Barth and the Christian Message*.[9] We shall also look at some of them later on in this sketch. The point I want to make here is not to try to solve them in five minutes, but to suggest that it is questions like these which constitute the real subject-matter of the philosophy of religion. The Reformers were not interested in philosophy as such. Their main concern was the reform of life, worship and teaching in the light of the Word of God. But their approach raises important philosophical questions. These demand careful attention for two reasons. On the one hand, critics of Christianity and would-be believers are entitled to an explanation of the grounds and nature of the Christian faith. And on the other hand, an investigation of them can in the long run serve only to deepen and enrich the faith of those who are already committed.

Before leaving the Reformers, one or two further observations may be made. The first is to underline what has just been said about the philosophy of religion. Pre-war British textbooks on the subject virtually took it for granted that what we have called the two-storey approach was the right one.[1] The job of philosophy of religion was to look around for objective proof, for non-Christian reasons for Christian faith. This was not really satisfactory. For one thing, it does not really work.[2] For another, it neglects the real grounds of Christian belief. The Christian faith has to stand on its own feet, and vindicate itself by itself, or not at all. Since the war there has been the growing belief amongst philosophers and theologians

[9] Tyndale Press, 1967. See especially Chapter 2, 'The Word of God and the Knowledge of God' and Chapter 3, 'The Bankruptcy of Natural Theology'.
[1] See above, p. 32; *cf.* below, pp. 167f.
[2] See above, pp. 21, 27f.

that this is the right approach. And, in fact, there is a real parallel here with other branches of philosophy. The philosophy of science investigates the nature, presuppositions and methods of scientific inquiry. It does not take over the actual research itself. Rather, it is concerned with the character and status of the techniques and results of that research. So it is with the philosophy of religion. It is concerned not so much with the content of religious experience as with its form and the questions raised by it. The proper starting-place, therefore, for the philosophy of the Christian religion is not outside it but within it. Its primary datum is the Christian experience of God in Christ.

This leads to our second observation which is that the approach to truth of the Reformers is essentially a continuation of that of Anselm and the authors of Scripture. It is summed up in Anselm's words: 'I believe so that I may understand.'[3] Without commitment to Christ in faith, the observer is not really in a position to appreciate the nature of Christianity. He can observe others from the outside. But he will not know what it is to believe himself. Again there is a partial parallel in the natural sciences. Understanding follows experiment and experience, rather than precedes it. Only here, of course, the experiment is open to public demonstration, and there is not the element of personal commitment and faith.

We encounter the same approach in the New Testament. Jesus did not hand out his message on a plate. To find out its truth demanded personal commitment. It is to those who follow him that he gives understanding.[4] It is through following him that men encounter the Father.[5]

Finally we must ask the question whether this approach does not land us in a vicious circle. 'Objective' proof seems to have been ruled out. God's existence is not a matter of logical or scientific demonstration but of inner awareness. The central truths of the Christian gospel are reached only by personal commitment. In reply it may be said that the argument is

[3] Cf. above, pp. 24, 32f.
[4] Cf. Mark 8:27-30; John 1:12f.; 7:17; 1 Corinthians 1:30.
[5] Cf. Matthew 11:27f.; John 14:6-11. On this see further Karl Barth and the Christian Message, pp. 28-32, 69ff.

circular, but not viciously so. There is indeed no independent vantage-point which would enable a man to stand outside himself and his experience and pass judgment. But to say that there is no such 'objective' proof is not to say that there is no proof at all.

Calvin compared Scripture with spectacles which put things into focus.[6] The value and use of the spectacles could only be appreciated by using them. So it is with Scripture. Its value emerges in the light of its capacity to interpret human existence and to convey knowledge of God. To change the picture, recognizing religious truth is like recognizing colours. How do we know that this object is yellow? We might say that it is like other yellow things. But how do we know that they are yellow? In the last analysis, we know yellowness by seeing it. We grasp it, when we see it.

Such analogies are limited. But when we talk about God, we can do no other than talk in limited analogies. For God is not an object of time and space. On the other hand, there is a genuine point of comparison. The truth of Christianity emerges in the act of living it out.[7]

III RATIONALISM

In everyday language rationalism has come to mean the attempt to judge everything in the light of reason. Bound up with this is the assumption that, when this is done, reason will have completely disposed of the supernatural, and that we are left with nothing but nature and hard facts. But in the more technical, philosophical sense of the term, rationalism denotes a more particular and certainly less atheistic approach. The rationalists of the seventeenth and eighteenth centuries differed widely among themselves in the way they worked out their different systems. But common to all was a belief in the rationality of the universe and the power of reason to grasp it. Behind all the complex machinery of nature there was a rational mind, and this could be known by the right use of reason. Given the right data, it was possible to draw up a map of reality, provided that one made the correct logical deductions.

[6] *Institutes*, I. xiv. 1.
[7] Cf. *Karl Barth and the Christian Message*, pp. 35–38.

The Reformers of the sixteenth century were dominated by a concern for God. They took as their starting-point God's action in Christ, as witnessed to by the Scriptures. From there they proceeded to think about the world. The rationalists of the seventeenth century were absorbed not so much by God but by the world. Many of them were scientists who had made notable contributions to mathematics, especially to geometry. Their starting-point was logic, and their techniques were derived from mathematics. They were not irreligious men. At any rate, the notion of God occupied a more or less important place in their thinking. But for them the problem was not one of their personal relationship with the one to whom all men have to give account. Rather, they were intrigued with the rational structure of the universe. And the view they took of the latter decided the role they assigned to God in their scheme.

Descartes

The first of the great rationalist philosophers was the Frenchman René Descartes (1596–1650). His dates make him a contemporary of Charles I and Oliver Cromwell, of Kepler, Galileo and Harvey. Descartes received his education not at a university but at a Jesuit college. But this proved no detriment, for he was given a better grounding in mathematics than he could have otherwise got at most universities at the time. Seeking a life of leisure, Descartes embarked upon a military career. He saw service in several European armies, always careful to transfer somewhere else when fighting broke out. He went to Sweden at the request of Queen Christina who (as Bertrand Russell has remarked[8]) thought that, as sovereign, she had the right to waste the time of great men. The queen could only spare the hour of five in the morning for her daily lessons, and this, coupled with the rigours of the Scandinavian winter, cut short the philosopher's life.

Descartes seems to have made a sustained effort to keep up the appearances of a gentlemanly amateur. He is said to have worked short hours and read little. He dabbled in various sciences, including medicine. But his main contributions were

[8] *History of Western Philosophy* (Allen and Unwin, 1946), p. 582.

made in the fields of geometry and philosophy. In the former he invented co-ordinate geometry. In the latter he pioneered rationalism and Cartesian doubt. His two chief philosophical works were his *Discourse on Method* (1637) and his *Meditations* (1641).[9]

In the *Discourse* Descartes recorded his intellectual testimony. He recalled how in the winter of 1619-20 he entered a stove[1] and spent the day in meditation. When he went in, his philosophy was half-baked. When he emerged, it was complete in basic essentials. As a first principle he resolved 'never to accept anything for true which I did not clearly know to be such'.[2] His ideal and method were modelled on mathematics. 'The long chains', he went on, 'of simple and easy reasonings by means of which geometers are accustomed to reach the conclusions of their most difficult demonstrations, had led me to imagine that all things, to the knowledge of which man is competent, are mutually connected in the same way, and that there is nothing so far removed from us as to be beyond our reach, or so hidden that we cannot discover it, provided only we abstain from accepting the false for the true, and always preserve in our thoughts the order necessary for the deduction of one truth from another.'[3]

And so were born Cartesian doubt and rationalism. The former excludes from serious philosophical consideration everything about which doubt may be entertained. The latter seemed to place within the philosopher's grasp the key that would not only guarantee modern scientific method, but also unlock the whole of reality. For whereas reliance upon observation and experience could prove deceptive, rational argument was unshakable.

With this in mind he set about probing the structure of the universe. Giving free rein to his doubts, he granted the possibility that everything in his mind might be no more than dreams and illusions. How then could he be sure that the

---

[9] Both works appear in a convenient English translation published by Everyman, (1912) 1949. References below are to this edition.
[1] *Discourse*, Part ii (p. 10). Commentators usually explain the remark to mean a room heated by a stove.
[2] *Ibid.*, p. 15.   [3] *Ibid.*, p. 16.

world existed? His answer had three main steps. First of all, he came to the realization that whatever else he could doubt, there was one thing that it was impossible to doubt – the fact that he was doubting. This, in turn, led him to his celebrated axiom: *Cogito ergo sum* ('I think, therefore I am'). The mere fact that he was having doubts and, therefore, thinking meant that he must exist.[4]

The next step in the argument was to show that God existed. This he attempted to take by a combination of the causal and ontological arguments. On the one hand, the idea of himself as a finite being implied the existence of an infinite being.[5] On the other hand, the very idea of a Perfect Being implied its existence.[6] The third and final step was to advance the claim that, since God is perfect, he would not deceive us. He would not allow us to think that our clear and distinct ideas were true, if they were not. We can thus rest assured that all our logical deductions about reality are valid.[7]

Descartes has been frequently taken to task for his philosophical blunders. We have already queried the validity of the ontological argument.[8] Once this goes, the whole system is bereft of its pivot. The celebrated *Cogito ergo sum* has also provided philosophers with ample shooting-practice. Bertrand Russell is among the many who have pointed out its fallacious character.[9] If Descartes is really wanting to start with *doubt*, his initial premise should have been 'There are doubts'. He is not entitled to infer from this the existence of a personal self, an 'I' with all the qualities we take for granted in everyday life. The latter is smuggled into the argument unnoticed. On the other hand, the phrase may well not be a logical deduction of personal existence from the mere fact that there are doubts but simply a disguised tautology, merely

---

[4] *Ibid.*, Part iv (pp. 26f.).   [5] *Meditations*, iii.
[6] 'I found that the existence of the Being was comprised in the idea in the same way that the equality of its three angles to two right angles is comprised in the idea of a triangle . . . and that consequently it is at least as certain that God, who is this Perfect Being, is, or exists, as any demonstration of geometry can be' (*Discourse*, Part iv, p. 30). On the ontological argument see above, pp. 20–23.
[7] *Discourse*, Part iv (pp. 31f.).   [8] See above, pp. 21f.
[9] *History of Western Philosophy*, pp. 589f.

repeating the same thing in different words.[1] In which case the phrase is simply a reaffirmation of his own existence.

But it is also questionable whether even an ultra-sceptic can honestly begin with nothing but doubt as his primary datum. However difficult it may be to formulate it, we are all profoundly conscious that we are not alone with our doubts. We live in a milieu, and that milieu is made up of other people, other things, and God. In short, Cartesian philosophy represents a false start.

Descartes is sometimes portrayed as the first modern philosopher. This is not quite correct. In refurbishing the medieval proofs of the existence of God he was drawing upon the legacy of the Middle Ages. Like the medieval philosophers he was interested in metaphysics. To the end of his life Descartes remained a nominal Catholic. But there is a sense in which Descartes represents a new departure. Descartes was interested in God not for his own sake, but for the world's. God is invoked as a kind of *deus ex machina* to guarantee the validity of our thoughts about the world. Apart from that he remains eternally standing in the wings. It is not surprising that, when later philosophers came along who shared Descartes's assumptions but not his methods, they could dispose entirely of this unwanted prop.

In one of his more speculative moments Archbishop William Temple was once tempted to ask himself which was the most disastrous moment in European history. The answer he came up with was the day Descartes shut himself up in his stove.[2] In saying this, Temple was not thinking so much about Descartes's view of God but about the trend he set in European thought. It epitomized a shift of concern. It symbolized a retreat into the individual self-consciousness as the one sure starting-point in philosophy. As a matter of fact, Temple went on to lump Luther together with Descartes as the spiritual

[1] *Cf.* A. J. Ayer, 'If I start with the fact that I am doubting, I can validly draw the conclusion that I think and that I exist. That is to say, if there is such a person as myself, then there is such a person as myself, and if I think, I think' (*The Problem of Knowledge*, Pelican, 1956, p. 46).

[2] *Nature, Man and God* (Macmillan, 1934), p. 57. The whole chapter (pp. 57-81) on 'The Cartesian Faux-Pas' is worth studying as a critique of Descartes.

counterpart to the latter's philosophical individualism.[3] But Luther and Descartes are ill-assorted bedfellows. The observation only serves to show how little the archbishop understood of Luther and the Reformers. For when Luther was confronted by the ecclesiastical authorities he took his stand, not upon his individual conscience, but upon the Word of God and his conscience simply as captive to it. Luther's ultimate authority was outside him. (And to that extent he has much more in common with the medievals.) But Temple is standing on surer ground when he pronounces upon Descartes. The French philosopher inaugurated a trend followed by many who rejected his actual system. He set up the individual consciousness as the final criterion of truth.

Descartes himself believed that he had firmly grasped objective reality with his doctrine of clear and distinct ideas which remained unshakable amid the shifting sands of experience. In fact, neither the *Cogito ergo sum*, nor the ontological argument, nor his method in general was anything like as dependable as he led himself to believe. The mere process of thinking thoughts (however logical their sequence) does not make them true. A thought may be said to be true when it corresponds with its object. This can only be done by checking it in experience. But this is precisely what Descartes tried to eliminate in philosophy. In effect, Descartes was driving a wedge between the mind and its thoughts on the one hand and the world and experience on the other. This approach was strongly (and rightly) opposed by the British empiricists.[4] But on the continent Descartes set the trend. Rationalism dominated continental, especially German, philosophy almost to the end of the eighteenth century. And even when rationalism was finally abandoned, there were many down to the present day who continued to take the individual self-consciousness as their starting-point and even as their sole reference-point.

Spinoza
Benedictus de (or Baruch) Spinoza (1632–77) was born in Amsterdam of Jewish parents. Some years before his birth

[3] *Ibid.*, pp. 62ff.   [4] See below, pp. 6off.; *cf.* p. 93.

the Netherlands had proclaimed freedom of thought and in so doing had turned themselves into a haven for all those who sought refuge from persecution or who had found that they could not get their books printed anywhere else. The young Spinoza made full use of his rights. Although brought up as a Jew, his free thought resulted in his expulsion from the synagogue. Later writings show him to have been a pioneer biblical critic.[5] But it was not only for biblical criticism that Spinoza made his name. In 1663 he published an exposition of Descartes set out in geometrical fashion, *Renati des Cartes Principiorum Philosophiae Pars I et II, More Geometrico Demonstratae per Benedictum de Spinoza*. It was the only book of his published during his lifetime that was to bear his name on the title page. It was followed in 1670 by a treatise on politics and religion, *Tractatus Theologico-Politicus*. But his chief life-work which was published posthumously and secretly in the year of his death was his *Ethics*,[6] or *Ethica Ordine Geometrico Demonstrata*. This too was written (as the Latin title suggests) in a quasi-geometrical form with definitions, axioms, propositions and proofs (to which Q.E.D. was duly appended).

Spinoza has been variously described as a hideous atheist and as God-intoxicated. In fact, he was a pantheist. But he was not the kind of pantheist of the romantic, poetical imagination. His was a rational pantheism, soberly worked out from premises akin to those of Descartes. Like the latter, he begins with clear and distinct ideas, notions which he thinks are self-evidently true. Their truth can be seen merely by stating them properly. His basic idea is that of Substance which he defines as 'that which exists by itself, and is conceived through itself; that is, something of which the conception needs for its formation no other thing'.[7] This idea is said to be self-evidently true. 'If anyone says, then, that he has a clear and distinct, that is a true idea of Substance and nevertheless doubts

[5] *Cf.* E. G. Kraeling, *The Old Testament since the Reformation* (Lutterworth Press, 1955), pp. 45f.
[6] A useful working edition of Spinoza is *The Chief Works of Benedict de Spinoza*, Eng. tr. by R. H. M. Elwes, 2 vols. (Bohn's Philosophical Library, 1883; reprinted by Dover Publications, New York, 1951).
[7] *Ethics*, Part I, Definition iii.

whether such Substance exists, he is like one who says that he
has a true idea and yet doubts whether it may not be false.'[8]
From here he goes on to argue that there is only one Substance,[9]
and that this Substance can be regarded as either God *or*
nature. For, 'Whatever is, is in God, and without God nothing can be, or be conceived.'[1]

At face value this last proposition could be taken in a
Christian theistic sense.[2] But Spinoza soon makes it clear
that he does not. For God does not exist outside nature but
within it. 'God is the indwelling and not the transient cause
of all things.'[3] Whether we say God or nature, we are really
talking about the same thing. The difference is really one of
emphasis. To speak of God draws attention to the cause; to
speak of nature points to the finished product, as it were.

Spinoza's teaching was worked out in considerable detail.
In the course of his argument he denied all free will,[4] and also
that God could love men in a personal way.[5] The whole system is as impersonal and as mechanical as a theorem. But
despite its apparently rigorous form, the argument is anything
but watertight. Apart from flaws in its outworking, the whole
system fails because Spinoza failed to establish the validity of
his definitions and procedure.

Nevertheless, Spinoza continued to fascinate continental
thinkers even when they broke with his particular philosophy. The idea of an all-embracing system, bringing together
God and man and accounting for everything in terms of a
single spiritual reality, dazzled nineteenth-century Idealists,
just as the Lorelei bewitched the boatmen sailing on the Rhine
below. Enthralled by the prospect, they plunged on heedless
of the rocks barely concealed beneath the torrent of ideas.
It mattered little whether the system could be harmonized

[8] *Ibid.*, Part I, Proposition viii, Note 2.
[9] *Ibid.*, Part I, Proposition xiv.   [1] *Ibid.*, Part I, Proposition xv.
[2] Theism may be defined as the belief that the ultimate ground of things is
a single supreme reality which is the source of everything other than
itself but which does not depend on them for its existence. This reality
is complete and perfect and, as a consequence, deserves unqualified
worship.
[3] *Ibid.*, Part I, Proposition xviii.   [4] *Ibid.*, Part V.
[5] *Ibid.*, Part V, Proposition xix.

with historic Christianity and religion as actually experienced
and practised. So much the worse for historic Christianity.
Where facts could be made to fit, so much the better. But where
not, the system could dispense with them. Even today the
bright prospect has not entirely lost its charms. In *Honest to
God* John Robinson re-echoed Tillich's wistful praise of Spinoza's idea of God existing not over and above things but in
them as 'the creative ground of all natural objects'.[6] But of
this more later.[7]

Leibniz

Descartes was a nominal Catholic, and Spinoza a free-thinking
Jew. An eminent Protestant philosopher who was indebted to
both was G. W. Leibniz (1646–1716). Leibniz was a universal
genius. He shares with Newton the honour of discovering the
infinitesimal calculus. His original work on symbolic logic,
lost for centuries, was brought to light again in the present
one. He invented a calculating machine (which earned him
membership of the Royal Society). The Prussian Academy was
largely his creation. He corresponded with and met many of
the most eminent minds in Europe. As well as being a philosopher, he was also an eminent diplomat. Leibniz wrote much,
but the nearest he came to a systematic account of his philosophy was his brief *Monadology* (written in 1714 and published
in 1720).[8]

According to Leibniz, the universe is made up of an infinite
number of *monads* or 'simple substances' without 'parts' and
without 'windows by which anything could come in or go
out'.[9] They are indivisible and ever active. Each monad
mirrors all existence. The monads form an ascending series
from the lowest which is next to nothing to the highest which is
God. By means of the ontological argument Leibniz deduced
the existence of God, or the *Necessary Being*, or 'the original
simple substance, from which all monads, created and

[6] *Honest to God* (SCM Press, 1963), p. 31.
[7] See below, pp. 194ff., 209ff.
[8] For a selection of his writings see Leibniz, *Philosophical Writings*, translated
by M. Morris (Everyman, 1934).
[9] *Monadology*, i, vii.

derived, are produced.'[1] The work concluded with a vision of the universe in which everything functioned as a perfect mechanism, where 'sins carry their punishment with them by the order of nature, and by virtue of the mechanical structure of things itself; and that in the same way noble actions will attract their rewards by ways which are mechanical as far as bodies are concerned, although this cannot and should not always happen immediately'.[2]

To elaborate further and appraise a thinker such as Leibniz would take us far beyond the scope of this sketch. When he died, Leibniz was in disfavour with his patrons. But his influence percolated through to his more immediate posterity through teachers such as C. Wolff (1679–1754),[3] albeit in a diluted and impure form. Thanks to such men rationalism became the philosophical orthodoxy in the German universities in the eighteenth century.

Today rationalism is discredited, whether we look at it from the viewpoint of philosophy or that of Christian theology. And, in the last analysis, for the same reason. For it is impossible to construct maps of reality, starting with mere concepts and *a priori* definitions, without looking to see whether the theories match experience. In the sphere of philosophy this means that the rationalists were on the wrong track in their endeavours to provide a metaphysical understanding of the natural order. But they were also on the wrong track theologically. The god of the rationalists was a hypothetical abstraction, a *deus ex machina*, invoked to make the system work, but not one who was encountered personally in history and present experience. His existence was, moreover, based upon arguments which we have already seen to be dubious. It is not surprising, therefore, that, when later thinkers rejected the rationalist approach and undermined the old proofs of the existence of God, they felt that God and religion had been disposed of alto-

---

[1] *Ibid.*, xlv; *cf.* xlvii. On the ontological argument see the present work, pp. 20–24, 51f., 97f.
[2] *Ibid.*, lxxxix.
[3] Wolff's *Preliminary Discourse on Philosophy in General* is available in the edition of R. J. Blackwell in the paperback Library of Liberal Arts, Bobbs-Merrill, Indianapolis and New York.

gether, and that there was no alternative to agnosticism or downright atheism.

Pascal

Before we leave rationalism, it is important to stress that not all continental scientists and thinkers were rationalists. Blaise Pascal (1623-62) was a slightly junior contemporary of Descartes. Like the latter, he was a scientist, mathematician and a Catholic. But his approach to religion was very different.

In 1646 Pascal came into contact with Jansenism, a Catholic movement with a strong Augustinian emphasis on man's need of divine grace, whose teaching was soon to be condemned by Pope Innocent X in 1653. And soon afterwards he became closely associated with the Jansenist centre at the convent of Port-Royal, Paris. For a time he continued his scientific pursuits and enjoyed Parisian society. But in November 1654 Pascal's 'definitive conversion' took place, when he discovered 'the God of Abraham, the God of Isaac, the God of Jacob, and not of the philosophers and men of science'. Between 1656 and 1657 he published his *Provincial Letters* in which he defended Jansenism against its Jesuit opponents, a work which was promptly placed upon the Index of forbidden books. But Pascal's chief work was his *Pensées*.[4]

Pascal had planned to write an apology, addressed to the free thinkers of his day who were indifferent to the claims of Christianity. The work was never finished. Pascal got no further than writing down his disconnected thoughts on scraps of paper which he had pinned together. The title of *Pensées* or *Thoughts* describes their character, but gives little idea of their strength and acuteness.

At times Pascal is arguing a case, as when he reflects on the fulfilment of prophecy and events in biblical religion. But often he looks deep into the human heart, and challenges man to consider his real situation, as when he writes: 'Nothing is more intolerable to man than a state of complete repose, without desires, without work, without amusements, without

[4] The quotations that follow are taken from the recent translation by Martin Turnell (Harvill Press, 1962).

occupation. In such a state he becomes aware of his nothing-ness, his abandonment, his inadequacy, his dependence, his emptiness, his futility. There at once wells up from the depths of his soul weariness, gloom, misery, exasperation, frustration, despair.'[5] Sport, pleasure, entertainment and society are so often pursued not because they bring pleasure, but because they take men's minds off themselves.[6]

Pascal was profoundly aware of the real nature of religion. His God was not the God of rationalist argument who is a mere hypothesis, invoked to make other hypotheses feasible. God is not known by reason in this way. 'The heart has its reasons which are unknown to reason . . . It is the heart which is aware of God and not reason. That is what faith is: God perceived intuitively by the heart, not by reason.'[7] To bring some men to the point of faith, Pascal knew that it was neces-sary to remind them of the odds that are at stake. Hence his celebrated wager, in which he challenges men to gamble their lives on the possibility that Christianity might be true. We cannot see God. We cannot prove the truth of the gospel to exclude every possible doubt. We can only find out the truth of Christianity by risking our whole lives on it. GOD OF JESUS

In direct opposition to the rationalists Pascal points out that, 'The metaphysical proofs of the existence of God are so remote from men's methods of reasoning and so involved that they produce little impact; and even if they did help some people, the effect would only last for a few moments while they were actually watching the demonstration, but an hour later they would be afraid that they had made a mistake. "What they had gained by their curiosity would be lost through pride" [St. Augustine, *Sermons*, CXLI]. That is the result of a knowledge of God which is reached without Jesus Christ, . . . Instead of which those who have known God through a mediator are aware of their own wretchedness.'[9]

Sometimes Pascal's teaching is classified as voluntarism, the implication being that he sets greater store by the will than by the intellect. It is even represented as a kind of self-inflicted brain-washing, in which the will to believe is allowed to

[5] *Ibid.*, p. 149   [6] *Ibid.*, pp. 175ff.   [7] *Ibid.*, p. 163.
[8] *Ibid.*, pp. 200ff.   [9] *Ibid.*, p. 212.

banish all intellectual considerations. But this is a caricature. It neglects to mention that the idea of the wager was addressed to the sporting men of the day, reminding them of a greater game played at infinitely greater odds. It does not take into account the fact that Pascal devoted a great deal of energy to rational argument.[1] At the same time he realized, 'What a vast distance there is between knowing God and loving him!'[2] He realized that the truth of Christianity lay deeper than arguments.[3] He was in fact trying to recall his age to the same biblical religion as the Reformers a hundred years previously. But he was a voice crying in the wilderness. Although today he is credited with being one of the profoundest thinkers of his day, he is also treated as being something of an oddity, outside the main stream of intellectual development.

IV EMPIRICISM

Rationalism was largely a continental movement. In Britain the movement which philosophers today regard as being the most significant among the philosophical trends of that age was empiricism.[4] Like rationalism, the term denotes not so much a well-defined school of thought as a general line of approach. In particular, the empiricists of the eighteenth century were especially concerned with the problems of knowledge. In contrast with the rationalists who tried to erect philosophical systems by means of reasoning on the basis of allegedly self-evident truths, the empiricists stressed the part played by experience in knowledge. They argued that we have no ideas at all other than those derived from experience which comes to us via our senses. Statements (apart from those of

---

[1] Cf. (e.g.) ibid., pp. 231ff., 281ff., 291.　　　　　[2] Ibid., p. 330.

[3] 'Do not be surprised at the sight of simple people who believe without argument. God makes them love him and hate themselves. He inclines their hearts to believe. We shall never believe with a vigorous and unquestioning faith unless God touches our hearts; and we shall believe as soon as he does so' (ibid.).

[4] The term derives ultimately from the Greek empeiria (= experience), empeirikos (= experienced) and their cognates. From the nineteenth century onwards it has been used to denote those kinds of philosophies which stress experience as the source of knowledge.

pure logic) can be known to be true or false only by testing them in experience.

It would scarcely be true to call empiricism an English movement. The three leading eighteenth-century representatives were, in fact, an Englishman, an Irishman and a Scotsman: Locke, Berkeley and Hume. Nor would it be true to brand the movement as uncompromisingly agnostic. Although Hume was a sceptic, Locke's theological writings show him to have been a man of sincere Christian faith, and Berkeley was an Anglican bishop. Even so, the movement is generally thought of as having made a great contribution to the general advance of modern agnosticism. For when Hume pushed empiricist techniques to their logical conclusions, he left no alternative to scepticism.

Locke

John Locke (1632–1704) was the son of a small country landowner and lawyer. He went up to Oxford when Puritanism was in its heyday and the university was under the vicechancellorship of the great John Owen. Among other things Locke studied medicine, and was eventually awarded an M.D. John Locke was also a semi-public figure. But in the last years of the Stuarts he found it prudent to live in Holland, and did not return until after the Glorious Revolution of 1688. While in Holland he had the time and leisure to complete his major philosophical treatise, *An Essay Concerning Human Understanding* (1690), and his first *Letter on Toleration* (1689). He subsequently published further letters on the same subject and treatises on education and civil government. *The Reasonableness of Christianity* (1695) was followed by the posthumous *Paraphrase and Notes on the Epistles of St. Paul* (1705–7) and *A Discourse on Miracles* (1706).[5]

Today Locke is chiefly remembered for pioneering the empiricist approach to knowledge. At Oxford he was impressed by reading Descartes, but his own approach struck out in a very different direction. He rejected the rationalist

[5] For Locke's theological opinions see *The Reasonableness of Christianity with a Discourse on Miracles and Part of a Third Letter concerning Toleration*, edited by I. T. Ramsey (Black, 1958).

idea that the mind had stamped on it from birth certain primary, self-evident notions.[6] Instead, he pictured the mind as a blank which received all its impressions from outside. 'Let us then suppose', he wrote in his characteristic seventeenth-century rhetoric, 'the mind to be, as we say, white paper, void of all characters, without any *ideas*; how comes it to be furnished? Whence comes it by that vast store which the busy and boundless fancy of man has painted on it, with an almost endless variety? Whence has it all the materials of reason and knowledge? To this I answer in one word, from *experience*: in that all our knowledge is founded, and from that it ultimately derives itself. Our observation employed either about *external sensible objects, or about the internal operations of our minds, perceived and reflected on by ourselves, is that which supplies our understanding with materials of thinking.* These two are the fountains of knowledge, from whence all the *ideas* we have, or can naturally have, do spring.'[7] In other words, what we know are either *ideas* (impressions in the mind of '*yellow, white, heat, cold, soft, hard, bitter, sweet,* and all those which we call sensible qualities')[8] or the mind's own *reflections* on them.[9] From this Locke drew the conclusion that the human mind 'hath no other immediate object but its own *ideas*',[1] and that 'Knowledge is the perception of the agreement or disagreement of two *Ideas*'.[2]

In arguing this, Locke was advancing what is sometimes called the representative theory of knowledge. The mind itself has no direct knowledge of the outside world, for it is never able to by-pass the senses and stand outside them. What the mind perceives is the data conveyed to it by the senses, upon which it then gets to work and interprets. Before we question the validity of this approach and turn to see how it was developed by later empiricists, it is worth while pausing to see how Locke defended Christianity against the doubters of his day.

Locke drew a distinction between faith and reason. He

---

[6] *An Essay Concerning Human Understanding*, I. i–iv.
[7] *Ibid.*, II. i. 2. Quoted from the Edinburgh edition of 1798.
[8] *Ibid.*, II. i. 3.   [9] *Ibid.*, II. i. 4–5.
[1] *Ibid.*, IV. i. 1.   [2] *Ibid.*, IV. i. 2.

defined the latter as 'the discovery of the certainty or probability of such propositions or truths, which the mind arrives at by deduction made from such *ideas*, which it has got by the use of its natural faculties, *viz.* by sensation or reflection. *Faith*, on the other side, is the assent to any proposition not thus made out by the deductions of reason, but upon the credit of the proposer, as coming from God, in some extraordinary way of communication. This way of discovering truths to men we call *Revelation*.'[3]

A page or two previously Locke had laid down the further distinction between that which was according to reason, that which was above and that which was contrary to reason. '1. *According to reason*, are such propositions whose truth we can discover, by examining and tracing those *ideas* we have from *sensation* and *reflection*; and by natural deduction find to be true or probable. 2. *Above reason*, are such propositions whose truth or probability we cannot by reason derive from those principles. 3. *Contrary to reason*, are such propositions as are inconsistent with, or irreconcilable to, our clear and distinct *ideas*. Thus the existence of one God is according to reason; the existence of more than one God contrary to reason; the resurrection of the dead, above reason.'[4]

Thinkers may disagree as to what should be put in each pigeon-hole. I myself would want to qualify further what I mean by reason and being reasonable. An idea is reasonable when one can prove its truth beforehand. It may also be called reasonable if it is warranted by experience. It may be that it contains implications which have not been fathomed or that we are incapable of examining at the moment. Nevertheless, if observation and experience warrant the conclusion, the idea may be said to be reasonable. It is in this sense that I would agree with Locke that the existence of God is according to reason. But there are many aspects of the Christian faith which, as Locke points out, are above reason. Locke's method was to accept such things on the authority of that which he could believe in by reason.

Reason is natural *revelation*, whereby the eternal Father of

---

[3] *Ibid.*, IV. xviii. 2.   [4] *Ibid.*, IV. xvii. 23.

light, and Fountain of all knowledge, communicates to mankind that portion of truth which he has laid within the
reach of their natural faculties; *Revelation* is natural *reason*
enlarged by a new set of discoveries communicated by GOD
immediately, which *reason* vouches the truth of, by the
testimony and proofs it gives that they come from GOD.[5]

For Locke the miracles of Christianity were not (as they
appear to be for many would-be apologists for Christianity
today) something to be apologized for. When their credibility
had been duly examined, miracles are evidence for the Christian faith. 'Where the miracle is admitted, the doctrine cannot
be rejected; it comes with the assurance of a divine attestation
to him that allows the miracle, and he cannot question its
truth.'[6] We shall return to the point when we discuss Hume.[7]

Berkeley

George Berkeley (1685–1753) was born in Ireland. He became
a Fellow of Trinity College, Dublin, when he was twenty-two,
and Dean of Derry in 1724. Four years later he made an
abortive attempt to establish a missionary college in Bermuda
for the evangelism of America. He subsequently became
Bishop of Cloyne. Nearly all his major philosophical work was
done by the time he was twenty-eight. His chief works include
An Essay towards a New Theory of Vision (1709), *A Treatise concerning the Principles of Human Knowledge* (1710), *Three Dialogues
between Hylas and Philonous* (1713) and *Alciphron or the Minute
Philosopher* (1732).

It is Berkeley's fate to be remembered chiefly for pushing
further the approach of Locke. He accepted the representative theory of perception, but gave it a novel twist. He agreed
that what we actually perceive is not the outside world of
material things, but ideas or perceptions. From here he went
on to argue that things exist in so far as they are perceived.
But this does not mean that objects simply cease to exist
when there is no-one around to perceive them. For they are
always perceived by the infinite mind, God.

---

[5] *Ibid.*, IV. xix. 4.   [6] *Cf.* Ramsey, *The Reasonableness of Christianity*, p. 82.
[7] See below, pp. 69f.

Berkeley's position is caricatured in the well-known limerick by Ronald Knox:

There was a young man who said, 'God
Must think it exceedingly odd
 If he finds that this tree
 Continues to be
When there's no-one about in the Quad.'

REPLY

Dear Sir:
 Your astonishment's odd:
I am always about in the Quad.
 And that's why the tree
 Will continue to be,
Since observed by
Yours faithfully,
GOD.

Berkeley himself put it rather more soberly. 'The table I write on, I say, exists, that is, I see and feel it; and if I were out of my study I should say it existed, meaning thereby that if I was in my study I might perceive it, or that some other spirit actually does perceive it.'[8] For Berkeley to exist meant either to be perceived (in the case of things) or to perceive (in the case of persons, including God).

Thus with one bold master-stroke Berkeley had ingeniously denied the existence of matter and proved the existence of God. It was novel and brilliant. But it was a thesis that was fraught with difficulties. Berkeley did not make clear (nor could he make clear) whether the objects perceived by our finite minds were the same as those perceived by the Infinite Mind. It made the objects of our perception hollow. There was nothing behind them. Nor was it clear how they came to be there in any case. It violated the common-sense assumption of all our everyday behaviour, that in some way or other matter does exist and that reality is not immaterial. The logical

[8] *The Principles of Human Knowledge*, I. iii. This work, together with the *Three Dialogues between Hylas and Philonous*, have been reprinted in *A New Theory of Vision and Other Select Philosophical Writings* (Everyman's Library), with an introduction by A. D. Lindsay.

C

conclusion of the representative view of knowledge is solipsism, that the only knowledge possible is that about oneself
and one's perceptions. For we cannot stand outside ourselves
and the data provided by our senses. We have no way of
showing that things or people have any existence independent
of our own minds.

At this point it would have been wiser, as E. L. Mascall
has suggested,[9] if philosophers had stopped to ask themselves
whether this view of knowledge was on the right track. Is it
really true that what we perceive are not objects but merely
sensations inside us which have made us jump to the conclusion that things really do exist outside us? Would it be not
more reasonable to treat the data of our senses not as a kind
of end in itself but as means through which the mind grasps
an intelligible reality? Contrasting his approach with that
of the empiricists, Mascall writes: 'Now against this assumption I wish to put forward the view, which has a very reputable
ancestry though its existence has been ignored by most modern
philosophers, that the non-sensory intellectual element in
perception does not consist simply of inference, but of apprehension. According to this view, there is (at any rate normally,
for we are not at the moment concerned with mystical experience) no perception without sensation, but the sensible
particular (the sense-object or sense-datum or, as the scholas-
tics would say, the sensible species) is not the terminus of
perception, not the *objectum quod*, to use another scholastic
phrase, but the *objectum quo*, through which the intellect
grasps, in a direct but mediate activity, the intelligible
extramental reality, which is the *real thing*.'[1] But neither Berkeley nor his immediate successors seem to have seriously entertained such a possibility. Berkeley developed his empiricism
in the direction of immaterialism and idealism. David Hume
was pushed by it into thorough-going scepticism.

Hume
David Hume (1711–76) was an odd mixture. A contemporary

[9] *Words and Images* (Longmans, 1957), pp. 29–45, gives an incisive appraisal
of empiricism.
[1] *Ibid.*, p. 34.

thought that he looked more like 'a turtle-eating Alderman than a refined philosopher'. In an obituary that he penned for himself he described himself as 'a man of mild disposition, of command of temper, of an open, social and cheerful humour, capable of attachment, but little susceptible of enmity, and of great moderation in all my passions. Even my love of literary fame, my ruling passion, never soured my temper, notwithstanding my frequent disappointments.' Doubtless, he was in a much better position to pass judgment than we are today.

He was born in Edinburgh and entered the university there at the age of twelve, leaving two or three years later. He enjoyed a chequered career which included tutorship to a lunatic, secretaryship to a general, and a librarianship in Edinburgh. For a time he was attached to the British embassy in France, and became a familiar figure in the Parisian scene. On returning to London, he brought over Jean-Jacques Rousseau, who rewarded him with charges that he was out to kill him.

In his lifetime Hume was more esteemed as a historian than as a philosopher. According to Bertrand Russell, Hume's multi-volume *History of England* was devoted to proving the superiority of Tories to Whigs and of Scotsmen to the English.[2] Hume's *Treatise of Human Nature* (1739-40)[3] proved a great disappointment to the author. He had hoped that it would stir up controversy. Instead, it 'fell dead-born from the press'. This was followed by the famous *Enquiry concerning Human Understanding* (1751), *An Enquiry concerning the Principles of Morals* (1751),[4] *Dialogues Concerning Natural Religion* (written before 1752 but published posthumously in 1779) and *The Natural History of Religion* (1757).[5]

[2] *History of Western Philosophy*, p. 686.
[3] The work is available in various editions including that of A. D. Lindsay (Everyman's Library, (1911) 1964).
[4] A convenient edition of both works is that of L. A. Selby-Bigge (OUP, (1902) 1961). The former work appeared in a first edition of 1748 as *Philosophical Essays concerning Human Understanding*.
[5] The former is available in a paperback version, edited and introduced by Norman Kemp Smith (Library of Liberal Arts, Bobbs-Merrill, Indianapolis and New York, 1947) and the latter appears in the Library of Modern Religious Thought, edited by H. E. Root (Black, 1956).

Perhaps the key to Hume is his scepticism. He used reason to the limits to demonstrate the limitations of reason. He pursued the representative theory of knowledge to the bitter end. For him this meant that you could prove the existence of neither things outside oneself nor even of oneself. For him the 'idea of a substance . . . is nothing but a collection of simple ideas, that are united by the imagination, and have a particular name assigned to them, by which we are able to recall, either to ourselves or others, that collection'.[6] We perceive the data of our senses, but we cannot know that there is anything beyond. The idea of the human self was equally elusive. 'For my part, when I enter most intimately into what I call *myself*, I always stumble on some particular perception or other, of heat or cold, light or shade, love or hatred, pain or pleasure. I never can catch *myself* at any time without a perception, and never can observe anything but the perception.'[7]

This might seem shattering to the unphilosophical reader who had always taken it for granted that there was such a thing as himself which was something more to him than his body. But Hume has even more explosive things in store. His greatest paradox, which he frankly admits that he would not believe himself, if he had not proved it, was his denial of causation.

Before we are reconciled to this doctrine, how often must we repeat to ourselves, *that* the simple view of any two objects or actions, however related, can never give us any idea of power, or of a connexion betwixt them: *that* this idea arises from a repetition of their union: *that* the repetition neither discovers nor causes anything in the objects, but has an influence only on the mind, by that customary transition that it produces: *that* this customary transition is therefore the same with the power and necessity; which are consequently qualities of perceptions, not of objects, and are internally felt by the soul, and not perceived externally in bodies?[8]

In other words, all that we are in the habit of thinking of as

⁶ *Treatise*, I. i. 6.   ⁷ *Ibid.*, I. iv. 6.   ⁸ *Ibid.*, I. iii. 14.

cause and effect is really a matter of sequence. It is not something that happens between objects. It is really a habit of mind.

Hume was never one to be overburdened with an anxiety for consistency. The whole point of a lot of what he was saying was that you just could not be rationally consistent. When he turned to the cosmological argument he accepted the common-sense view of causation, but only to deny that it could be of use in rational proof of God. He rightly doubted whether it was possible 'for a cause to be known only by its effect'.[9] And as we saw when discussing Aquinas, Hume pointed out that we are not entitled to attribute to a cause any capacities other than those necessary to produce the effect in question.[1] In other words, we are not entitled to say that the ultimate cause of one thing is the same as that of another. We are not entitled to say that this is the same as the Christian God. And we are not entitled to attribute to a first cause (even if such a thing could be established) moral attributes. Hume was making a valid point when he pronounced the idea of a first cause to be 'useless; because our knowledge of this cause being derived entirely from the course of nature, we can never, according to the rules of just reasoning, return back from the cause with any new inference, or making additions to the common and experienced course of nature, establish any new principles of conduct and behaviour'.[2] But as we have also seen, he was on less sure ground when he ridiculed the notion of design in the universe.[3]

Hume was also sceptical about miracles. It might have been thought that someone who denied the rationality of causation and in this way undermined the basis of scientific law would hardly presume to invoke scientific law as an ally. But such considerations did not deter Hume. In his classic attack on miracles in Section x of his *Enquiry* he argued that miracles contradicted the laws of nature, and were therefore improbable. Belief must be proportioned to the evidence. A hundred instances of one happening as opposed to only one of the contrary created the presumption that the

[9] *Enquiry*, xi. 115.
[2] *Enquiry*, xi. 110.
[1] See above, p. 27.
[3] See above, p. 29, n. 9.

one was somehow wrong. He concluded: 'A miracle is a viola-
tion of the laws of nature; and as a firm and unalterable experience has established these laws, the proof against a miracle
from the very nature of the fact, is as entire as any argument
from experience can possibly be imagined.'[4]

Turning (though in a rather wholesale way) to the evidence
for miracles, Hume pronounced it to be weak. There was a
general lack of discerning, competent witnesses who had sufficient gumption not to be taken in by frauds.[5] Then we must
take into account the notorious propensity of human nature to
exaggerate, which is bound to shake our confidence in so
many of the tales.[6] We ought also to ask why miracles do not
happen in our own day.[7] Finally, we should remember that
all religions claim miracles, but they cannot all be true.[8]
Thus miracles can never be appealed to as the foundation of
a religion.[9] They can never be used to establish faith. They
can be swallowed only by those who have enough faith
already.[1]

Hume was not yet done with religion. In *The Natural History of Religion* he again took up the cudgels to attack the view
that the original religion of mankind was a rational, moral
monotheism. Hume was no more of an anthropologist than
his opponents. What he did was to suggest a kind of evolutionary hypothesis. By dint of drawing on his knowledge of the
classics, he argued that the gods and goddesses of polytheism
(who were simply magnified human beings) were progres-
sively credited with different attributes until they were eventually rolled into one and credited with infinity. Side by side
with this process went a growth in fanaticism. The more unique
God became, the more bigoted were his devotees (whether
Mohammedan or Christian).

Commenting generally on Hume, Bertrand Russell observes
that 'Hume's philosophy, whether true or false, represents
the bankruptcy of eighteenth-century reasonableness'.[2] It
undermines all rational thought, even though having done
so Hume proceeded to use reason to belabour others. On his

---

[4] *Enquiry*, x. 90.　　　　[5] *Ibid.*, x. 92.　　　　[6] *Ibid.*, x. 93.
[7] *Ibid.*, x. 94.　　　　[8] *Ibid.*, x. 95.　　　　[9] *Ibid.*, x. 99.
[1] *Ibid.*, x. 100, 101.　　　　[2] *History of Western Philosophy*, p. 698.

premises, he is not entitled to say that fire warms, or that water refreshes. This may be a matter of belief but not of reason. For the sceptic about causation there can be no rational grounds for pronouncing about anything.

Hume himself had his own ways of handling his doubts. To quote his own words, 'Most fortunately it happens, that since reason is incapable of dispelling these clouds, Nature herself suffices to that purpose, and cures me of this philosophical melancholy and delirium, either by relaxing this bent of mind, or by some avocation and lively impression of my senses, which obliterate all these chimeras. I dine, I play a game of backgammon, I converse, and am merry with my friends; and when, after three or four hours' amusement, I would return to these speculations, they appear so cold, and strained, and ridiculous, that I cannot find in my heart to enter into them any further.'[3]

No doubt Hume was right in saying, 'There is nothing in any object, considered by itself, which can afford us a reason for drawing a conclusion beyond it'.[4] But when (for example) we have encountered fire so many times that when we touch it, it burns us, we are rationally entitled to say more than simply that burning follows contact with fire. Fire actually causes the burning.

Hume gives the appearance of being disarmingly frank when he acknowledges that 'Nature is always too strong for principle'.[5] At face value it is a salutary warning to both system-builders and system-destroyers against being cocksure in either their sweeping affirmations or their sweeping denials. But Hume's observation here is an implicit claim that his approach (difficult though it be) is the only valid one. In fact, Hume's scepticism is suspect at every major point.

We have already suggested that there is a better alternative to the representative theory of perception, the logical conclusion of which is solipsism.[6] When Hume protested that he could never observe himself, he was assuming that the self was an object that could be observed in the same way that material objects could be perceived. But, in fact, he gives the

[3] *Treatise*, I. iv. 7.   [4] *Ibid.*, I. iii. 12.   [5] *Enquiry*, xii. 128.
[6] See above, pp. 65f.

game away by his repeated use of the word 'I'. The fact that
he is a conscious *subject* capable of introspective reflection
ought to have put him on his guard against a cavalier dis-
missal of the self.

In his treatment of miracles Hume was right to insist that
belief should be proportioned to evidence. The trouble is not
that Hume was too empirical; he was not empirical enough.
At first sight his essay is very plausible. But his technique
is more a case of demolition by bluff and insinuation than of
precise argument. Certainly his warnings against credulity
should be heeded. Even so, we need to be equally on our
guard against accepting uncritically Hume's line of reasoning.
It should not be allowed to pass unnoticed that Hume adroitly
avoids discussion of any actual test-case, say, the physical
resurrection of Jesus, by which Christianity stands or falls.
Instead, he talks in general terms, all the time building up the
impression that no self-respecting intelligent person could
take miracles seriously.

In so doing Hume started a trend which has virtually
established itself as intellectual orthodoxy, thus relieving people
of the need to think about miracles for themselves. Locke had
argued that miracles provide evidence for faith. Hume inverted the procedure. Miracles are so preposterous that only
those who have faith already can accept them.[7] This line of
thought has been accepted not only by agnostics but by many
would-be advocates of the Christian faith down to the present
day. But it was not the point of view of the first Christians
who would have found themselves agreeing with Locke on this
matter.[8] In dealing with an alleged miracle like the resurrection of Jesus, what is needed is not generalizations but a hard
look at the historical evidence and the alternative theories. If
we approach the subject with preconceived ideas (as Hume
virtually admits that he does in making the point that miracles

[7] For a survey of the great debates on miracles see J. S. Lawton, *Miracles
and Revelation* (Lutterworth Press, 1959). B. B. Warfield, *Miracles: Yesterday
and Today, True and False* (Eerdmans, 1953), gives a detailed discussion of
alleged post-biblical miracles. See also C. S. Lewis, *Miracles: A Preliminary
Study* (Bles, 1947, and many reprints), for discussion of criteria.
[8] *Cf.* (*e.g.*) the Gospel accounts of Jesus' resurrection and Luke 24:19;
John 2:11, 23; 3:2; 20:31; Acts 2:22; 4:10; 13:30ff.; Romans 1:4.

violate the laws of nature), then no amount of historical evidence will avail. But if we are willing to take evidence seriously, the result is very different.[9]

But miracles are not the only item on which many thinkers have taken their cue from Hume. It is merely part and parcel of his aversion to the supernatural, of his defiant insistence that our thoughts must not stray beyond the physical realm. David Hume has become almost the patron saint of contemporary agnostic philosophers. In one of his more purple passages, which has become something of a favourite with modern empiricists, he asked: 'When we run over libraries, persuaded of these principles, what havoc must we make? If we take in our hand any volume; of divinity or school metaphysics, for instance; let us ask, *Does it contain any abstract reasoning concerning quantity or number*? No. *Does it contain any experimental reasoning concerning matter of fact and existence*? No. Commit it then to the flames: for it can contain nothing but sophistry and illusion.'[1] The young A. J. Ayer saw in these words already an outline of the programme of Logical Positivism.[2] But on this we shall have more to say presently.[3] Suffice it to say for the present that Hume is important less for any conclusions that he reached than for his historical significance as a patriarch of modern scepticism.

V THE ENGLISH DEISTS AND THEIR OPPONENTS

Hume's half-melancholy, half-jubilant pessimism about the limitations of human thought was not shared by the majority of his contemporaries. As Hume himself was painfully aware, his philosophical writings did not meet with the desired acclamation. Although he is now regarded as the outstanding British philosophical mind of the age, Hume attracted less

[9] The best historical evaluation of the evidence for the resurrection and modern views is probably still James Orr, *The Resurrection of Jesus* (Hodder, 1908). In *History: Sacred and Profane* (Bampton Lectures for 1962, SCM Press, 1964) Alan Richardson gives a massive review of approaches to history and defends the historicity of the resurrection of Jesus on the grounds that the existence and history of the early church are inexplicable without it.
[1] *Enquiry*, xii. Pt. 3, 132. The passage is, in fact, the conclusion of the work.
[2] *Language, Truth and Logic* (Gollancz, 1936, 1946[2]), p. 54.
[3] See below, pp. 168–173.

attention in his day than many who have long since been forgotten. And if to many students empiricism was *the* philosophy
of the eighteenth century, it was not so to most of those who
lived in that age. Among the various philosophies which
clamoured for attention (and indeed got it) was Deism.

The revival of natural theology
In so far as the term Deism is used in common parlance today, it has come to denote the sort of thinking which believes
in a God but which treats him as an absentee landlord. In the
beginning God made the world and set it in motion. But he
has now left it to its own devices, running of its own accord
rather like a clockwork toy. God exists. But he is too remote to
be personally involved in the day-to-day events of his creation.

The Deism of the seventeenth and eighteenth centuries
was very different, at least in its early days. In the hands of a
man like Lord Herbert of Cherbury (1583-1648), who is usually
credited with the creation of Deism, it was more like a revival
of the natural theology of Thomas Aquinas. At any rate, it
adopted what we earlier called the two-storey approach to
theology.[4] In his main work *On Truth* (published in Latin in
Paris, 1624) Lord Herbert argued that certain *common notions*
were imprinted upon the human mind by the hand of God.
They are independent of particular creeds and revelations,
and as such form the basis of all true religion. They included
the belief that God exists, that it is a duty to worship him, that
the practice of virtue and piety are an important part of religion, that sin is evil and must be expiated by repentance and
that there will be rewards and punishments after death.[5]
These ideas have a status comparable with the clear and distinct ideas of Descartes and Spinoza.[6] But, unlike the latter,
Lord Herbert attempted to relate them to the Christian experience of revelation.[7]

Similar ideas were soon to be re-echoed (though in differing
tones) by the Cambridge Platonists. The latter were a small
but not uninfluential group of Anglican divines who flourished
roughly between 1633 and 1688. The most important of them

[4] See above, pp. 32f.   [5] *On Truth*, ix.
[6] See above, pp. 50f., 54.   [7] *On Truth*, x.

were Benjamin Whichcote (1609–83), N. Culverwel (1618?–51?), John Smith (1618–52), Ralph Cudworth (1617–88) and Henry More (1614–87). They were indebted to Platonism, the Neo-Platonists and to Descartes. Human reason was a gift of God. It enabled men to judge the truth of both natural and revealed religion. The Cambridge Platonists combined a distaste for fanaticism and Calvinism with an enthusiasm for Plato. To them the God of Calvinism was highly arbitrary. Their God was essentially rational. To be a good Christian was to share in God's rationality. 'To go against Reason', wrote Whichcote, 'is to go against God; it is the selfsame thing, to do that which the Reason of the case doth require; and that which God Himself doth appoint: Reason is the Divine Governor of Man's Life; it is the very Voice of God.'[8] Not all of their number were prepared to go so far. But the ethos of the group was determined by a common interest in philosophic contemplation and a distrust of fanatical, revealed religion.

A lofty confidence in the powers of reason was also shared by the most eminent scientist of the day, Sir Isaac Newton (1642–1727). Newton was a Cambridge scholar, Master of the Mint and President of the Royal Society from 1703 to his death. Among his scientific achievements were the formulation of the law of gravitation, the discovery of the differential calculus (apparently simultaneously but independently of Leibniz), and the first correct analysis of white light. For Newton, rational reflection upon phenomena led to the conclusion that 'there is a being, incorporeal, living, intelligent, omnipresent'.[9] This conviction was worked out in his *Mathematical Principles of Natural Philosophy* (written in Latin in 1686–87). It rested chiefly upon the admirable order of the universe.

This interest in natural theology continued right through the eighteenth century. It was shared by many who had little in common with Deism proper. And it continued long after both Deism and empiricism had flared up and died down. One of the most celebrated exponents of natural theology in his own day and for some time afterwards was Archdeacon Paley. William Paley (1743–1805) was a Fellow of Christ's

[8] *Aphorism*, 76.   [9] *Optics* (1704), 344.

College, Cambridge, and a popular lecturer in mathematics. After a few years in a north-country parish he became Archdeacon of Carlisle. It was said that it was only latitudinarian views of his younger days that debarred him from even greater preferment.

In later life Paley wrote several works which established themselves as theological textbooks. *The Principles of Moral and Political Philosophy* (1785) was at once adopted at Cambridge. The celebrated *View of the Evidences of Christianity* first appeared in 1794. A Prebendary of Lichfield Cathedral furnished it with suitable essay and examination questions on each page. Paley's last book was *Natural Theology; or, Evidences of the Existence and Attributes of the Deity, Collected from the Appearances of Nature* (1802). By 1820 it had already gone through twenty editions.

Today Paley's name crops up in discussions of philosophical theology as a kind of joke in rather poor taste. The present study has already queried the validity of the traditional proofs of divine existence. But in fairness it must be said that Paley's writings cram in a good deal of hard thinking. The *Evidences* looks frankly at historical evidence and the *Natural Theology* piles up scientific data from nature which point to a creative mind as the author. Paley was no fool. And even though his arguments are not quite so conclusive as he urged, we cannot honestly shrug them off without more ado.

Sceptical Deism

With Lord Herbert, the Cambridge Platonists and Sir Isaac Newton, natural theology was designed to support the Christian religion. The end-product may have been somewhat unorthodox in places, but it was recognizably Christian in intention. But as time went on a different and discordant note began to make itself heard. Instead of being a prop to the Christian faith, natural religion became a rational alternative to irrational, revealed religion. This was the theme of John Toland (1670–1722) whose chief claim to fame was his *Christianity Not Mysterious, Showing that there is Nothing in the Gospel contrary to Reason nor above it, and that no Christian Doctrine can properly be called a Mystery* (1696). A recent historian has described Toland as an Irishman of facile gifts who 'passed through most stages of thought from Romanism to pantheism. His most celebrated work owed its fame less to its intrinsic merits than to its remarkable ability to crystallise views already in the ascendent'.[1] The work was condemned by the Irish Parliament, and the Convocation of Canterbury was deterred from taking legal action only by a technicality. Subsequent writings were even more openly opposed to orthodox Christianity. His *Tetradymus* (1720) contained a natural explanation of the biblical miracles. And in the same year Toland published his *Pantheisticon*, a kind of pagan liturgy, imitating Christian worship but propagating a pantheistic creed.

Natural religion was to receive its most authoritative statement from the pen of Matthew Tindal (1655–1733). This Oxford scholar was already past seventy when he published the work which became known as 'the Bible of Deism', *Christianity as Old as the Creation; or, the Gospel a Republication of the Religion of Nature* (1730). It was not without significance that the title was drawn from a sermon of the orthodox Thomas Sherlock. Similar statements abounded in the utterances of the learned divines of the day. But whereas Sherlock and his colleagues proceeded to draw inferences akin to those of Locke,[2] Tindal inverted the argument. The gospel, he insisted, must not be made to teach anything beyond the grasp of reason and nature. Since orthodox Christianity and rational religion are not coextensive, Tindal proposed to jettison certain expendable doctrines of the former. High on the list were those of the Fall and original guilt,[3] and the atonement.[4] True religion consisted of moderation and of acting according to one's nature.[5]

While Toland was making his pilgrimage from Romanism to pantheism and Tindal was quietly simmering his natural religion, there were others who used Deism as a springboard from which to launch attacks on the veracity of the Bible. The Deists were among the pioneers of radical biblical criti-

[1] Gerald R. Cragg, *Reason and Authority in the Eighteenth Century* (CUP, 1964), p. 67.
[2] See above, pp. 62 ff. [3] *Christianity as Old as the Creation*, p. 340.
[4] *Ibid.*, p. 379. [5] *Ibid.*, p. 14.

cism. In *The Scheme of Literal Prophecy* (1727) Anthony Collins (1676–1729) argued that the book of Daniel must be dated late. Three years earlier the same writer had published *A Discourse of the Grounds and Reasons of the Christian Religion* which provoked no fewer than thirty-five replies in the interval between the two works. In this work he had claimed that the prophecies of the Old Testament do not really fit Christ, and that the New Testament interpretation of them is forced. A kind of sequel to Collins's work was written by Thomas Woolston (1670–1733) in his six *Discourses on the Miracles of our Saviour* (published between 1727 and 1729). Each of the tracts was ironically dedicated to a bishop of the established church, and the argument regularly took the form of a discussion between an imaginary friend and a learned rabbi. Equally regularly the latter gets the best of the argument. Many of the events of Jesus' life are patently absurd if given a literal interpretation. Hell, Satan and the devil are really states of mind. Fifteen Gospel miracles are explained away. But the climax comes in the final *Discourse* where the resurrection of Jesus is depicted as a gigantic piece of fraud, perpetrated by the disciples who in fact stole the body of Jesus.

Replies to Deism

Unlike many arm-chair philosophers, Woolston was a martyr to his beliefs. In 1729 he was tried for blasphemy by the Lord Chief Justice in the Guildhall and sentenced to a year's imprisonment and a fine of £100. Unable to pay the fine, he spent the remainder of his days in prison. But there were others who replied less savagely and more effectively. Among them was Thomas Sherlock (1678–1761), Bishop of Bangor (and later of Salisbury and London). Sherlock was a kind of eighteenth-century C. S. Lewis. His *Trial of the Witnesses of the Resurrection of Jesus* (1729) went through many editions both in England and on the Continent. The book reopens Woolston's case in the form of a private discussion of gentlemen of the Inns of Court. His argument is scrutinized point by point. The motives and the plausibility of the actions of the chief participants are subjected to close questioning. The conclusion is drawn that, whatever else they were, the disciples were sincerely testifying to their experience. The attempt to get round the resurrection of Jesus must either ignore the evidence or explain it away in a manner that raises more difficulties than it solves. Apart from this, one cannot ignore the claims of Christian testimony down the ages to present experience of Christ.

Among those who felt that a philosophical reply to Deism was called for was Joseph Butler (1692–1752) who was successively Bishop of Bristol (1738) and Durham (1750). Today Butler is remembered by his admirers for his *Analogy of Religion* (1736)[6] written amid the pastoral duties of a northern parish, and by his detractors for his curt treatment of John Wesley whom he forbade to preach in his diocese. The bishop saw Wesley as an enthusiast. He sent him away on the grounds that pretending to have extraordinary revelations and gifts of the Holy Spirit was 'a very horrid thing'. But Wesley stayed, on the grounds that his business here on earth was to do what good he could wherever he could; and at the time he thought he could do it most in the bishop's diocese. Perhaps the two men were talking at cross purposes.[7] There are indications that the bishop's personal faith was in the end nearer to Wesley's than this dialogue suggests.[8] But at least it typifies two attitudes to Christianity shared by its adherents and correspondingly two attitudes to Deism.

The full title of Butler's *magnum opus* indicates its scope – *The Analogy of Religion, Natural and Revealed, to the Constitution and Course of Nature.* In his Introduction he admitted that his case could not be proved beyond all doubt. But 'probability is the very guide of life'.[9] And on this basis his book was an attempt to show that there was a real likeness between the beliefs of Christianity and the workings of nature amd providence, and that therefore there was but one single Author of

[6] This has been reprinted numerous times including an Everyman's Library edition (1906 and several reprints). This has a brief but useful introduction and is the edition used here.

[7] For an account of the episode see Rupert E. Davies, *Methodism* (Pelican, 1963), pp. 75f.

[8] *Cf.* Alexander Whyte, *Bishop Butler* (Oliphant, 1903), especially on Butler's deathbed confession (pp. 86ff.).

[9] *The Analogy of Religion*, p. xxv.

both.[1] In a sense, the book was thus the coping-stone of the two-storey view of philosophy and faith.[2] On the other hand, it took for granted the existence of God,[3] and thus for us today begs the crucial question. Although the book did not mention the Deists, there are those who hold that, more than any other single work, it contributed to their downfall. (It may be added that there are those today who see in Butler a guide to show us the way out of the present philosophical and theological morass.[4]) But already Deism was past its peak. It fell to Hume to knock in a coffin nail with his *Natural History of Religion*[5] by pointing out that savages are not enlightened Deists. By this time Deism was dead. It never had been a popular movement. It was made superfluous by the fresh awareness of the living God which had come to light again in the Evangelical Revival.

A perusal of Butler's *Analogy* shows him to have been a man of sincere Christian convictions.[6] But all too often they appear smothered beneath the weight of abstract argument and pedantic verbiage. Two years after the work was published John Wesley was converted. He had already been a missionary in America, and had long been a clergyman of the Church of England. At the same time he was deeply aware of his sin and his remoteness from God. On 24 May 1738 he found peace with God. It was at a meeting which he rather reluctantly attended where someone was reading Luther's Preface to the Epistle to the Romans. 'About a quarter before nine', he later wrote, 'while he was describing the change which God works in the heart through faith in Christ, I felt my heart strangely warmed. I felt I did trust in Christ, Christ alone, for salvation; and an assurance was given me that He had taken away my sins, even mine, and saved me from the law of sin and death.'[7]

As with Luther, so with Wesley and the many who had

---

[1] *Ibid.*, pp. xxviii, 245–253.   [2] See above, pp. 32f..
[3] *The Analogy of Religion*, p. xxviii.
[4] *Cf.* David Jenkins, *Guide to the Debate about God* (Lutterworth Press, 1966), pp. 21ff., 108f.
[5] See above, pp. 67, 70.
[6] *Cf. The Analogy of Religion*, pp. 115, 119–135, 249f.
[7] *Cf.* R. E. Davies, *Methodism*, pp. 43–64, for a brief account of John and Charles Wesley.

similar experiences of God in the Evangelical Revival, this meant that the whole of life must be looked at in the light of this continued experience. The guide to life was the Word of God. Philosophy was set aside. There were more important things to do. No doubt this was true. All the same, it was a pity that no-one in the Evangelical Revival attempted to work out the philosophical implications of their faith (a notable exception was Jonathan Edwards (1703–58) in America). In the meantime, the opponents of Christianity were not inactive, especially on the Continent where secular thinkers eagerly devoured translations of the Deists and where Deism soon entered the bloodstream of philosophy.

VI ENLIGHTENMENT AND SCEPTICISM ON THE CONTINENT

On the Continent rationalism was the new philosophy of the seventeenth century and the orthodoxy of the eighteenth. But already inquiring minds were questioning its methods and results, and seeking alternative, though none less rational, views of reality. In this section we shall mention four: Rousseau, Voltaire, Lessing and Kant. The first two were French, the second two German. In their different ways all four were seeking enlightened views of human knowledge, conduct and religion. All four rejected traditional Christianity. All four pressed further along the course charted by the English Deists.

Rousseau

Jean-Jacques Rousseau (1712–78) was man of many parts. He was in turns a Protestant, a Catholic and a Deist (after his own style). In the course of his restless life he devised a new system of musical notation, wrote an opera which was performed before Louis XV, and tried his hand as an educationist, political theorist, novelist and man of letters. He made and broke numerous friendships with the famous and the not-so-famous. To many he was and is an enigma. He was one of the most eloquent exponents of the dignity of man, and yet his personal relationships were pathetically sordid. His educational theories have found considerable applause in recent years,

and yet Rousseau deposited his own five illegitimate children
in a foundlings' hospital.

Rousseau's literary career began in 1750 with his *Discourse
on the Sciences and the Arts*, a prize essay for the University of
Dijon, in which he argued the thesis that progress corrupts
human morals. This theme was amplified and elaborated in
various subsequent writings. *Julie, or the New Heloïse* (1760)
attacked the conventions of society which divorced love from
marriage. It also contained a defence of natural religion
based upon an allegedly undogmatic interpretation of the
Gospels.

Émile, or On Education (1762)[8] was a philosophical romance.
It sketched an ideal programme of education based upon
natural instincts, free from the corrupting influence of society.
The young Émile is to be brought up in a kind of quarantine
where harmful influences are kept well at bay. Among these
latter are toy soldiers and church bells. Both are symbols of
decadent society, through which the evils of war and established religion might corrupt the young. Émile himself is to
be brought up in the country under the watchful eye of a
private tutor who will see to it that his natural instincts are
naturally led in the right direction.

The fourth book of *Émile* contains a lengthy excursus on religion entitled 'The Creed of a Savoyard Priest'. It was a kind of
eighteenth-century *Honest to God*. Rousseau is not opposed to
religion as such – only to the encrustations of orthodoxy.
It sweeps aside rational, natural theology on the one hand and
revealed religion on the other in favour of a natural religion
based upon feeling. The old priest summons his hearers
to 'seek honestly after truth' and to bring all that they have
ever been taught 'to the bar of conscience and of reason'.[9]
They are left in no doubt what the desired result will be. To
place any reliance upon miracles and events in the past plunges
everything into uncertainty.[1] God is not, in the last analysis, a
fit subject for argument and debate. He is known already in

[8] A handy edition is the translation of Barbara Foxley with an introduction
by A. B. de Monvel (Everyman's Library, (1911) 1966). References below
are to this edition.
[9] *Ibid.*, p, 261.   [1] *Ibid.*, p. 261.

the depths of our being. It is dangerous to speculate; it is much better to repose in God.

> If I have succeeded in discerning these attributes of which I have no absolute idea, it is in the form of unavoidable deductions, and by the right use of my reason; but I affirm them without understanding them, and at bottom that is no affirmation at all. In vain do I say, God is thus, I feel it, I experience it, none the more do I understand how God can be thus.
> In a word: the more I strive to envisage his infinite essence the less do I comprehend it; but it is, and that is enough for me; the less I understand, the more I adore. I abase myself, saying, 'Being of beings, I am because thou art; to fix my thoughts on thee is to ascend to the source of my being. The best use I can make of my reason is to resign it before thee; my mind delights, my weakness rejoices, to feel myself overwhelmed by thy greatness.'[2]

In the same year that he published *Émile* Rousseau also published *The Social Contract*,[3] setting out his theory of the state. The laws of the state were not a matter of divine appointment. They were not to be based upon divine law but upon the will of the people. The only valid basis for a society is for its members to agree to a social pact which will combine freedom with just government in the interests of the majority. The essay was a seminal work of modern secular, democratic thinking and played no small part in paving the way for the French Revolution.

Rousseau's last main works were his *Confessions* (1772)[4] and *The Reveries of the Solitary Stroller* (1778). In a sense, the two were complementary. The former is a massive, introspective piece of autobiography, a striking secular counterpart to Augustine's work of the same title. The latter was his spiritual testament.

[2] *Ibid.*, p. 249.
[3] *Cf. The Social Contract, 1762 and Other Essays* translated by G. D. H. Cole (Everyman's Library, 1913).
[4] A handy edition is that of J. M. Cohen (Pelican, (1953) 1965).

Both the *Émile* and *The Social Contract* were condemned and Rousseau fled from France, though he later managed to return. After his death he exerted tremendous influence on continental literature and politics. He popularized nature, the natural and natural religion in a way far beyond the powers of the English devotees of natural religion. His writings have a persuasive quality about them, making the reader feel that he is not unreasonable in either what he demands or what he throws overboard. He makes man his central point of reference, and yet does not abandon religion. Indeed, his approach to God has the advantage over the older natural theology of taking seriously man's experience of God in the depths of his consciousness, rather than becoming embroiled in merely abstract speculation.

In his approach to religion Rousseau showed himself to be more modern than his immediate successors. His was the pattern followed by the more radical elements in the nineteenth century and the ostensibly *avant garde* today.[5] It also suffers from the same basic weaknesses: an almost naïvely optimistic view of human nature and a bland unwillingness to take seriously Christ and the Christian revelation.

Voltaire

A contemporary of Rousseau's who was, if possible, even more hostile to the church was François-Marie Arouet (1694–1778) who is better known by his pen-name, Voltaire. His life was scarcely less colourful. In 1717 he was imprisoned in the Bastille for ridiculing the Regent. He found himself in prison again after a quarrel, and was exiled in London from 1726 to 1729. Here he came into contact with English Deism which left its profound mark on all his later thinking. Back in Paris he was forced to flee again, and spent the best part of the next fifteen years in Lorraine in the company of the learned Mme. du Châtelet. For a time he was received back in favour under the patronage of Mme. de Pompadour and was named historiographer of France and elected to the French Academy. From 1750 to 1752 he served as philosopher-poet at the court of Frederick the Great of Prussia. In 1755 he moved to Geneva.

[5] See below, pp. 110ff., 194ff., 209ff.

From 1759 to the end of his life he lived on an estate at Ferney over the border in France. The details that filled these years read more like a romance than history.

For fifty years Voltaire dominated the French stage. He wrote close on sixty pieces including some which exist only as fragments or sketches. His tragedies broke new ground in continental literature. Among them was *Zaïre*, where love was admitted as a motive for action (something that was a dramatic novelty in the eighteenth century). His poems include a blasphemous epic on Joan of Arc, *La Pucelle*. His historical writings, though bulky, were undistinguished. But his tales, such as *Candide*, exhibit Voltaire's inimitable irony. Voltaire's largest philosophical work was his *Philosophical Dictionary*, a medley of articles most of which he had written for Diderot's *Encyclopedia*. The latter, which was intended to be a complete review of the arts and sciences of the day, proved to be a major revolutionary intellectual force. Between 1751 and 1780 thirty-five volumes appeared. Contributors included Rousseau and other anti-Catholics, and it was a notable organ for free thought.

Throughout his life Voltaire was bitterly opposed to the Catholic Church against whom he directed his slogan *Écrasez l'infâme*. He saw in its institutions and representatives nothing but deceit and corruption. Nevertheless, he preserved its natural theology. 'I shall always be convinced', he wrote in a letter of 1741, 'that a watch proves a watch-maker, and that a universe proves a God.'[6] Voltaire preferred to call himself a *Theist*, and the nearest he came to setting out what he believed appears under that entry in his *Dictionary*.

He is a true Theist who says to God: 'I adore Thee and serve Thee', and to the Turk, the Chinese, the Indian and the Russian, 'I love you' . . . The Theist is firmly persuaded of the existence of a supreme Being as good as He is powerful, who formed all extended beings, perpetuates their kinds, punishes crime without cruelty, and recompenses virtuous actions with bounty. The Theist does not know how God punishes, or how He favours and pardons, and is not rash

[6] *Cf.* H. N. Brailsford, *Voltaire* (OUP, (1935) 1963), p. 122.

enough to flatter himself that he knows how God acts, but that God acts and that He is just, this he knows. The difficulties that tell against the idea of Providence do not shake his faith, because they are merely difficulties, and not demonstrations ... He is submissive to Providence, and ... believes that it extends to all places and centuries ... To do good is his worship, to submit to God his doctrine.[7]

The dividing-line here between Theism and Deism is scarcely perceptible. Nor does it matter. Voltaire had no use for precise theological definition. In his enlightened view of religion deeds counted more than words. With him humanity weighed more than divinity.

Lessing

The name of Gotthold Ephraim Lessing (1729–81) is one which figures more often in histories of German literature than in histories of philosophy.[8] Lessing played a leading part in founding German national drama with plays like *Emilia Galotti* (1772), *Minna von Barnhelm* (1767) and *Nathan the Wise* (1778–79). He helped free German drama from slavish imitation of French classical tragedy, and introduced the novel practice of writing plays about middle-class people instead of kings and nobility. But Lessing's contribution to the rising tide of scepticism was no smaller than, even though quite differerent from, that of Rousseau and Voltaire.

It was Lessing who published the anonymous, posthumous *Fragments* of H. S. Reimarus (1694–1768), and thus, according to Albert Schweitzer, set in motion the nineteenth-century quest of the historical Jesus.[9] Reimarus's work was originally written for private consumption only. Lessing resorted to the device of pretending that he had accidentally stumbled across them in an ancient manuscript in the course of his duties as

---

[7] *Cf. ibid.*, pp. 123f.

[8] The most important of Lessing's writings on philosophical theology have been translated and given a valuable historical introduction by Henry Chadwick in Lessing's *Theological Writings* (Black, 1956).

[9] *Cf.* Albert Schweitzer, *The Quest of the Historical Jesus: A Critical Study of its Progress from Reimarus to Wrede*, Eng. tr. by W. Montgomery (Black, (1910) 1954), pp. 13–26.

librarian to the Duke of Brunswick at Wolfenbüttel. The true identity of the author was only disclosed long after Lessing's death. Reimarus depicts Jesus as a ranting enthusiast who came to grief at the hands of the political authorities. After his death the disciples, who realized that they had been on to a good thing, lay low for a time and then pretended that Jesus had been raised from the dead and ascended into heaven. Christianity was thus a gigantic fraud, and it was high time that it should be exposed.

Albert Schweitzer regarded the work as 'perhaps the most splendid achievement in the whole course of the historical investigation of the life of Jesus', after which later theology 'appears retrograde'.[1] Reimarus focused attention on eschatology, the nearness of the kingdom of God in Jesus' message. This was the essential. The miraculous and all testimony to the divinity of Christ could be discounted as later embellishment. The result – the picture of a good man who had enthusiasm for life, but whose message was distorted almost beyond recognition by his followers – was curiously like Schweitzer's own conclusions.[2] Organized Christianity is a great mistake, but it is still possible to catch some of Christ's enthusiasms.

In their own day both Reimarus and Schweitzer created a stir. But today it is impossible to share the latter's rosy views of the former's achievements. For one thing they were hardly as novel as Schweitzer makes out. Unsuspecting readers of Schweitzer's eulogistic pages would hardly guess that Reimarus was largely repeating the views of the English Deists, views which were already widely canvassed on the Continent through translations of their works. Nor would they gain any fair impression of the strength of the replies, least of all of that of J. S. Semler, which was a massive point-by-point examination of Reimarus's case. Today few, if any, scholars can be found who are willing to endorse the conclusions of Reimarus, or for that matter of Schweitzer. Reimarus's work was no piece of careful historical investigation. It was written on the assumption that the intervention of the supernatural is impossible in history. But it was by no means the last

[1] *Ibid.*, p. 23.   [2] *Ibid.*, pp. 396–401.

work of this kind to do so. The history of subsequent theology is the history of the debates between those who have wanted to discount the supernatural and those who have insisted that it must be taken into consideration in any assessment of Christianity and the biblical records. Rahmation

Lessing published the notorious *Fragment: On the Intentions of Jesus and his Disciples* in 1778. In the ensuing uproar he endeavoured to sit upon the fence, doing his best to keep the controversy alive without actually committing to print his own personal views. But the previous year he had already entered the general fray provoked by earlier *Fragments* with a pamphlet of his own, *On the Proof of the Spirit and of Power*.[3] Here he endeavoured to outflank the question of history by denying its relevance. If he had lived in the time of Christ, then the fulfilment of prophecy and the performance of miracles would have weighed with him. But now we have only *reports* of such fulfilments and such phenomena. There was now no way of demonstrating their truth. This led Lessing to his celebrated axiom that *accidental truths of history can never become the proof of necessary truths of reason*.[4]

Evidently Lessing was content that he had made a real score here. In fact, he was not saying anything new. On the one hand, he was simply unearthing a rather obvious truism, that historical statements are not of the same order as, say, the statement that *two plus two equal four*. The latter is self-evident. Once we understand the meaning of the word *two* and the other words in the statement we can see its truth. The truth of historical statements depends upon the credibility of the evidence supporting them. On the other hand, in enunciating this axiom Lessing was doing no more than reiterating the basic dogma of continental rationalism since Descartes, that only self-evident, clear and distinct ideas may serve as the basis for a system of thought.[5] Therefore, since history was not of the same order as mathematics it could not provide the basis of a system. Between the two there was an 'ugly, broad ditch' which Lessing pronounced himself in-

[3] Eng. tr. by H. Chadwick in Lessing's *Theological Writings*, pp. 51–56.
[4] *Ibid.*, p. 53.   [5] See above, pp. 50, 54.

capable of jumping.[6] But fortunately, there was no need to attempt the leap. For the truth of religion does not depend upon the accidents of history but upon the truth of its *teaching*.[7] And this can be experienced in life here and now.

Before we leave Lessing it is worth while pausing to reflect upon this claim. For one thing, it exemplifies a trend in continental theology which has persisted from Lessing in the eighteenth century to Bultmann in our own. It argues that, however much we might have to scrap Christianity as history, it is still possible to salvage it by appealing to its teaching. In the nineteenth century liberal rewriters of the life of Jesus tried to do it by appealing to the high moral teaching of Jesus. While Bultmann regards the Gospels as historically dubious productions couched in thoroughly mythical language, the gospel still vindicates itself by means of its existential teaching,[8] *i.e.*, its capacity to illuminate the meaning of life. Lessing himself adopted a combination of the two. The value of any religion (Christian or otherwise) depends upon its capacity to transform life through love. This comes out in the appended dialogue which Lessing called *The Testament of John* and also in his celebrated parable of the three rings in *Nathan the Wise*.[9] There was once an ancient ring which had the power to bestow upon its owner the gift of being loved by God and man. This was passed on down many generations until it came into the possession of a father who had three sons equally dear to him. To resolve the dilemma, he had two replicas made and gave a ring to each son. After his death all three claimed to possess the true ring. But as with religion, the original cannot be traced. Historical investigation is of no avail. But a wise judge counsels each son to behave as if he had the true ring and prove it by deeds of love. Thus in the end it will not matter who had the original. The three sons represent Judaism, Christianity and Islam. One day they will transcend themselves and become united in a universal religion of love.[1]

[6] Lessing's *Theological Writings*, p. 55. [7] *Ibid.*
[8] See below, pp. 186ff. [9] Act III, Scene 7.
[1] This theme reappears in *The Education of the Human Race*, 1780 (*Theological Writings*, pp. 82–98).

As Lessing said elsewhere, 'Religion is not true because the evangelists and apostles taught it; on the contrary, they taught it because it was true. The written traditions must be interpreted by their inward truth and no written traditions can give religion any inward truth if it has none.'[2] Lessing's theme has a lofty ring about it. It re-echoes the refrain of Matthew Tindal.[3] But it must be asked whether it is as true as it appears at first sight. It makes the gratuitous assumption that religions are all about the same thing, and that they all equally possess the power to reconcile men to God. It assumes (as Lessing and the rationalists have done all along) that history cannot be of decisive importance for religion, that no person or event in time can affect the central questions of religion. It fails to recognize that historical evidence has its own compulsion. To fail to recognize it incurs the same charges of intellectual obscurantism and evasion of evidence that failure to take seriously any other kind of evidence involves. Of course, religion is not true merely because the evangelists and apostles taught it. They taught it because it was true. But what they taught was not a kind of general truth equally accessible to all regardless. They were bearing witness to what God was saying and doing and had done in Christ. Lessing talked about this. He even wrote what he considered to be his best theological work on the study of the Gospels.[4] But in the last analysis Lessing's philosophical theology was not an attempt to grapple with the event of Christ, but a massive exercise in evasive tactics, all designed to avoid taking that event seriously.

Kant

It is arguable whether Immanuel Kant should be placed in the eighteenth or the nineteenth century. His dates (1724–1804) put him in both. And so does his thought. In some ways it

[2] Lessing's *Editor's Counter-Propositions* appended to the *Fragment* on Jesus (*cf. Theological Writings*, p. 18).
[3] 'The Christian Deists . . . believe not the Doctrines because contain'd in Scripture, but the Scripture on account of the Doctrines' (*Christianity as Old as the Creation*, 1730, p. 336). See above, p. 77.
[4] *New Hypothesis Concerning the Evangelists Regarded as Merely Human Historians*, 1778 (*cf. Theological Writings*, pp. 65–81).

represents the climax of eighteenth-century rationalism and empiricism. In other ways it is curiously modern. His scepticism cast a long shadow over the nineteenth century. Kant personifies modern man's confidence in the power of reason to grapple with material things and its incompetence to deal with anything beyond.

Kant's life was outwardly uneventful. He was born and died at Königsberg in East Prussia. He was the son of a saddler of Scottish ancestry and had a pietistic upbringing. He was a student at the University of Königsberg and, apart from a period as a private tutor, spent well-nigh the rest of his life there. In 1755 he became an unsalaried lecturer and continued in that capacity for the next fifteen years. In 1770 he was elected professor of logic and metaphysics, and despite a weak constitution continued active in the post until a year or two before his death. His private life presents a curious, paradoxical picture. He was fond of books on travel, but never travelled far. He enjoyed company, but never married. The pattern of his life was strictly regulated.

The idea of the world coming of age is frequently attributed to Dietrich Bonhoeffer as if it were some brilliant new insight of the twentieth century. In fact, it goes back to Kant. In 1784 in a magazine article Kant asked himself the question: *What is Enlightenment?*[5] The answer that he gave was that enlightenment was man's emergence from his self-inflicted immaturity – from his reliance upon external authorities and his reluctance to use his own understanding. The motto of enlightenment was: Dare to use your own understanding. This applies especially to religion. No generation should be bound by the creeds and dogmas of bygone generations. To be so bound is an offence against human nature whose destiny lies in progress. We do not yet, Kant admitted, live in an enlightened age. But we do live in the age of enlightenment, the age of Frederick the Great! Mankind is in the process of coming of age, refusing to take external authorities and judging everything by its own understanding.

Kant's life and thought were a series of variations on this

[5] 'Beantwortung der Frage: Was ist Aufklärung?' *Berlinische Monatsschrift*, December 1784 (*Gesammelte Schriften*, Berlin, VIII, p. 35).

single theme. By the time he had written this article he had
already published his *Critique of Pure Reason* (1781),[6] a work
in which he had attempted to set out an enlightened approach
to human knowledge. A dozen years later he wrote to the
Göttingen professor of theology, C. F. Stäudlin, of his great
plan for an enlightened reappraisal of the main areas of
human activity.

> My longstanding plan for the reappraisal, incumbent upon
> me of the field of pure philosophy centred upon dealing
> with three tasks: (1) What can I know? (Metaphysics) (2)
> What should I do? (Ethics) (3) What may I hope? (Reli-
> gion); upon which the fourth should now follow: What is
> man? (Anthropology . . .). With the accompanying work
> . . . I have tried to complete the third part of my plan. In
> this work conscientiousness and true respect for the Christian
> religion but also the principle of a proper freedom of thought
> have led me to conceal nothing. On the contrary, I have
> presented everything openly, as I believe I see the possible
> union of the latter with the purest practical reason.[7]

The work in question was *Religion within the Limits of Reason
Alone* (1793).[8] It was a work which drew upon Kant the
personal censure of the king of Prussia. This in turn constrained
from Kant an ambiguous declaration to the effect that his
purpose was not to condemn but to commend Christianity.[9]
But the reason for its commendation was rather a backhanded
compliment. He pronounced the Bible to be the best vehicle
for the instruction of the public in a truly moral religion.

In the meantime Kant had duly turned his attention to
ethics, first in his *Fundamental Principles of the Metaphysic of
Morals* (1785) and then in the great *Critique of Practical Reason*

---

[6] A second revised edition was published in 1787. The best English
translation is that of Norman Kemp Smith (Macmillan, (1929) 1964[9]).
Page numbers given in subsequent footnotes are to this edition.

[7] Letter dated 4 May 1793 (*Gesammelte Schriften*, XI, p. 429, No. 574).

[8] Eng. tr. with introduction and notes by T. M. Greene and H. H. Hudson
and essay on 'The Ethical Significance of Kant's *Religion*' (1934, Harper,
New York, 1960). Page numbers given below are to this edition.

[9] *Ibid.*, p. xxxv.

(1788).[1] These were followed in 1790 by the *Critique of Judgment*[2] which handled questions of aesthetics and purpose in the universe. The long-awaited inquiry into *Anthropology* (on which Kant had lectured for more than twenty years) finally appeared in 1798. By this time he had retired from active lecturing.

In a historical survey of these proportions it is impossible to give more than the barest outline of a man's thought. The difficulties are made many times more acute in the case of a thinker of the stature of Kant. We shall therefore confine attention to four aspects of his thought: (a) Kant's view of knowledge, (b) his rejection of the traditional proofs of the existence of God, (c) his moral approach to God and (d) his evaluation of Christianity.

a. Kant's view of knowledge. Kant's view of knowledge was a mixture of rationalism and empiricism. He had been educated in the rationalist tradition, but fairly early on he had read Hume who (in his own phrase) had awoken him from his dogmatic slumbers.[3] For a time he swung over to Hume and became convinced that all speculation about the great metaphysical themes of God, freedom and immortality was a waste of time.[4] But over the years he worked out his own critical philosophy which investigated the nature and scope of human knowledge. Kant agreed with the empiricists in saying that 'all our knowledge begins with experience', but differed from them in insisting that 'it does not follow that it all arises out of experience'.[5] The 'raw material' of knowledge comes from outside us.[6] But the mind also played a part in processing that material by means of its own built-in concepts. Kant's aim in the *Critique of Pure Reason* was to examine this processing.

[1] Eng. tr. of both works by T. K. Abbott (Longmans, (1909[6]) 1963). This edition includes other moral writings including parts of *The Metaphysic of Morals* (1797).
[2] Eng. tr. by J. C. Meredith (OUP, (1928) 1964[5]).
[3] The phrase occurs in the introduction to the *Prolegomena to Any Future Metaphysics* (1783), a shorter work designed to act as an introduction to the *Critique of Pure Reason*.
[4] Cf. *Dreams of a Ghost-Seer, elucidated by Dreams of Metaphysics* (1766).
[5] *Critique of Pure Reason*, Introduction, p. 41.   [6] *Ibid.*, p. 42.

The general reader who has no special interest in Kant's view of knowledge may be advised to skip the next few paragraphs. But others may welcome some elucidation of Kant's terminology, for it is impossible to go far in Kant without some understanding of his vocabulary.[7]

Kant formulated the central question of the *Critique of Pure Reason* in the following words: 'How are *a priori* synthetic judgments possible?'[8] To grasp what he means, one has also to grasp the basic meaning of two sets of terms. The first is the distinction between *synthetic* and *analytic*.

> In all judgments in which the relation of a subject to the predicate is thought . . . this relation is possible in two different ways. Either the predicate B belongs to the subject A, as something which is (covertly) contained in this concept A; or B lies outside the concept A, although it does indeed stand in connection with it. In the one case I entitle the judgment analytic, in the other synthetic.[9]

Thus, to say that 'a rainy day is a wet day' is to make an *analytic* statement. The notion of 'wet day' is already contained in that of 'rainy day'. Such a statement is also said to be *necessary*. It is necessarily true. To deny it would involve a contradiction in terms. But to say that 'Tuesday was a wet day' is to make a *synthetic* statement. Such statements are not necessarily true. For Tuesday could have been a dry day, or any other kind of day. In synthetic statements the predicate says something about the subject which is not already contained in the notion of the subject. To deny it is not to involve oneself in a contradiction in terms. Its truth or otherwise depends on whether what is said corresponds with facts. In other words, to test whether a *synthetic* statement like 'Tuesday was a wet day' is true, you have to check on what people remember about Tuesday.

The other set of terms which require definition is *a priori* and *a posteriori*. *A priori* knowledge was knowledge which was

---

[7] See the Introductions and Prefaces to the *Critiques* where Kant himself defines his terms.
[8] *Critique of Pure Reason*, Introduction, p. 55.   [9] *Ibid.*, p. 48.

'absolutely independent of all experience'. This contrasts with *a posteriori* knowledge which is empirical knowledge, knowledge which is 'possible only . . . through experience'.[1] As an example of the former we might instance the sum $2+2 = 4$. Although we might work out the answer by doing it on our fingers, the truth of it does not ultimately depend upon experience.[2] On the other hand, *a posteriori* knowledge – knowledge of people, places and things – depends upon experience.

To some extent these pairs of concepts overlap. Analytic knowledge is also *a priori* knowledge. It is a matter of logical definition of terms and concepts. Synthetic knowledge is also *a posteriori*. It involves observation and experience through the senses. But Kant believed that knowledge was also both synthetic and *a priori*. Hence the central question of his book. His aim was to examine the factors involved in this kind of knowledge. It affected both metaphysical and physical knowledge. For before one could safely embark upon these enterprises it was necessary to embark upon a *critique of pure reason*, to examine the scope and limitations of human thought.[3] Having done so, Kant ventured to claim 'that there is not a single metaphysical problem which has not been solved, or for the solution of which a key at least has not been supplied'.[4] As we shall see in a few moments, this triumphal cry is to be taken not as an indication that all metaphysical problems are soluble. It was in fact the reverse. In effect, Kant is saying, 'Hands off metaphysics!' For metaphysics are completely beyond the grasp of the human mind.

Kant's view of knowledge may be summed up by saying that its raw material consists of the outside world perceived by the senses (the synthetic element), but that this is inevitably processed by the human mind (the *a priori* element). In perceiving the raw material the mind employs the Forms of Intuition

[1] *Ibid.*, pp. 42f.
[2] It should be noted that Kant himself regarded mathematical judgments as synthetic (*ibid.*, pp. 52–55). On this point see A. J. Ayer, *Language, Truth and Logic* (1946[2]), p. 78.
[3] *Ibid.*, Preface to First Edition (p. 9). By the term *pure* Kant meant containing 'no admixture of anything empirical' (p. 43).
[4] Preface to First Edition, p. 10.

of time and space.[5] It also makes use of Categories or the Pure Concepts of the Understanding, such as quantity and quality.[6] The result is that the mind does not actually perceive things as they are in themselves. For 'while much can be said *a priori* as regards the form of appearances, nothing whatsoever can be asserted of the thing in itself, which may underlie these appearances'.[7] It is as if we look at everything through rose-tinted spectacles. We see things, but they are always coloured. Just so, Kant argued, the mind looks at everything through its Forms of Intuition and Categories of Understanding. Inevitably, the mind conditions everything that it encounters.

This doctrine had far-reaching consequences. It was intended to be a safeguard against Hume's scepticism, but the price that it paid for this defence was further scepticism. It has often been remarked that Hume gave Kant the problem of knowledge and Kant gave it back as if it were the solution. What Kant has achieved is in fact a more sophisticated form of the representative theory of knowledge. And apart from the fact that it is not a comprehensive theory of knowledge,[8] it is open to the same basic objections.[9]

Thus, what we call knowledge of things is to some extent illusory. When the scientist (or, for that matter, the proverbial man in the street) talks about time and space or cause and effect, he is not talking about something which is actually there or happens. He is really talking about his own habits of mind. He cannot help talking in this way. But if Kant is right, there is no way of knowing whether such concepts are really applicable to things-in-themselves. In the last analysis. the latter remain strictly unknowable.

If Kant was sceptical about the possibility of knowing material things as they are in themselves, he was doubly so

[5] *Ibid.*, 'Transcendental Aesthetic', pp. 67–91.

[6] *Ibid.*, 'Transcendental Analytic', pp. 111–119. Kant listed twelve such categories in four groups of three: *Quantity* (Unity, Plurality, Totality), *Quality* (Reality, Negation, Limitation), *Relation* (Inherence and Subsistence, Causality and Dependence, Community) and *Modality* (Possibility-Impossibility, Existence-Non-existence, Necessity-Contingency).

[7] *Ibid.*, 'Transcendental Aesthetic', p. 87.

[8] *Cf.* S. Körner, *Kant* (Pelican, 1955), pp. 22ff.

[9] See above, pp. 66, 68.

about realities which allegedly transcend the material. The Forms of Intuition are 'valid only for objects of possible experience'.[1] As soon as the human mind tries to press beyond the material order it lands itself in *Antinomies* or irreconcilable self-contradictions.[2] The lesson to be learnt from this is that the mind cannot attain to rational knowledge of anything beyond its immediate experience of the world.

b. Kant's rejection of the traditional proofs of the existence of God. In view of all this, it is not surprising that Kant goes on to subject the traditional proofs of natural theology to merciless criticism. He points out that these are three in number and only three: the *ontological*, the *cosmological* and the *teleological* (or, as he calls it, the *physico-theological*) proof.[3] And he tackles them in this order.

In dealing with the *ontological* argument, he points out that it just will not do to assume (as Descartes did[4]) that the mere definition of a necessary being implies its existence in the same way that the definition of a triangle implies that it has three angles. The proof only works in this way if we assume that such a being exists in the first place.[5]

If we speak of God as the most real being, the *ens realissimum*,

---

[1] *Critique of Pure Reason*, 'Transcendental Aesthetic', p. 91.
[2] Kant expounded four main Antinomies (corresponding to the four main types of Categories): that the world was both finite and infinite, that every substance is made up of simple parts and that nothing is made up of simple parts, that there is freedom and that there is no freedom, that the world posits a necessary being and that no such being exists (*ibid.*, 'Transcendental Dialectic', pp. 396–421).
[3] *Ibid.*, 'Transcendental Dialectic', p. 500.
[4] See above, p. 51.
[5] 'The absolute necessity of the judgment is only a conditioned necessity of the thing, or of the predicate in the judgment. The above proposition does not declare that three angles are absolutely necessary, but that, under the condition that there is a triangle (that is, that a triangle is given), three angles will necessarily be found in it. So great, indeed, is the deluding influence exercised by this logical necessity that, by the simple device of forming an *a priori* concept of a thing in such a manner as to include existence within the scope of its meaning, we have supposed ourselves to have justified the conclusion that because existence belongs to the object of this concept . . . we are also of necessity . . . required to posit the existence of its object' (*ibid.*, pp. 501f.).

D

and then claim that his existence is involved in this definition, we must ask whether we are making an *analytic* or a *synthetic* statement.

> If it is analytic, the assertion of the existence of the thing adds nothing to the thought of the thing ... (it) is nothing but a miserable tautology ... But if, on the other hand, we admit, as every reasonable person must, that all existential propositions are synthetic, how can we profess to maintain that the predicate of existence cannot be rejected without contradiction? This is a feature which is found only in analytic propositions, and is indeed precisely what constitutes their analytic character.[6]

In short, the argument no more proves the existence of God than the thought of having a hundred thalers in the bank implies that one must actually have such an amount.[7] We can no more extend our stock of insight 'by mere ideas, than a merchant can better his position by adding a few noughts to his cash account'.[8]

Turning to the *cosmological* argument, Kant formulates it like this: 'If anything exists, an absolutely necessary being must also exist. Now I, at least, exist. Therefore an absolutely necessary being exists.'[9] The argument is plausible, but it is fraught with many 'pseudo-rational principles'.[1] In particular it makes tacit use of the worthless ontological argument in order to convert the mere notion of a necessary being into an actually necessary being.[2] Furthermore, 'The principle of causality has no meaning and no criterion for its application save only in the sensible world.'[3] Nor is it possible to conceive what such a being is like. There are many forces in nature which 'manifest their existence through certain effects, [but which] remain for us inscrutable; for we cannot track them sufficiently far by observation'.[4]

---

[6] *Ibid.*, p. 504. For the distinction between *analytic* and *synthetic* statements see above, p. 94. An 'existential proposition' is a statement about something or someone whose existence is implied in what is said.
[7] *Ibid.*, p. 505.   [8] *Ibid.*, p. 507.   [9] *Ibid.*, p. 508.
[1] *Ibid.*, p. 509.   [2] *Ibid.*, p. 511.   [3] *Ibid.*
[4] *Ibid.*, p. 514.

The *teleological* argument, Kant admits, commands respect. It gives purpose and meaning to life and to scientific investigation. In the world we find clear signs of order and purpose. They are such that the things in this world could not have devised themselves. They point beyond themselves to a wise, intelligent free being. In view of the reciprocal relations existing between different parts of the world, it may be inferred that there is only one such being and not several.[5] But in the last analysis Kant believes that this argument is really only another form of the cosmological proof, and the latter 'is only a disguised ontological proof'.[6] They do not, therefore, afford rational, compelling proof of the existence of God.

But if the objective reality of God cannot be proved, it 'also cannot be disproved by merely speculative reason'.[7] Although Kant pronounces the efforts of natural theology to be 'null and void',[8] he does not close the door altogether on God. He believes that his work has shown not only that speculations 'which profess to lead us beyond the field of possible experience are deceptive and without foundation; it likewise teaches us this further lesson, that human reason has a natural tendency to transgress these limits, and that transcendental ideas are just as natural to it as the categories are to understanding'.[9] This tendency can be both good and bad. It is bad when it leads us to think of God, freedom and immortality as if they were real objects knowable by reason. In fact, they are Regulative Ideas which are not objects as such, but which give purpose and meaning to our thought and our lives. As Kant suggests, in winding up his discussion of the existence of God in the *Critique of Pure Reason*, they have their place not in the realm of speculative thought but in the realm of ethics.[1]

c. Kant's moral approach to God. Kant subjected ethics to the same enlightened, rational scrutiny that we have just seen him bringing to the question of knowledge and natural theology. If modern man is really to live as if he has come of age, he

---

[5] For the above points see *ibid.*, p. 521.   [6] *Ibid.*, p. 524.
[7] *Ibid.*, p. 531.   [8] *Ibid.*, p. 528.   [9] *Ibid.*, p. 532.
[1] *Ibid.*, pp. 528, 531.

must throw away all external and pseudo authorities. He must do what his own reason tells him is right. He has no need of God in the capacity of either a heavenly adviser or provider of incentives. He must do what his own reason tells him is right. This is the theme of the opening words of *Religion within the Limits of Reason Alone*.

> So far as morality is based upon the conception of man as a free agent who, just because he is free, binds himself through his reason to unconditioned laws, it stands in need neither of the idea of another Being over him, for him to apprehend his duty, nor of an incentive other than the law itself, for him to do his duty.[2]

Nevertheless, Kant believed that this conception of ethics pointed towards God.

Before we ask how Kant was pointed in this direction and whether he was justified in being so pointed, it is worth while stopping to look at Kant's ethics. For even though few people would take it over today in its neat form, it has passed unconsciously into the blood-stream of the secular humanitarianism which believes in doing duty for its own sake.

Kant drew a distinction between what he called the *hypothetical* and *categorical* imperatives.[3] An imperative is an objective moral principle formulated in the form of a command. 'The former represent the practical necessity of a possible action as means to something else that is willed.'[4] In other words (though they are not Kant's): 'If you want to learn judo, get an expert teacher.' Characteristic of this kind of imperative is the fact that not everybody wants it. Nor is it binding upon all. It is relative to individual needs and circumstances.

The *categorical* imperative is very different. Kant believed that it was a rational principle, valid under all circumstances. He formulated it in two ways:

[2] Preface to First Edition (Eng. tr. by Greene and Hudson, p. 3).
[3] *Fundamental Principles of the Metaphysic of Morals* (Eng. tr. by T. K. Abbott, pp. 30ff.).
[4] *Ibid.*, p. 31.

Act only on that maxim whereby thou canst at the same time will that it should become a universal law.

Act as if the maxim of thy action were to become by thy will a universal law of nature.[5]

It was not a case of acting according to conscience. It was a matter of coldly and deliberately following a rational principle. The *categorical* imperative has with Kant the same status that the clear and distinct ideas have for Descartes and the rationalists. Kant accepts it as self-evidently true.

As instances of how it works out Kant mentions suicide, lying, laziness and self-seeking.[6] If everyone did these, life would be impossible. Whether it gives a really adequate basis for ethics is another matter. It would need restatement to cater for various contingencies such as that of the melancholic who wished the whole world to come to an end. But it has the merit of making the virtue of an action not dependent upon its results. For an action could be well meant and yet misfire. It recognizes the sense of obligation that people feel, that it is right to love and serve others as themselves. This obligation does not depend upon circumstances and personal likes and dislikes. But in the last analysis it does not say *why* we should act in this way. It appears to take it for granted.

If the reply to this is that we should obey the *categorical* imperative because it makes life a lot more pleasant for everyone, then it must be said that the *categorical* imperative is only a disguised form of the *hypothetical* imperative. The only difference is that it operates on a grander scale. And if this is the case, it is not universally binding, but simply an expression of what the speaker happens to think desirable. But if it be said that we should obey the *categorical* imperative for its own sake, then we are guilty of oversimplification. For it is not enough simply to ask what we should do. The imperative also raises the question, what kind of authority is it that stands over and above me and which demands that I should behave like this? In other words, we are confronted with the transcendent. It is

[6] *Ibid.*, pp. 38, 39. In Kant's language a *maxim* is a moral principle that one adopts for oneself as distinct from a *law* which is valid for everyone.
[6] *Ibid.*, pp. 47ff.

not, as Kant told his readers, an *autonomous* principle of the will,[7] but something which comes to man from outside.[8]

It is worth while comparing Kant and Jesus at this point. Jesus taught that the second great commandment was to love one's neighbour as oneself.[9] In saying this he was extending the teaching of the Old Testament revelation.[1] He was also giving expression to an awareness of an obligation which men feel generally, whether they are religious or not and whether they in fact meet it or not. But Jesus reminded his hearers of an even higher obligation – to love God with the whole of their being.[2] This too was part of the Old Testament revelation to Israel.[3] But again men generally have an awareness of obligation towards God. This is true not only of Christianity but of other religions. It is true whether men take this obligation seriously or not. It is something which is there at the back of their minds, and it is something which Kant and many others have discreetly ignored in working out their philosophical systems.

In his *Critique of Practical Reason*[4] Kant explained how God fitted into his picture. God is given (together with the notions of freedom and immortality) the status of a Postulate of Pure Practical Reason.[5]

The fact of human freedom cannot be proved. From a scientific point of view, Kant argues, our actions are subject to laws of causality. But moral obligation introduces a new factor. Obligation implies freedom to obey or disobey the moral law.

---

[7] *Ibid.*, p. 51.

[8] This point was clearly seen by J. A. T. Robinson in *Honest to God*, p. 113. But Robinson rejects Kant's ethics as a hangover from Christianity, a piece of 'secularized deism'.

[9] Matthew 22:39; *cf.* 19:19; Mark 12:31; Luke 10:27.

[1] Leviticus 19:18; *cf.* the last six of the Ten Commandments (Exodus 20:12–17; Deuteronomy 5:16–21).

[2] Matthew 22:37f.; Mark 12:29f.; Luke 10:27.

[3] Deuteronomy 6:4–9; *cf.* the first four of the Ten Commandments (Exodus 20:1–11; Deuteronomy 5:6–15).

[4] In Kant's terminology *practical* reason is concerned with the rational grounds on which the will acts, as distinct from *pure* reason, which is the mind's capacity to know things.

[5] For a brief summary of Kant's position see *Critique of Practical Reason* (Eng. tr. by T. K. Abbott, pp. 229f.).

Ought implies can. In this sense we transcend our spatio-temporal existence. But the notion of freedom does not entitle us, Kant believes, to erect a complete metaphysical system upon it. Freedom is a presupposition of ethics. It is a postulate of practical reason.

Kant discusses God and immortality in the context of what he calls the *summum bonum*, or ultimate good. It is the ideal state where virtue and happiness coincide.[6] However, it is all too painfully obvious that the two do not coincide in this life. Moreover, human attainment of it is conceivable only if man is granted an infinite existence.[7] And to unite happiness and virtue, we must also assume 'the existence of a cause of the whole of all nature, distinct from nature itself, and containing the principle of this connexion, namely, of the exact harmony of happiness with morality'.[8] In other words, God.

d. Kant's evaluation of Christianity. This view of God is re-echoed in *Religion within the Limits of Reason Alone*. Morality does not need religion, but it points to it. It leads to 'the idea of a highest good in the world for whose possibility we must postulate a higher, moral, most holy, and omnipotent Being which alone can unite the two elements of this highest good' (duty and happiness).[9]

This is the starting-point for Kant's reappraisal of Christianity. As his title suggests, his aim is to strip Christianity of such extras as faith and belief in a supernatural God who personally intervenes in human affairs. In its place he wants to put a sober religion, ready for use by the modern enlightened man. The result is a fully attenuated Deism.

The Christian view of revelation – of God revealing himself in history and personal experience through events and his Word – is replaced by reason. Bible stories are all right for the ignorant masses. They present a graphic way of teaching them morality. But in the last analysis it is 'universal human reason' which is 'the supremely commanding principle'.[1]

The Christian view of grace and salvation – that God does for man what man cannot do for himself by blotting out his

---

[6] *Ibid.*, p. 206.   [7] *Ibid.*, pp. 218 ff.   [8] *Ibid.*, p. 221.
[9] *Religion within the Limits of Reason Alone*, pp. 4f.   [1] *Ibid.*, p. 152.

sins and restoring him to fellowship with himself out of pure
love – is replaced by an unbending religion of self-help.

> True religion is to consist not in the knowing or considering
> of what God does or has done for our salvation but in what
> we must do to become worthy of it . . . and of its necessity
> every man can become wholly certain without any Scriptural
> learning whatever.[2]
> Man himself must make or have made himself into whatever,
> in a moral sense, whether good or evil, he is or is to become.[3]

In Kant's religion Jesus is 'the personified idea of the good
principle', the incarnation of moral good who 'has come down
to us from heaven'.[4] Curiously enough, neither here nor anywhere in his writings does Kant seem to have been able to
bring himself to pronounce the name of Jesus. Instead, he
talks abstractly about one who represents 'the ideal of a
humanity pleasing to God' and who thus sets men an example
to follow.[5]

It would be interesting to pursue this theme and see how
at every end and turn Kant attempts to rationalize and
secularize the Christian faith.[6] But it is high time to bring to a
close this discussion of Kant and with it our account of philosophy and faith from the Reformation to the Age of Enlightenment.

Few contemporaries were so openly consistent in pursuing
the ideals of enlightenment. Kant put into print his own programme for bringing Christian faith into line with what he
conceived to be modern secular thought. He had no time for
organized religion. When the University of Königsberg
solemnly processed to the university church, Kant would duly
take his place in its ranks. But when the procession reached
the church door, he quietly dropped out and went off home
around the back.

Kant was not ready to jettison religion completely. Yet for

[2] *Ibid.*, p. 123; *cf.* p. 110.   [3] *Ibid.*, p. 40.
[4] *Ibid.*, p. 54.   [5] *Ibid.*, p. 55.
[6] For a brief comparison see Jacques de Senarclens, *Heirs of the Reformation*,
Eng. tr. by G. W. Bromiley (SCM Press, 1963), pp. 55–64.

all practical purposes, his was a religion without God, and indeed a religion without religion. It involved no worship. Its central ideas could be practised by any, whether they were religious or not. God is relegated to the status of a secondary hypothesis.

Kant rightly rejected natural theology. His acute mind was quick to spot flaws in the traditional proofs of God. But what he put in their place was scarcely more seaworthy. His Postulates of Practical Reason look suspiciously like pieces of wishful thinking. The fact that we as men fail to reach perfection in this life gives us no grounds to expect a second chance to do better. The fact that virtue and happiness do not perfectly coincide in this life is of itself not sufficient grounds to expect a future state of affairs where they will.

Earlier on we suggested that Kant's view of the role of reason in ethics is really a hangover from seventeenth-century rationalism. He believed that reason itself prescribed the course of duty. He behaves as if the *categorical* imperative were a clear and distinct, self-evident idea. But as we saw, it is not.[7] It is either a disguised form of the *hypothetical* imperative, or it is the rational expression of an awareness of an obligation which comes to man from outside himself. But in this case reason does not prescribe, but recognizes a reality which is above reason. Man is not the source of his own authority. There is something over and above him which impels him to think and act in this way.

It is hardly to be wondered at that those who found congenial Kant's view of man's autonomy could readily dispense with his view of God. But are we compelled to accept Kant's starting-point? In making man and human reason his central point of reference Kant was simply following the course charted by Descartes. What Kant does and, in their different ways, all the thinkers in the rationalist, enlightened tradition do, is to work out a framework of thought and then try to fit religion into it. If the Christian faith does not quite fit, then so much the worse for it. Philosophy becomes a Procrustean bed. Whatever is made to lie on it has either to be stretched or chopped about to be made to fit. The difficulty is that one

[7] See above, p. 101.

cannot always get at truth by means of such preconceived ideas. Hume once observed in a moment of candour that nature is always too strong for principle.[8] He might equally have said that religion is too strong for preconceived philosophies.

When one has a theory that does not fit all the facts, one has the choice of modifying (or even dropping) the theory or of ignoring the facts. In dealing with religion Kant (like so many philosophers of the seventeenth and eighteenth centuries) opted for the latter. His philosophy takes no account of Christian experiences of God and of the historical testimony of the Bible. His method was rather like writing a book about the Himalayas with the deliberate intention of ignoring Everest. Kant was not the first to do this. And though there were others in the nineteenth century, like Schleiermacher and Kierkegaard, who raised their voices in protest, he was by no means the last.

[8] See above, p. 71.

3 THE NINETEENTH-CENTURY FERMENT

In popular imagination the Victorian Age was an era in which all and sundry conformed to the same rigid moral code and practised the same unbending, joyless religion. In fact, the nineteenth century was an age of belief and an age of unbelief. It witnessed unparalleled missionary expansion, and saw religious revivals in various quarters of the globe. The church pews of the western world were still filled with the ranks of the devout. But outside the churches there was no lack of strident voices assuring the faithful that they were deluding themselves. And even inside the churches could be heard the cultured tones of those who had reached the conclusion that Christianity could no longer be believed in quite the same way ever again.

The nineteenth century has passed through the portals of history into the realms of examination syllabuses and academic research. At present the nineteenth-century church is undergoing extensive reappraisal. The output of scholarly studies of its institutions, characters and ideas has stepped up appreciably over the past decade not only here but also on the Continent and in the United States. It was not all that long ago that lecturers used to speak as if the entire intellectual landscape of the nineteenth century was dominated by the twin figures of Kant and Hegel. Today the scene looks less like two mountains (surrounded of course by their foothills) than a jungle in which over-all patterns are not easy to discern.

Modern scholars no longer talk of Kant as *the* philosopher of Protestantism,[1] or of Hegel as if he had worked out the

[1] This was the view of Kant's disciple, Julius Kaftan, in *Truth of the Christian*

philosophy to end all philosophies. The two giants have been cut down to life-size, and others have been noticed in their shadows who have scarcely less claim to fame. One of the most curious features of the nineteenth century is its novelty. Many of its ideas have a kind of evergreen quality which (whether true or false) have a habit of being discovered in our own day as something startlingly new. Much of what is aired today in books like *Honest to God* was, in fact, first tried out not only upon our grandfathers but upon theirs as well.

In this chapter we shall try to take a fresh look at this century which has so much influenced our own. Some of the names that we shall consider were already world-figures. Others were little known outside their own country and their immediate circle. Some founded schools of thought; others were great individualists. If they have anything in common, it is not on what they agree. It is their common desire to reinterpret Christianity in the light of what they deem to be modern knowledge and their own particular philosophies.

I SCHLEIERMACHER

Few people in England were aware of the significance of Schleiermacher in the nineteenth century. For many years he was known only by a rather undistinguished essay on Luke,[2] and almost a century elapsed after his death before his most important work, *The Christian Faith*, was translated into English.[3] But on the Continent it was a very different story. It is with justice that Karl Barth has applied to Schleiermacher some words which the latter first applied to Frederick the Great: 'He did not found a school, but an era.'[4] Only now are we, in the English-speaking world, beginning to appreciate Schleiermacher's real significance for better or for worse.

Religion, Eng. tr. by G. Ferries (Edinburgh, 1894), I, pp. 351f. On this see James Richmond, *Faith and Philosophy* (Hodder, 1966), pp. 44ff.; Werner Schultz, *Kant als Philosoph des Protestantismus* (Reich, Hamburg-Bergstedt, 1960).
[2] *Critical Essay on the Gospel of St. Luke* (1821), Eng. tr. by Connop Thirlwall, 1825.
[3] Eng. tr. edited by H. R. Mackintosh and J. S. Stewart (T. and T. Clark, Edinburgh, (1928) 1960).
[4] *From Rousseau to Ritschl*, p. 306.

Life and works

Friedrich Daniel Ernst Schleiermacher (1768–1834) was the son of an army chaplain in Upper Silesia. Both his grandfathers were pastors, and his father, who had strong pietistic leanings, sent him to the Moravian seminary at Barby in the hope that these leanings would be fostered in his son. Curiously enough, he once advised him to read Kant as an antidote to modern liberalism. The young Schleiermacher read Kant, but reacted differently. He also reacted against his pietistic upbringing. In later life Schleiermacher could describe himself as a Moravian only of a higher order. By this time his thought had gone through many vicissitudes, and had now endeavoured to combine the stress on religious experience of the evangelical pietists with the newer liberal attitude to Christianity advocated by the intelligentsia of his day.

In the meantime Schleiermacher studied at Halle (then the centre of radical thought in Germany) and Berlin. After a spell as a private tutor he returned to Berlin as chaplain of the Charity Hospital, and soon became an accepted member of a brilliant circle of Romantic writers and poets. The group rebelled against the rationalistic views of the Enlightenment, and stressed the role of mystery, imagination and feeling. It was in this period that Schleiermacher published the celebrated *On Religion: Speeches to its Cultured Despisers* (1799).[5] In 1804 he returned to Halle as a professor. But the Napoleonic wars soon obliged him to settle in Berlin, for the Peace of Tilsit severed Halle from the rest of Prussia. In Berlin Schleiermacher established himself as one of his country's leading intellectuals. He played a foremost part in the founding of the University of Berlin in 1810 and thereafter dominated its theological faculty. But theology was by no means his only interest. His several-volume translation of Plato was for long the standard edition in German. A steady stream of learned articles flowed from his pen, many of them first appearing in the shape of papers delivered to the Prussian Academy of Sciences. And all the while Schleiermacher ministered regularly at the fashionable Trinity Church in Berlin.

[5] Eng. tr. by John Oman (1893) reissued with an introduction by Rudolf Otto (Harper, New York, 1958).

Schleiermacher's posthumous collected works in German fill thirty volumes (almost equally divided between sermons, theological works and philosophical works). Many of them were first only put into print by his devoted students who wrote them down at lectures. These include a *Life of Jesus*. But the most important work of all was the one which attempted to set out systematically Schleiermacher's new approach to Christianity, *The Christian Faith* (1821–22, 1830–31[2]).[6]

Schleiermacher's approach

So far, we have noticed two broad avenues of approach to the knowledge of God. There was that of the Reformers who based their teaching on the biblical revelation. And there was that of the philosophers who tried to work out a natural theology based upon various logical deductions about the nature of the world (or, in the case of the ontological argument, upon the very idea of God). From Thomas Aquinas onwards there were those who tried to combine the two by the simple process of adding them together. And there were philosophers like Kant who held that the two cancelled each other out. Because natural theology was rotten at the foundations, it was incapable of bearing the superstructure of Christian theology. Schleiermacher tried to get the best of both worlds by steering a middle course between them. He developed what is sometimes called *positive theology*.

Natural theology in the old sense of the term was a blind alley up which Schleiermacher did not care to venture. Kant had exposed its specious arguments for what they were. But Kant's own alternative was little better. It missed the point of real, live religion. On the other hand, Schleiermacher felt that he could no longer treat the Bible as a narrative of divine interventions and a collection of divine utterances. But it was a record of religious experience, and the idea of religious experience was a key which Schleiermacher grasped with both hands. It seemed to him capable of unlocking every theological question (except those bolted on the inside which were

---

[6] The definitive critical edition is *Der Christliche Glaube*, edited by Martin Redeker, 2 vols. (de Gruyter, Berlin, 1960). For Eng. trs. see above, p. 108, n. 3.

insoluble to the human mind in any case). It meant that he no longer needed to take the Bible seriously in every detail. It seemed to open a new door to apologetics by leading both the believer and the unbeliever on to the common ground of their common experiences. What, therefore, Schleiermacher endeavoured to do was to analyse religious experience and extract from it the essence of religion. Having done this, he could then reinterpret the Christian faith in terms that were acceptable to modern man, whether he be inside or outside the church.

Religion involves all kinds of things. There are religious acts like taking part in worship and doing good. There is also an element of knowledge which may be classified under the general heading of theology (whether it be a learned discourse or a Bible story in Sunday school). Schleiermacher concluded that the essence of religion was neither activity nor knowledge but something common to both.[7] In the *Speeches* he defined it as 'sense and taste for the Infinite'.[8] By the time he came to write *The Christian Faith* he was able to be a little more precise: 'The common element in all howsoever diverse expressions of piety . . . is this: the consciousness of being absolutely dependent, or, which is the same thing, of being in relation with God.'[9] The essence of religion lies in our *sense of absolute dependence*.[1]

In Schleiermacher's hands this idea becomes a sort of common denominator of religious experience and also a yard-stick for measuring all other Christian teaching. Armed with it, Schleiermacher set about reinterpreting the whole range of Christian doctrine. He sums up his approach to the nature of God by saying, 'All attributes which we ascribe to God are to be taken as denoting not something special in God, but only something special in the manner in which the feeling of absolute dependence is to be related to him.'[2] Sin is construed in the same way. It is not so much transgression of divine law

---

[7] *The Christian Faith*, pp. 5–12.   [8] *On Religion*, p. 39.
[9] *The Christian Faith*, p. 12.
[1] Schleiermacher's term *das schlechthinnige Abhängigkeitsgefühl* is usually translated as *feeling of absolute dependence*. But the word *feeling* is perhaps too strong and positive. What he is trying to analyse often seems to be more a profound awareness or sense of utter dependence.
[2] *The Chrisitan Faith*, p. 194.

as 'an arrestment of the determinative power of the spirit, due to the independence of the sensuous functions'.[3] It is man's lower nature wanting to be free, when he should be dependent. It is a clouding over of our *sense of absolute dependence*. In its extreme form it may be called '*Godlessness (Gottlosigkeit)*, or, better, *God-forgetfulness (Gottvergessenheit)*'.[4]

Redemption is accordingly construed as the restoration of our *sense of dependence*. It so happens that Christian experience relates this to the person of Christ.

> Indeed, working backwards we must now say, if it is only through Him that the human God-consciousness becomes an existence of God in human nature, and only through the rational nature that the totality of finite powers can become an existence of God in the world, that in truth He alone mediates all existence of God in the world and all revelation of God through the world, in so far as He bears within Himself the whole new creation which contains and develops the potency of God-consciousness.[5]

Now this is precisely what constitutes the uniqueness of Christ. We are not to think of him in terms of the creeds of the early church with all their overtones of Greek metaphysical speculation.

> The Redeemer, then, is like all men in virtue of the identity of human nature, but distinguished from them all by the constant potency of His God-consciousness, which was a veritable existence of God in Him.[6]

In other words, we are not to think of Jesus as the God-man of Christian orthodoxy, the divine Word who took human nature upon himself. Jesus was a man who walked so closely with God that you could say that God dwelled in him.

The redemptive work of Jesus was to assume 'believers into the power of His God-consciousness'.[7] It was not to bear their sins on their behalf, but so to move men that 'His motive principle becomes ours also'.[8] Schleiermacher retains some of

---

[3] *Ibid.*, p. 273.   [4] *Ibid.*, p. 54.   [5] *Ibid.*, p. 388.
[6] *Ibid.*, p. 385.   [7] *Ibid.*, p. 425.   [8] *Ibid.*, p. 457.

the vocabulary of the older Christian theology and even something of its contents. But the meaning he gives it is considerably stretched or all but completely changed. Thus his teaching about reconciliation still bears some resemblance to Protestant orthodoxy. He can still write: 'Assumption into living fellowship with Christ, regarded as a man's changed relation to God, is his Justification; regarded as a changed form of life, it is his Conversion.'[9] But when he talks about the Trinity, the term remains but the meaning is no longer the same. He can still call it 'the coping-stone of Christian doctrine'.[1] He can still scour around for reasons for retaining the idea.[2] But he gives the game away when he insists that we must avoid the dualism of speaking about 'unity of Essence and trinity of Persons'.[3] He admits that 'the assumption of an eternal distinction in the Supreme Being is not an utterance concerning the religious consciousness, for there it could never emerge'.[4] In other words, Schleiermacher's approach leads to a form of Unitarianism. He believes in God. For God is that upon which we feel dependent. But Jesus is a man who had this experience in a supremely high degree, and the Holy Spirit is really a way of describing our experience of God in the church.[5]

Comment

When we pick up Schleiermacher's *Christian Faith* today and plough through its 750 pages, it is like trying to cut through an undergrowth of abstract ideas. For this the team of British translators must bear some responsibility. The language is sometimes dry and the renderings wooden. But the fault lies

---

[9] *Ibid.*, p. 478.   [1] *Ibid.*, p. 739.

[2] 'For unless the being of God in Christ is assumed, the idea of redemption could not be concentrated in His Person. And unless there were such a union also in the common Spirit of the Church, the Church could not thus be the Bearer and Perpetuator of the redemption through Christ. Now these exactly are the essential elements in the doctrine of the Trinity, which, it is clear, only established itself in defence of the position that in Christ there was present nothing less than the Divine Essence, which also indwells the Church as its common Spirit' (*ibid.*, p. 738).

[3] *Ibid.*, p. 739.   [4] *Ibid.*

[5] *Cf. ibid.*, pp. 738–751 and especially see above, n. 2.

largely with Schleiermacher himself. Nevertheless, much of it has a familiar modern ring. For consciously or unconsciously a good deal of it has found its way into *Honest to God* and the writings of Paul Tillich. The basic approach of all three is essentially the same. Whereas Schleiermacher explained to the men of his generation that God was the object of our *sense of absolute dependence*, Tillich[6] and Robinson[7] (following suit) have tried to make God meaningful for people today by describing him as the object of *ultimate concern* or as *depth* or the *ground of being* from whom we have become alienated.

In each case the writer has attempted to cut away from both biblical theology and the older natural theology in favour of an analysis of religious experience. In each case we have a kind of common denominator which is used to reinterpret traditional ideas. And in particular, the common denominators of all three make use of the idea of dependence. It is not therefore very surprising that the resultant theologies of all three bear marked family resemblances.

They no longer speak the language of traditional Christian Theism which regarded God as one who exists over against the world, who is complete in himself, who is the creator and sustainer of all things, who is actively concerned for the world and in it, but who is also independent of it. To Schleiermacher the dividing-line between Theism and Pantheism is a very fine one.[8] Whereas Tillich prefers to speak of God not as *a* being outside the world but as *being itself* or the *ground of being*, Robinson can write a chapter on 'The End of Theism?' and answer his question by endorsing Tillich's approach.

Sin, for Schleiermacher, is that which disturbs our sense of absolute dependence, the desire to be free when we should be at one with God. Tillich changes the vocabulary but retains the basic idea. Sin, for him, is lack of ultimate concern and estrangement from the ground of our being. The Christ who saves from sin plays the same role in the thought of all three.

---

[6] For a formal statement of Tillich's position see his three-volume *Systematic Theology* (Nisbet, 1953–64). Volume I outlines his approach. See also below, pp. 191–200.
[7] J. A. T. Robinson, *Honest to God*, pp. 21f., 29–83. See also below, p. 209.
[8] *The Christian Faith*, p. 39.

They are all sceptical of the New Testament picture of Christ as it stands. They have no time for the Christ of the creeds who was both truly God and truly man. In his place they set a perfect man who is variously described as distinguished from all others 'by the constant potency of His God-consciousness' (Schleiermacher), 'the bearer of the final revelation' (Tillich),[9] and 'a window into God at work', one who 'reveals God by being utterly transparent to him, precisely as he is nothing "in himself" ' (Robinson).[1] His significance for all three is not that he bore punishment for sin on man's behalf,[2] but that having this unique awareness of God, he is able to mediate it to others.[3] Not far beneath the skin of Tillich's 'bearer of the New Being' and Robinson's 'man for others' is the early-nineteenth-century Christ of Schleiermacher.

But in comparing Schleiermacher with Paul Tillich and the Bishop of Woolwich, we have been jumping ahead. We shall have to look at the latter two more closely in the next chapter. We must now ask how satisfactory is this new approach of Schleiermacher's. In answer to this question it must be said that it was a genuine attempt to restate the truth of the Christian message in terms that are valid and relevant for modern man. It is, moreover, only right that such attempts should be made. The difficulty here, as all too often, is that the proverbial baby is thrown out with the proverbial bath water.

Schleiermacher is attempting to be empirical in his approach, rejecting abstract speculation in favour of analysis of religious experience. The difficulty is not that he was too empirical, but that he was not empirical enough. Nowhere do we find in his work any precise analysis of particular religious experiences such as we find, for example, in William James's *The Varieties of Religious Experience* (1902). Nor did Schleiermacher attempt any detailed discussion of religious experience in the New Testament. Instead, the *sense of absolute dependence* is assumed to be the common factor of religious experience without further

---

[9] *Systematic Theology*, I, p. 148.   [1] *Honest to God*, pp. 71,73.
[2] *The Christian Faith*, p. 459; *Systematic Theology*, II, pp. 196–203; *Honest to God*, pp. 78f.
[3] *Cf.* above, pp. 112f. with *Systematic Theology*, II, pp. 136–159, 174–190; *Honest to God*, pp. 75–83.

ado. It virtually enjoys the status of the clear and distinct ideas of seventeenth-century rationalism. Admittedly, it has a certain air of plausibility, for the simple reason that religious experience does involve a sense of dependence upon God. But Schleiermacher never pauses to ask whether there might not be more to it than that. And having got so far, he proceeds to use it like a Procrustean bed. Anything that he finds in Christian teaching which does not fit is either stretched or lopped off. He is thus prevented from paying due attention to what the New Testament actually says about God, Christ, sin and salvation by his preconceived method which demands that everything should be interpreted in the light of a preconceived principle.

All this raises the vital question of theological method. Schleiermacher approaches the Christian faith in the light of his general world view, armed with certain rigid principles of interpretation. The same is true of Tillich and Robinson. They then proceed to examine Christianity accordingly. Where they cite evidence it is more by way of illustration than as proof. In evaluating their work, it is important that they should be judged not only by what they put in but also by what they leave out.

By contrast, Christian orthodoxy (whether Protestant or Catholic) has adopted a rather different approach. By and large, its exponents have been willing to accept as a working hypothesis the world views of their age. But they have also asked that any particular world view should not be allowed to prejudge the issue. Theological method, like scientific method, cannot be decided *a priori*. It must be determined by the evidence that it is dealing with. Schleiermacher, Tillich and Robinson have the appearance of being modern in virtue of their willingness to jettison traditional teaching in favour of ideas which are apparently more acceptable to modern man. But novelty is not necessarily the same as truth. And it must be asked whether more conservative scholars, who were willing to follow the historical evidence presented by the New Testament where it led them, were not in fact much closer to modern scientific methods.

II   HEGEL AND IDEALISM

For many philosophers and theologians of the older generation
Idealism was *the* modern philosophy. Schleiermacher remained
buried in the decent obscurity of German, a language which
few English theologians bothered to learn in the nineteenth
century. And even on the Continent Schleiermacher was for
long eclipsed by the Idealist philosophers. This was painfully
brought home to Schleiermacher at the height of his powers by
an interview with the young D. F. Strauss who was soon to
make a name for himself as the author of the most radical life
of Jesus of the century.[4] In the autumn of 1831 Strauss went
to Berlin to sit at the feet of the greatest scholars of the day.
He had scarcely attended his first lectures when Hegel died in
a cholera epidemic. He learnt the news from Schleiermacher
and blurted out to the latter's discomfort, 'It was for his sake
that I came here.'[5]

Idealism

The term Idealism is an elastic one.[6] In its widest sense it
denotes the view that the mind and spiritual values are more
fundamental than material ones. As such, it is opposed to
naturalism which explains the mind and spiritual values in
terms of material things and processes. The term was first
applied as a technical term in philosophy in the eighteenth
century. And soon it was used to describe the teaching of
Berkeley, that nothing could be known to exist or did exist
except ideas in the mind of the percipient.[7] Berkeley himself
preferred to call his philosophy *immaterialism*. But the term
Idealism stuck, and was soon applied to other philosophies.
Kant adopted it, carefully distinguishing his own teaching
which he called 'Transcendental Idealism' from that of
Descartes and Berkeley which he called problematic and
dogmatic idealism. As we have already seen, Kant held that it
was impossible to gain knowledge of the world by rational

[4] See below, p. 152.
[5] *Cf.* Eduard Zeller, *David Friedrich Strauss*, Eng. tr. 1874, p. 33.
[6] A very useful anthology of idealistic writings is contained in A. C. Ewing,
ed., *The Idealist Tradition, from Berkeley to Blanshard* (Allen and Unwin, 1958).
[7] See above, pp. 64–66.

thought alone. On the other hand, he believed in a transcendental self and postulated the existence of God, freedom and immortality.[8]

It was partly in reaction to Kant and partly owing to inspiration from him that the next generation of German philosophers developed what came to be known as Absolute Idealism. The most important of them were Fichte, Schelling and Hegel. We shall not be able to go into any detail with the first two, but shall merely try to state their general positions.

Like Kant, J. G. Fichte (1762–1814) believed that strict determinism was incompatible with morality, and therefore we must presuppose the freedom of the will. For, according to determinism, all our thoughts and actions are determined entirely by natural, physical processes, and thus freedom of thought and action is illusory. In 1792 Fichte dedicated to Kant his *Critique of All Revelation*. Taking his cue from Kant, he argued that revealed religion is an expression of our recognition of a spiritual, moral imperative over and above us. Belief in God is essentially recognition of a fundamental and sovereign moral dynamic. It was the first of a series of works whose central theme has been variously described as 'moral idealism' and 'ethical pantheism'. Certainly, it was far from clear whether Fichte believed in a personal deity. In any case, he was no advocate of orthodoxy. His Sunday lectures proved a rival attraction to church services for the students at Jena. In the uproar which was sparked off by his alleged atheism Fichte was obliged to resign his philosophical chair. But from 1810 to his death he occupied the chair of philosophy and various administrative posts in the University of Berlin.

'The kind of philosophy which one adopts', wrote Fichte, 'depends upon the sort of man one is; for a philosophical system is not a lifeless piece of furniture that one might take or discard . . . but it is animated by the soul of the man who has it.'[9] Fichte himself opted to base his philosophy upon the notion of a free, intelligent Ego or self or 'I' from which everything else must be deduced. Our physical universe is the outworking of the spiritual Ego.

F. W. J. von Schelling (1775–1854) began his philosophical

_____
[8] See above, pp. 95f., 102f.   [9] *Werke*, I, p. 434.

career as a disciple of Fichte, as is shown by the title of his early work, *On the I as a Principle of Philosophy* (1795). Here he acknowledged only one reality, the infinite and absolute Ego of which the universe was the expression. But this was later modified in favour of Nature Philosophy in books like *Ideas towards a Philosophy of Nature* (1797) and *On the World Soul* (1798). Nature was now the absolute being which works itself out unconsciously, albeit purposively. A few years later this was developed into Identity Philosophy which was deeply indebted to Spinoza. Nature and spirit are but manifestations of the same being, the absolute identity being the ground of all things. Later on he came under the influence of Neo-Platonism[1] and the theosophy of Jakob Boehme.[2] In his last years, while lecturing at Berlin, he tried to reconcile Christianity and his philosophy. But the result could hardly be called successful from a Christian point of view. Nevertheless, he exercised considerable influence on German thought, and his earlier teaching provided the point of departure for the greatest of the German Idealist philosophers, G. W. F. Hegel.

Hegel

By common consent Georg Wilhelm Friedrich Hegel (1770–1831) is regarded as the greatest and also the most difficult exponent of nineteenth-century German Idealism. After a career as a private tutor, a newspaper editor and a headmaster, Hegel accepted the chair of philosophy at Heidelberg in 1816 and succeeded Fichte at Berlin (1818) where he remained until his death. His collected works in German fill twenty volumes. They include *The Phenomenology of Mind* (1806),[3] *Science of Logic* (1812–16),[4] and his *Encyclopedia of Philosophy* (1817).[5] After his death devoted students put

[1] See above, p. 16.
[2] In its general sense theosophy denotes a variety of embracing pantheism and natural mysticism in which the divine is claimed to be intuitively known. The very involved teaching of Boehme (1575–1624) appears to be an attempt to combine Christianity with pantheism.
[3] Eng. tr. by J. B. Baillie (Allen and Unwin, (1910) 1931²).
[4] Eng. tr. by W. H. Johnston and L. G. Struthers, 2 vols. (Allen and Unwin, 1929).
[5] Eng. tr. by G. E. Mueller (New York, 1959).

together their lecture notes which were sometimes collated
with their master's own and these were subsequently published. Such volumes include *The Philosophy of History*,[6] *The
History of Philosophy*[7] and *The Philosophy of Religion*.[8] In his
youth Hegel also wrote several essays on Christianity. But,
as a recent writer has remarked, Hegel was not like Schelling,
who carried out his philosophical education in public.[9] The
essays, which show a marked Kantian influence in places, were
put into a drawer and remained unpublished until 1907.[1]

The basic idea in all Hegel's mature teaching is denoted by
the German word *Geist*. The word may be translated as *Mind*
(emphasizing its rational aspect) or *Spirit* (emphasizing the
immaterial – or better, the supermaterial and religious –
aspect of reality). Perhaps it is best to let Hegel state his
meaning in his own words. At least it will enable the reader to
capture something of the flavour of his writing.

> Spirit is alone Reality. It is the inner being of the world,
> that which essentially is, and is *per se*; it assumes objective,
> determinate form, and enters into relations with itself – it
> is externality (otherness), and exists for itself; yet, in this
> determination, and in its otherness, it is still one with itself –
> it is self-contained and self-complete, in itself and for itself
> at once. This self-containedness, however, is first something
> known by us, it is implicit in its nature; it is Substance
> spiritual. It has to become self-contained *for itself*, on its own
> account; it must be knowledge of spirit, and must be con-
> sciousness of itself as spirit. This means, it must be presented
> to itself as an object, but at the same time straightway
> annul and transcend this objective form; it must be its own
> object in which it finds itself reflected. So far as its spiritual

---

[6] Eng. tr. by J. Sibree (1861, reprinted Dover Publications, New York,
1956).
[7] Eng. tr. by E. S. Haldane and F. H. Simson, 3 vols. (Routledge, 1892–96).
[8] Eng. tr. by E. B. Spiers and J. Burdon Sanderson, 3 vols. (1895, reprinted
by Routledge and Kegan Paul, 1962).
[9] Walter Kaufmann, *Hegel: Reinterpretation, Texts, and Commentary* (Weidenfeld and Nicolson, 1965), p. 64. The remark is a repetition of Hegel's own.
Kaufmann's work is the best anthology and introduction to Hegel.
[1] *On Christianity: Early Theological Writings*. Eng. tr. by T. M. Knox with
introduction by R. Kroner (Chicago, 1948; Harper, New York, 1961).

content is produced by its own activity, it is only *we* the thinkers who know spirit to be for itself, to be objective to itself; but in so far as spirit knows itself to be for itself, then this self-production, the pure notion, is the sphere and element in which its objectification takes effect, and where it gets its existential form. In this way it is in its existence aware of itself as an object in which its own self is reflected. Mind, which, when thus developed, knows itself to be mind, is science. Science is its realization, and the kingdom it sets up for itself in its own native element.[2]

In other words – at the risk of oversimplification – all reality is the outworking of Spirit. This is true, says Hegel, whether we think of nature, history or thought. The sum total of human knowledge is none other than the Absolute Spirit thinking out its thoughts through human minds. Or it may be put another way around. History, nature and human thought are really aspects of the Absolute Spirit coming to self-consciousness.

It is customary to describe Hegel's view of the outworking of Spirit as a Dialectic (which is simply another word for process or dynamic pattern) of Thesis, Antithesis and Synthesis. But it has been pointed out that although Hegel makes occasional use of these latter terms, they are in fact more characteristic of Fichte.[3] However, the basic idea is there, and the notion of Dialectic is paramount. Hegel saw the Dialectic of the Spirit in everything. He detected it in the broad patterns of history:

The History of the World is the discipline of the uncontrolled natural will, bringing it into obedience to a Universal principle and conferring subjective freedom. The East knew and to the present day knows only that *One* is Free; the Greek and Roman world, that *some* are free; the German World that *All* are free. The first political form therefore

[2] *The Phenomenology of the Mind*, p. 86. It may be pointed out that the word *science* in the last two sentences is the German *Wissenschaft* which denotes not merely the natural sciences but systematized knowledge in general. The word *kingdom* (*Reich*) in the last sentence is better translated as *realm*.
[3] J. N. Findlay, *Hegel: A Re-examination* (Allen and Unwin, 1958), p. 70.

which we observe in History, is *Despotism*, the second *Democracy* and Aristocracy, the third *Monarchy*.[4]

In other words, the grand climax of world history was the emergence of the Prussian monarchy from Graeco-Roman and even earlier antiquity. Whether any historian could be found today to endorse this view is somewhat doubtful.

But history was only a particular manifestation of the Spirit. The same ideas are invoked in religion which is even more fundamental. Religion is in fact 'the self-consciousness of God'.[5] It is God coming to self-consciousness through human activity. Perhaps we had better let Hegel explain it again in his own words.

> We define God when we say, that He distinguishes Himself from Himself, and is an object for Himself, but that in this distinction He is purely identical with Himself, is in fact Spirit. This notion or conception is now realised, consciousness knows this content and knows that it is itself absolutely interwoven with this content; in the Notion which is the process of God, it is itself a moment. Finite consciousness knows God only to the extent to which God knows Himself in it; thus God is Spirit, the Spirit of His Church in fact, *i.e.*, of those who worship Him. This is the perfect religion, the Notion become objective to itself. Here it is revealed what God is; He is no longer a Being above and beyond this world, an Unknown, for He has told men what He is, and this not merely in an outward way in history, but in consciousness.[6]

Hegel, then, presents us with a picture of reality which is ultimately spiritual. Everything that we experience is, in fact, part and parcel of the divine evolution. We are not to think of God as over and above our world but as immanent in it. This is also the key to the incarnation, which is a particular manifestation of the Spirit in one particular human being.[7]

In working out this all-embracing philosophy of Spirit,

---

[4] *The Philosophy of History*, p. 104.
[5] *The Philosophy of Religion*, II, p. 327.   [6] *Ibid.*, II, pp. 327f.
[7] *Ibid.*, III, pp. 74ff. See further, below, p. 139, n. 5.

Hegel believed that he discovered the philosophy to end all philosophies. He had not only salvaged Christianity from modern attacks. He had found the key to its inner meaning. In a moment or two we shall ask whether he was right, but before we do so it is worth while going on to look at some later thinkers who thought that he was, or nearly so.

The progress of Idealism

Hegel soon found posthumous disciples among the ranks of the German theologians who made Hegelianism the philosophical basis of their teaching.[8] Hegelianism reached the shores of Britain and North America about the middle of the century. It was made known to the larger British public through James Hutchinson Stirling's *The Secret of Hegel* (1865), though there were some who said that he had managed to keep it rather well.

In the second half of the century Idealism found a firm foothold in the British universities, especially Oxford. Among its advocates were T. H. Green (1836–82), Benjamin Jowett (1817–93), Edward Caird (1835–1908), A. S. Pringle-Pattison (1856–1931), and F. H. Bradley (1846–1924). In pre-1914 Britain Idealism seemed as firm and enduring as the British Empire.

Part of the reason for this was that this was (in one shape or another) the doctrine taught by all these leading lights in the philosophical firmament. But if we probe further, and ask why it should be so, then a number of reasons suggest themselves. One is that British education in those days consisted of a staple diet of the classics, which in turn introduced students to Plato as the philosopher *par excellence*. And it was not a far cry from Plato's doctrine of the Forms to Hegel's Absolute Idealism. Moreover, Hegel had the edge on Plato in so far as his view was more dynamic and seemed to harmonize better with evolution. Finally, Idealism seemed to present a spiritual bulwark against the rising tides of materialism and secularism. It seemed to offer a rational basis for Christianity when theologians, one after another, became embarrassed by its historical claims.

At the turn of the century the ranks of the ecclesiastical

[8] See below, pp. 152, 158.

advocates of Idealism were joined by such statesmen as
A. J. Balfour, R. B. Haldane and J. C. Smuts. But the early
years of the twentieth century saw the beginning of the end.
Among the more vociferous of its assailants were the British
philosophers, G. E. Moore and Bertrand Russell.[9]

The big difficulty about Idealism is its lack of proof. The
Idealist philosophers talk on and on at enormous length. But
what they say seems not only contrary to common sense but
indemonstrable. It is one thing to build up a system of ideas;
it is something else entirely to show that the ideas are true.
In an article on 'The Conception of Reality' Moore accused
Idealists of falling into the basic error of not distinguishing
between ideas and reality. It was like not seeing the difference
between saying 'Unicorns are thought of' and 'Lions are
hunted'. Russell took Berkeley and his successors to task for
'confusing the thing apprehended with the act of apprehension'.
When 'Berkeley says that the tree must be in our minds if
we can know it, all that he really has a right to say is that a
thought of a tree must be in our minds. To argue that the
tree itself must be in our minds is like arguing that a person
whom we bear in mind is himself in our minds'.[1]

There were also those who were uneasy about the alliance
between Idealism and Christianity. Although not a believer
himself, J. M. E. McTaggart pointed out that Hegelianism
was 'an enemy in disguise – the least evident but the most
dangerous'.[2] As the twentieth century wore on, some churchmen were alarmed at the revival of empiricism which was
soon to swamp the philosophical faculties of the British
universities. They need not have bothered. At least modern
empiricism has helped to bring the crucial issues back into
focus. But in fact, there were already strong protests in the
nineteenth century against Idealism on the Continent. The
most important of these came from the shrill voice of the
eccentric Dane, Søren Kierkegaard, a thinker whose stature
is only now beginning to be assessed although he died more
than a hundred years ago.

[9] For extracts from their criticisms see Ewing, *The Idealist Tradition*, pp.
289-316.
[1] *Ibid.*, p. 312.   [2] *Studies in Hegelian Cosmology* (Macmillan, 1901), p. 250.

III KIERKEGAARD
Life and works

To some readers, Kierkegaard's excruciating analysis of human reactions throws a brilliant light on personal behaviour. To others he is a boring windbag. In the minds of some, ✝ Kierkegaard's Existentialism occupies the place vacated by Idealism as the philosophical basis of Christianity. To others Kierkegaard represents the bankruptcy of western philosophy.

In its own way Kierkegaard's writing is no less difficult to follow than Hegel's, but for a different reason. Hegel just did not bother to express himself plainly. Kierkegaard deliberately sets out to be tortuous. For to him truth is not something objective that can be handed out on a plate. It is only discovered personally and subjectively in the course of long and sometimes painful self-analysis. And in order to bring his reader to the desired goal, Kierkegaard often found it necessary to be devious. Kierkegaard is at his plainest and most poignant in his *Journals*,[3] and it is here that the beginner is best advised to begin his study of him. Certainly, without any knowledge of his turbulent life, it is very difficult to understand what Kierkegaard is driving at.

Søren Aaby Kierkegaard (1813–55) was born at Copenhagen, the son of a well-to-do, Lutheran businessman. After a secluded and unhappy childhood he became a student at the University of Copenhagen, and intended eventually to enter the ministry. He passed his theological examination in 1840[4] and became engaged the following year. But he could not bring himself to go through with either ordination or marriage. Some time previously in 1835 he experienced what he called 'the great earthquake'. The searing question entered his mind

[3] The handiest version is the Fontana paperback, *The Journals of Soren Kierkegaard*, selected, edited and translated by Alexander Dru (1958). This is based on the larger version also produced by Dru published by OUP under the same title (1938, 1959[3]). These have been further supplemented by *The Last Years: Journals 1853–1855*, edited and translated by Ronald Gregor Smith (Collins, 1955). Except where otherwise stated, references here are to the paperback edition.

[4] In 1841 he submitted his master's dissertation, *The Concept of Irony with Constant Reference to Socrates*, Eng. tr. by Lee M. Capel (Collins, 1966) which also contains attacks on Hegel.

whether his family's outward prosperity was not perhaps the sign of God's curse rather than his blessing.[5]

In the years that followed Kierkegaard plunged into an extravagant social life, half hoping that it would distract his mind. At the same time he was not entirely idle. A steady stream of books flowed from his pen. All bore the marks of a brilliant, but tortured, mind. It was a mind that was cynical about the world, human behaviour, and philosophical orthodoxy, alias Hegelianism. In a number of these works Kierkegaard masked his own opinions under pseudonyms.[6] In others he lampooned Hegel. The very titles of books like *Philosophical Fragments* (1844)[7] and *Concluding Unscientific Postscript* (1846)[8] were designed to parody the grandiose pretensions of Absolute Idealism. The titles of two earlier works *Fear and Trembling* (1843)[9] and *The Concept of Dread* (1844)[1] are pointers to where Kierkegaard thought that the real concerns of human existence lay. As early as 1835 he had written in his *Journal*, 'The thing is to understand myself, to see what God really wishes *me* to do; the thing is to find a truth which is true *for me*, to find *the idea for which I can live and die*.'[2] Real truth was not a matter of detached, abstract speculation. It was a matter of painful heart-searching.

In Holy Week 1848 Kierkegaard went through an experience of conversion.[3] The *Journals* record him as saying, 'My whole being is changed', and shortly afterwards, 'But belief in the forgiveness of sins means to believe that here in time the sin is forgotten by God, that it is really true that God forgets.' Both before and after this experience Kierkegaard wrote a number of works dealing with aspects of Christianity. They include *Purity of Heart is to Will One Thing* (1846),[4] *Works of*

[5] *Journals*, pp. 39ff.

[6] *Johannes Climacus or, De Omnibus Dubitandum Est* (1842), Eng. tr. T. H. Croxall (Black, 1958); *Either/Or: A Fragment of Life* edited by Victor Eremita, Eng. tr., 2 vols, by D. F. and L. M. Swenson and W. Lowrie (Princeton, 1944).

[7] Eng. tr. by D. F. Swenson, revised by H. V. Hong, with introduction and commentary by N. Thulstrup (Princeton, 1962).

[8] Eng. tr. by D. F. Swenson and W. Lowrie (Princeton, (1941) 1963[7]).

[9] Eng. tr. by W. Lowrie (1941, Doubleday, New York, 1954).

[1] Eng. tr. by W. Lowrie (Princeton, 1944).   [3] *Journals*, p. 44.

[2] *Ibid.*, pp. 137ff.   [4] Eng. tr. by D. Steere (Fontana, 1961).

Love (1847),[5] and *Christian Discourses* (1848).[6] Whilst they contain ruthless self-analysis, they are much less hostile to the frailties of others than his previous writings.

Kierkegaard's last years were marred by bitter quarrels with the established church. In January 1854 the leading ecclesiastic of Denmark, Bishop Mynster, died. In an impressive oration, Bishop Martensen (who shortly succeeded Mynster) extolled the virtues of the deceased primate. Kierkegaard could no longer suppress his withering scorn of official religion, and published an article against Martensen, 'Was Bishop Mynster a Witness to the Truth?' Controversy pursued Kierkegaard to the grave. He felt deeply the attacks on himself made by the satirical journal *The Corsair*. On his deathbed he declined to receive communion 'from the King's official', even though the minister concerned was his oldest friend. He died at the age of forty-two.

Truth and Christianity

Kierkegaard's criticism of Hegelianism can be summed up with great brevity: it was no good, and it was untrue. He graphically compared the value of Hegelianism with the difficulty of trying to travel through Denmark with the aid of a small map of Europe in which Denmark shows up no bigger than a pin-point.[7] He went on to ridicule the abstract arguments of speculative metaphysics. Hegel's reality bears no relation to the reality of human existence.

Kierkegaard has another charge to bring against Hegel. In a sense it is a variation on the same basic theme, that we have already noticed as we looked at Hegel. But it is worth while to draw attention to it, partly because of the light that it sheds upon Kierkegaard himself, and partly because of the way that the same complaint has been taken up in the twentieth century by Kierkegaard's secular successors (the Existentialists) against Hegel's secular successors (the Marxists). I quote Kierkegaard's summary of it that he made in his *Journals* in 1850.

[5] Eng. tr. by H. and E. Hong (Collins, 1962).
[6] Eng. tr. by W. Lowrie (1940, OUP, New York, 1961).
[7] *Concluding Unscientific Postscript*, p. 275.

How often have I shown that fundamentally Hegel makes men into heathens, *into a race of animals gifted with reason.* For in the animal world 'the individual' is always less important than the race. But the peculiarity of the human race is that just because the individual is created in the image of God 'the individual' is above the race.

This can be wrongly understood and terribly misused: *concedo.* But that is Christianity. And *that* is where the battle must be fought.[8]

It is tempting to go on and quote page after page of the *Journals* at this point. They sum up so well Kierkegaard's private crusade against Hegel in the name of Christianity. But Hegel is not the sole victim. The real objective of his attacks is the modern gratuitous assumption that truth is impersonal, that it can be attained simply by thinking dispassionately. The latter may be all right in the realms of natural science. It is of no use at all when it is a question of finding God. For here it is a matter of choice, a choice which has to be made in 'fear and trembling'.[9] In short, 'Christianity begins more or less where Hegel leaves off.'[1] But even religion can be a danger here. For it is possible to obtain a certain superficial satisfaction in religion which stops short of really throwing oneself without reserve upon the mercy of God, and thus failing to allow God to meet one's deepest needs.[2]

Kierkegaard's view of truth is often discussed under the heading of *Subjectivity.* It is a term which he used frequently himself, as for example in his *Concluding Unscientific Postscript* where he contrasts the objective approach with the subjective. But it is also vividly illustrated in the *Journals* where he writes: 'It is perfectly true, isolated subjectivity is, in the opinion of the age, evil; but "objectivity" as a cure is not one whit better. The only salvation is subjectivity, *i.e.* God, as infinite compelling subjectivity.'[3] He then proceeds to discuss what he calls 'The dialectic of becoming a Christian'.

[8] *Journals*, p. 187.
[9] 'Now how are the sciences to help? Simply not at all, in no way whatsoever. They reduce everything to calm and objective observation – with the result that freedom is an inexplicable something. Scientifically Spinoza is the only one who is consistent' (*ibid.*, p. 188). See above, pp. 53–56.
[1] *Ibid.*, p. 189.   [2] *Ibid.*, p. 190.   [3] *Ibid.*, p. 184.

He begins by citing (with approval) the example of Socrates and the famous dictum of Lessing. Socrates did not first gather proofs of immortality and then live on the strength of them. The reverse was the case. He staked his life on the belief and his life was the proof. This for Kierkegaard is the life of the *spirit*, as contrasted with that of the 'cowardly, effeminate natures' who lead second- and even tenth-hand lives. Lessing had said that one cannot base eternal happiness upon something historical.[4] How then does Christianity fit in, seeing that it is a historical religion? Kierkegaard's reply is that the results of historical research are uncertain, and that in any case they do not really help. For what matters is the subjective choice, the leap of faith, one's commitment to the absurd. In other words, it follows the same pattern as Socrates' belief in immortality.

And so I say to myself: I choose; that historical fact means so much to me that I decide to stake my whole life upon that if.* Then he lives; lives entirely full of the idea, risking his life for it: and his life is the proof that he believes. He did not have a few proofs, and so believed and then began to live. No, the very reverse.

That is called risking; and without risk faith is an impossibility. *To be related to spirit means to undergo a test*;† to believe, to wish to believe, is to change one's life into a trial; daily test is the trial of faith.

* That occurs, too, in Christ's words: if anyone will follow my teaching, *i.e.* live according to it, *i.e.* act according to it, he shall see etc. That means to say, there are no proofs beforehand – nor is he satisfied that the acceptance of his teaching should mean: I assure you.

† That is because man is a synthesis of body-soul and spirit. But 'spirit' sows dissension – whereas effeminate men always want to include what is lower in every relationship, and to have its consent. Hence the dread of 'risking'. The unspiritual man always desires 'probability'. But 'spirit' will never grant it, for 'spirit' is the test: do you wish to avoid probability, do you wish to deny yourself, give up the world etc.[5]

4 See above, pp. 88ff.   5 *Journals*, pp. 185f.

E

It is difficult to read Kierkegaard without mixed feelings. He is obviously grappling with an important aspect of life from which so many analytic philosophers (and, for that matter, preachers) have shut themselves off. But he often gives the impression of making necessity into a virtue and of shouting loudest when his argument is at its weakest. At times his view of God seems to have a good deal in common with the Wizard of Oz. It is not so much his existence that counts but the *thought* of his existence. In the American fairy story Dorothy, the straw man, the tin man and the cowardly lion take a course of action because they believe in the Wizard of Oz. Their lives are transformed because of their belief in him. But in the end the Wizard turns out to be a fraud. He is not a Wizard at all, but an ordinary man. So it often appears with Kierkegaard that it is the thought of God that prompts him to react in the way he does, rather than encounter with God himself.

This appears to be endorsed by the celebrated remark in the *Philosophical Fragments*:

> If the contemporary generation had left nothing behind them but these words: 'We have believed that in such and such a year the God appeared among us in the humble figure of a servant, that he lived and taught in our community, and finally died,' it would be more than enough. The contemporary generation would have done all that was necessary; for this little advertisement, this *nota bene* on a page of universal history would have been sufficient to afford an occasion for a successor, and the most voluminous account can in all eternity do nothing more.[6]

For Kierkegaard the paradox of faith means that belief must be proportioned in inverse proportion to the evidence. The less evidence, the better. Faith and reason are mutually exclusive opposites. With Kierkegaard, what counts is not *what* you know, but *how* you react.[7] And the end-product is not

---

[6] *Philosophical Fragments*, p. 130.
[7] 'What makes the difference in life is not what is said, but how it is said. As for the "what", the same thing has already been said perhaps many times before – and so the old saying is true: there is nothing new under the sun, the old saying which is always new . . . ' (*Journals*, p. 190).

more factual knowledge, but an enlarged understanding of oneself and human existence. This last point could be amply illustrated from works like *Christian Discourses* and *Works of Love*. But perhaps the tersest and most poignant example occurs in an entry in the *Journals* in 1846.

> To-day an accusing memory passed by. Supposing, now, the accusation came to light. I could go far away, live in a foreign country, a new life far from the memory, far from every possibility of its being revealed. I could live hidden – No, I must remain on the spot and continue to do everything as usual, without a single prudential measure, leaving everything to God. Terrible, how it can develop a man to remain on the spot, formed only by possibility.[8]

In his own peculiar way Kierkegaard sees much deeper into life than most philosophers. His understanding of certain aspects of human experience is much more profound than that of his more orthodox opponents. And yet, there are times when he seems to miss the point of the Christian gospel. The apostolic kerygma cannot be reduced without remainder to the paradoxical *story* of an alleged incarnation. A gospel story without the resurrection of Jesus is the melancholy tale of a dead Christ who is helpless to save. The absolute antithesis which Kierkegaard draws between the objective and the subjective is one which no biblical writer or speaker ever drew. The biblical writers summon men to faith not because it is absurd but because there are good grounds for committing oneself to Christ. These occur, for example, in the signs he performed and the fact that God raised him from the dead.[9]

Kierkegaard once described his work as a corrective, 'Just a bit of cinnamon.'[1] He could scarcely have realized that a hundred years later he would have come to be regarded as the

---

[8] *Ibid.*, p. 97.
[9] *Cf.* John 20:30f.; Acts 2:22–24; 4:33; Romans 1:4; 1 Corinthians 15:4ff., 14, *etc.* For further discussion of faith and its object with reference to Kierkegaard and modern theology, see my *Karl Barth and the Christian Message*, pp. 44ff.
[1] *Cf.* H. Diem *Kierkegaard's Dialectic of Existence*, Eng. tr. by H. Knight (Oliver & Boyd, 1959), p. 157.

great-grandfather of theological and atheistic Existentialism.[2] But, certainly, his teaching already contains within it the elements of a system, which in its own way was no less a system than Hegel's for all its irrationalism. If we follow certain of its lines to their logical conclusion, there can be no rational grounds for preferring belief to unbelief, and objective knowledge of God must be replaced by subjective knowledge of the human condition. But perhaps the most generous thing to do is to let Kierkegaard have the last word. As a corrective to something else, cinnamon can be pleasant. But you cannot live for ever on a diet of it.

IV ATHEISM AND AGNOSTICISM

Atheism means disbelief in, or denial of, the existence of God. It is a term which has been current since the late sixteenth century. The word agnosticism is of much more recent coinage. It is generally ascribed to T. H. Huxley, the Victorian scientist and friend of Charles Darwin, who devised it to describe his own state of mind. He used it, not to deny God altogether, but to express doubt as to whether knowledge could be attained, and to protest ignorance on 'a great many things that the -ists and the -ites about me professed to be familiar with'.[3]

But if the word was new, the idea was not. Moreover, it caught on rapidly. By the end of the century more and more people found that it was the term agnosticism which best described their beliefs about religion. No doubt, Kant's metaphysical agnosticism had percolated down to the more general reading and thinking public via his disciples, ecclesiastical or otherwise. But more important was the place that science had come to assume in popular imagination. As scientists explained more and more about the workings of the universe, God seemed to be relentlessly elbowed out of life.

[2] See below, pp. 181ff.
[3] *Cf.* C. Bibby, *T. H. Huxley* (Watts, 1959), p. 60. The word ultimately derives from the Greek. In his address to the Athenians Paul spoke of an altar dedicated to an Unknown God (*agnostos theos*) (Acts 17:23). But here the sense is rather different. Bibby has also edited *The Essence of T. H. Huxley* (Macmillan, 1968).

The point is underlined by the story of the celebrated, but probably apocryphal, conversation between Napoleon and the French astronomer Pierre Simon Laplace. Napoleon remarked that Laplace had eliminated God from his astronomy. Whereupon he was greeted with the reply: 'Sire, I have no need of that hypothesis.' God was no longer a term of scientific explanation. For many this meant that the words *nature* and *science* explained everything.

To some the intellectual history of the nineteenth century is the story of the final overthrow of God and the subsequent search for philosophies which would fill the place vacated by him. In this section we shall look at half a dozen of the more important atheistic and agnostic philosophies of the nineteenth century.

Feuerbach

Curiously enough, two of the most important anti-religious movements of the nineteenth century took Hegel as their starting-point. They are the philosophies of Feuerbach and Marx. Ludwig Feuerbach (1804–72) studied theology at Heidelberg, and then went to Berlin to read philosophy and sit at the feet of Hegel. He became an unsalaried lecturer at the University of Erlangen in 1828. Such a position was usually the first step to a professional academic career in Germany. But the prospects never materialized, and Feuerbach retired to a life of private reading and writing.

The titles of several of Feuerbach's principal works have a definite theological slant: *The Essence of Christianity* (1841),[4] *The Essence of Religion* (1845), and *Lectures on the Essence of Religion* (1851). They scarcely betray their author's intention to abolish the Christian idea of God and put nature in his place. Feuerbach did not want to dismiss religion as mere superstition. He wanted people to recognize it for what he believed it really was. Whereas Hegel had said that all reality was a manifestation of the Absolute Spirit, Feuerbach calmly

---

[4] Eng. tr. by George Eliot (1854), new edition with introductory essay by Karl Barth and foreword by H. Richard Niebuhr (Harper, New York, 1957).

told his readers that this spirit was none other than nature. 'Nature is thus the ground of man.'[5] Feuerbach could also agree with Schleiermacher that the core of all religion is a sense of absolute dependence, but 'that on which man depends and feels himself dependent is none other than nature'.[6]

In religion man objectifies and projects his nature. 'The divine being is nothing else than the human being, or, rather, the human nature purified, freed from the limits of the individual man, made objective – *i.e.* contemplated and revered as another, a distinct being. All the attributes of the divine nature are, therefore, attributes of the human nature.'[7] From here it was but a short step to the celebrated equation: 'theology is nothing else than anthropology – the knowledge of God nothing else than a knowledge of man!'[8]

As a footnote to all this, it is interesting to note that Feuerbach's pleas received a sympathetic hearing in *Honest to God*.[9] As Bishop Robinson pointed out, Feuerbach (like Nietzsche) was not so much an atheist as an *antitheist*. He was protesting against the idea of a God out there, over and above the universe. Taking Hegel as his starting-point, he came to the conclusion that Hegelianism must be transcended.[1] He was left with nature which he proceeded to deify and indeed treat as personal in so far as nature erupts into personal self-consciousness in the guise of man. Given his premises, Feuerbach's system is fairly logical. It demands that everything must be interpreted in the light of his system. The difficulty with it is that Christianity presents an obstinate lump that just will not be dissolved into the system. It speaks of a God who is other than nature. Modern man is left therefore with a choice, whether to follow Feuerbach to his logical conclusion or whether to take seriously the obstinate lump that refuses to dissolve.

[5] *Preliminary Theses Towards Reform of Philosophy* in *Sämtliche Werke*, edited by W. Bolin and F. Jodl (1903–11) 1959, II, p. 240.
[6] *The Essence of Religion* in *Sämtliche Werke*, VII, p. 434.
[7] *The Essence of Christianity*, p. 14.
[8] *Ibid.*, p. 207.   [9] *Honest to God*, pp. 41, 49–53.
[1] 'Hegelian philosophy is the last resort, the last rational prop of theology' (*Preliminary Theses* in *Sämtliche Werke*, II, p. 239).

Marx and Dialectical Materialism

Karl Marx (1818–83) was born in the Rhineland of Jewish parents who later became Lutherans. As a student at Bonn Marx studied law, but he then went to Berlin to read philosophy and history. He eventually received a doctorate at Jena for a study of the ancient Greek philosophers.

Hegel had died five years before Marx went to Berlin, but, as Marx later said, his intellectual legacy 'weighed heavily on the living'. The young Marx associated himself with a group of deviationist Hegelians who called themselves free spirits. From time to time Marx turned to journalism, but often his efforts proved abortive. The *Rheinische Zeitung*, which he edited, was suppressed by the authorities for its radicalism. His *Neue Rheinische Zeitung* met with a similar fate in the revolution of 1848. Marx was arrested, tried for sedition, acquitted, but expelled from Germany. He lived the rest of his life in London, dwelling in comparative poverty, and spending a good deal of his time in the British Museum gathering material for his great analysis of capitalism, *Das Kapital* (1867).

In the 1840s Marx met Friedrich Engels (1820–95). Together they wrote an enormous number of pamphlets and polemical works.[2] Engels was not only a literary collaborator. His prosperous textile business proved a useful means of support to Marx, who never had regular work. It was Engels who completed *Das Kapital* from Marx's posthumous papers.

Marx was both consciously and unconsciously indebted to Hegel.[3] But whereas Hegel regarded all reality as the outworking of the Absolute Spirit, Marx followed Feuerbach.

[2] The definitive editions of their joint works published in East Berlin and Moscow fill many volumes. For an abridged edition see Karl Marx and Frederick Engels, *Selected Works in Two Volumes* (Foreign Languages Publishing House, Moscow, 1950). There are two handy Pelican editions of Marx: *Karl Marx: Selected Writings in Sociology and Social Philosophy*, edited by T. B. Bottomore and Maximilien Rubel (1956, 1965) and *Marx on Economics*, edited by Robert Freedman (1962, 1963). There is an Everyman edition of *Capital* translated by Eden and Cedar Paul which first appeared in 1930. For Engels see W. O. Henderson (ed.), *Engels: Selected Writings* (Pelican, 1967).

[3] Although Marx consciously deviated from Hegel in his later writings, *Capital* contains a handful of appreciative references. Moreover, as Jean Hyppolite has shown in his *Études sur Marx et Hegel* (Paris, 1955), Marx's

He credited Feuerbach with having 'founded *genuine materialism* and *positive science* by making the social relationship of "man to man" the basic principle of his theory'.[4] But instead of reinterpreting religion Marx went on to denounce it as the enemy of all progress. 'Man makes religion, religion does not make man. Religion is indeed man's self-consciousness and self-awareness as long as he has not found his feet in the universe. But man is not an abstract being, squatting outside the world. Man is the world of men, the State, and society. This State, this society, produce religion which is an inverted world consciousness, because they are an inverted world. . . . Religious suffering is at the same time an expression of real suffering and a protest against real suffering. Religion is the sigh of the oppressed creature, the sentiment of a heartless world, and the soul of soulless conditions. It is the opium of the people. The abolition of religion, as the illusory happiness of men, is a demand for their real hapiness.'[5] This last quotation from an early unpublished work shows that already in 1843 Marx had formulated the basic programme from which he never afterwards deviated.

The vacuum left by religion was to be filled by materialism. But it was a dynamic materialism modelled along the lines of Hegelian dialectic. It fell to Engels, Lenin and others to work out the full orthodox doctrine of Dialectical Materialism, but the elements are there in Marx. Reality is not static. It follows a course of upward progress, though the latter is sometimes of necessity rather jerky. In *Capital* Marx announced that in the economics of society, 'just as in the natural sciences, we find confirmation of the law discovered by Hegel in his *Logic*, that, at a certain point, what have been purely quantitative changes become qualitative'.[6] In context Marx was discussing the point at which the small property owner became a capitalist. He proceeded to draw various illustrations from chemistry. But the classic Communist illustration of the way society evolves by sudden dramatic leaps is drawn from the

---

Capital retains a good deal of the substance of his earlier Hegelianism, even though the Hegelian vocabulary has been dropped.

[4] *Economic and Philosophical Manuscripts* (1844) in Bottomore and Rubel, p. 85.
[5] *Ibid.*, pp. 41f.　　　　　　　　[6] *Capital*, p. 319.

way water turns into steam or ice at certain temperatures.[7] Such is the scientific justification of the evolution of society from feudalism to capitalism, from capitalism to socialism, and from socialism to Communism. In each case the change came about through class struggles. As the opening words of *The Communist Manifesto* (1848) announce: 'The history of all hitherto existing society is the history of class struggles.'[8] The next step involves the abolition of all property in land, the centralization of credit, communication, industry, agriculture and education.[9] To that end, the *Manifesto* closes with the call: 'Working men of all countries, unite.'[1]

Bertrand Russell, who for the best part of this century has been one of the intellectual leaders of the left in politics, has scathingly commented: 'Marx professed himself an atheist, but retained a cosmic optimism which only theism could justify. Broadly speaking, all the elements in Marx's philosophy which are derived from Hegel are unscientific, in the sense that there is no reason whatsoever to suppose them true.'[2] In the last analysis, the remedies that Marx prescribed for the evils of society had little to do with their philosophic dress. As Russell says, they must be judged on their own merits. Nevertheless, the fact remains that large numbers of intellectuals, both professional and self-made, have been influenced by his thinking. And in the Communist bloc today Marxist-Leninist materialism is the official creed of millions, whether they understand it or not.

Nietzsche

Another continental thinker who was bitterly opposed to religion and whose thought has also been utilized in the twentieth century for political purposes was Friedrich

---

[7] *Cf.* R. N. Carew Hunt, *The Theory and Practice of Communism* (1950, Pelican, 1963), p. 44.
[8] Marx and Engels, *Selected Works*, I, p. 33. Although it was first printed in London, the work was written in German. The translation of Samuel Moore (1888) has been republished as a Pelican Book (1967) with a full and critical introduction by A. J. P. Taylor.
[9] *Ibid.*, p. 50.   [1] *Ibid.*, p. 51.
[2] *History of Western Philosophy*, p. 816.

Nietzsche (1844–1900).[3] Under the Nazis expurgated editions of his works were used to bolster their doctrines. But, in fact, Nietzsche seems to have less in common with National Socialism than he has with modern Humanism and Existentialism. At the present time, Nietzsche is being feted as the founder-member of the Death of God school in theology.[4]

Friedrich Nietzsche was the son and grandson of a family of Lutheran pastors. He was born in Prussia, and studied theology and philology at Bonn, later transferring to Leipzig. He enjoyed a brilliant reputation as a student. He was made an associate professor at Basel without having written the customary qualifying theses, and was awarded a doctorate by Leipzig in 1869 without having to produce a dissertation. He became a full professor in 1870, but resigned nine years later through ill-health. Illness dogged him throughout his life. Scholars disagree over the causes. Insanity ran in the family. He may have contracted syphilis. But early in 1889 Nietzsche became insane, and remained in mental darkness until his death.

Nietzsche has been described as a prophet rather than a systematic thinker. Certainly his numerous writings were fragmentary. Many of his books, including his chief work, *Thus Spoke Zarathustra*, consist entirely of aphorisms. They are written in a bitterly ironic and intensely personal manner. They include *Human, All too Human: A Book for Free Spirits* (1878), *The Joyful Wisdom* (1882), and *Beyond Good and Evil* (1886). Other works include *The Twilight of the Idols* (1888) (a title which parodied Wagner's opera), *Towards a Genealogy of Morals* (1887), *The Antichrist: Attempt at a Critique of Christianity* (1895) and *Ecce Homo* (1888).

But if Nietzsche was a prophet, he was a self-appointed spokesman on behalf of man. And the object of his attack was

---

[3] The standard English edition of Nietzsche is that of *The Complete Works*, edited by Oscar Levy (Allen and Unwin, 18 vols., 1909–13). The handiest edition is the paperback one, edited by Walter Kaufmann, *The Portable Nietzsche* (The Viking Press, New York, 1966[18]). His most important work *Thus Spoke Zarathustra* is available in a Penguin paperback edition in the translation of R. J. Hollingdale (1961).

[4] See below, pp. 218f.

God. In *The Joyful Wisdom* he gave almost poetic expression
to his militant atheism when he exulted:

> The most important of more recent events – that 'god is
> dead', that the belief in the Christian God has become
> unworthy of belief – already begins to cast its first shadows
> over Europe. . . . In fact, we philosophers and 'free spirits'
> feel ourselves irradiated as by a new dawn by the report
> that the 'old God is dead'; our hearts overflow with gratitude,
> astonishment, presentiment and expectation. At last the
> horizon seems open once more, granting even that it is not
> bright; our ships can at last put out to sea in face of every
> danger; every hazard is again permitted to the discerner;
> the sea, *our* sea, again lies open before us; perhaps never
> before did such an 'open sea' exist.[5]

Nietzsche's starting-point is the non-existence of God. Man is
therefore left to fend for himself. Since God does not exist,
man must devise his own way of life. Admittedly, Nietzsche
found it necessary to shout from time to time at those who
still believed. And the reader of the above passage may
discern a certain wistful note among the more jubilant strains.
For if God no longer exists, man must go it alone. While this
brings a certain sense of relief, it also brings anxiety about the
future.

Nietzsche's prescription for the human predicament lay in
the complementary doctrines of the will to power, the revalua-

---

[5] *The Joyful Wisdom*, No. 343, p. 275. As this quotation in fact suggests,
Nietzsche was not the first to speak of the 'death of God'. The Romantic
poet Jean Paul (1762–1825) had already sounded the death-knell in his
Siebenkäs (1796–97) which contained a 'Discourse of the dead Christ from atop
the cosmos: there is not God'. The poet considers the loneliness and meaninglessness of the universe without God. G. W. F. Hegel had also spoken about
the death of God in his *Phenomenology of Mind* (1807, 1841², Eng. tr., pp.
781ff.). But here the thought is that traditional theism is now obsolete, and
must give way to Absolute Idealism. Curiously enough, Hegel dresses his
thought up in the language of Christian theology, and speaks of 'the event
of God's emptying Himself of His Divine Being through His factual Incarnation and His Death' (p. 780). On Hegel see above, pp. 119–123.
The thought is similar to that of Thomas Altizer today (see below, pp.
219–221).

tion of all values, and the superman. This last idea has been the frequent victim of caricature and misunderstanding. The superman (German: *Übermensch*) has nothing to do with Nazi doctrines of racial superiority. Still less does the term imply a Batman-type comic-strip figure of space fiction. The superman is the man who realizes the human predicament, who creates his own values, and who fashions his life accordingly. He himself is no stranger to anguish, but he triumphs over weakness, and despises it in others.

These combined elements in Nietzsche's teaching stand out clearly, for example, in the poem.

> Souls that lack determination
> Rouse my wrath to white-hot flame![6]

and also the aphorism on *What Belongs to Greatness:*

> Who can attain to anything great if he does not feel in himself the force and will *to inflict* great pain? The ability to suffer is a small matter: in that line, weak women and even slaves often attain masterliness. But not to perish from internal distress and doubt when one inflicts great suffering and hears the cry of it – that is great, that belongs to greatness.[7]

It is not difficult to see why Nietzsche was adopted as the philosopher of National Socialism. Of all the nineteenth-century atheists he was the most consistent. He had nothing but scorn for those who denied the Christian idea of God but sought to salvage Christian morality.[8] For Nietzsche there must be a clean sweep. Man must start from scratch, deciding what is right and wrong by his own will.

Nietzsche's influence upon European literature and philosophy has been incalculable. Among the poets and writers indebted to him are Rainer Maria Rilke, Stefan George, Gottfried Benn, Thomas Mann, Hermann Hesse,

---

[6] *The Joyful Wisdom*, p. 364.   [7] *Ibid.*, No. 325, p. 250.
[8] *Cf. The Antichrist*, Nos. 15ff. and *Twilight of the Idols*, Nos. 4ff. (Kaufmann, *The Portable Nietzsche*, pp. 515ff. and 581ff.).

André Gide, André Malraux, Shaw and Yeats. Camus, Sartre, Scheler, Spengler, Tillich and Buber are among the philosophers who in one way or another have been influenced by Nietzsche. The discerning reader who has the patience to wade through the torrents of bitter diatribe will encounter a mind which in its moments of lucidity clearly grasped the implications of the premise that God is dead. For those who accept this premise Nietzsche is *the* prophet and philosopher of the nineteenth century. But for those who do not, his writings present interesting case-material.

Comte and Positivism

Before we leave atheism and agnosticism on the Continent, mention must be made of the French Positivist philosopher Auguste Comte (1798-1857). Among other things he is said to have invented the term 'sociology'. Certainly, he did pioneer work in the subject, and did much to set it on a scientific basis.

Comte was born into a Catholic family, but at the age of fourteen he announced that he had 'naturally ceased believing in God'. At the same time he seems to have abandoned his family's traditional attachment to royalism in favour of republicanism. After studying in Paris, he earned his living by tutoring in mathematics. In 1826 Comte began to give private lectures on his new philosophy. From these emerged his major six-volume work, *Cours de la Philosophie Positive* (1830–42) which appeared in English as *The Positive Philosophy of Auguste Comte, Freely translated and condensed* by Harriet Martineau (2 volumes, 1853). In later works, such as *The System of Positive Polity* (1851–54)[9] and *The Catechism of Positive Religion* (1852),[1] Comte tried to work out a religion of humanity.

Comte believed that the history of the human race revealed three main stages of development, 'the Theological, or fictitious', 'the Metaphysical, or abstract' and 'the Scientific, or positive'. In the first the human mind looks for first causes and 'supposes all phenomena to be produced by the immediate

[9] Eng. tr. in 4 volumes by J. H. Bridges, F. Harrison and others (1875–77).
[1] Eng. tr. by R. Congreve (1858).

action of supernatural beings'. The second is a transitional stage where the mind searches for 'abstract forces' behind phenomena. But in the third and ultimate stage man's mind applies itself to the scientific study of the laws according to which things work. God and the supernatural are left behind as irrelevant superstition. Having announced all this by way of introduction,[2] Comte's *Positive Philosophy* went on to review various scientific ideas and to dabble in history and sociology. The great goal was a kind of humanitarian, European commonwealth which is perhaps best left described in Comte's own words:

> The five elements of this great process will each bring their own special contribution to the new system, which will inseparably combine them all. France will bring a philosophical and political superiority; England, an earnest predilection for reality and utility; Germany, a natural aptitude for systematic generalization; Italy, its genius for art; and Spain, its familiar combined sense of personal dignity and universal brotherhood. By their natural co-operation, the positive philosophy will lead us on to a social condition the most conformable to human nature, in which our characteristic qualities will find their most perfect respective confirmation, their complete mutual harmony, and the freest expansion of each.[3]

Much to the disgust of thoroughgoing atheists like Nietzsche, Comte proposed a religion of humanity in which God was dethroned and humanity, 'the great being', put in his place. He even adapted Catholic worship, priests and sacraments to his secular purposes. A 'Positivist Calendar' was produced in which the names of secular scientists and scholars replaced those of the saints. And in 1848 a 'Positive Society' was founded which endeavoured to apply Positivist principles to the reformation of society. But the new religion never really caught on. The really important social reforms of the nineteenth century were carried out either by convinced Christians

[2] *Positive Philosophy*, I, p. 2.   [3] *Ibid.*, II, p. 467.

or by those who were committed to less grandiose political programmes.

Mill and Utilitarianism

Consciously or unconsciously Utilitarianism has become absorbed into the bloodstream of much modern thinking. Utilitarian ideas tend to be regarded as a more rational alternative to Christianity as the basis for political and social action. In its simplest and crudest form Utilitarianism teaches that the right action is the one that promotes (or at least tries to promote) the greatest happiness of the greatest number.

Modern Utilitarianism dates from Thomas Hobbes in the seventeenth century, but it is arguable that its antecedents go back to classical times in the shape of Epicureanism. It was revived in the late eighteenth century by Jeremy Bentham (1748–1832), but it was John Stuart Mill (1806–73) who popularized the term and produced the classical Victorian exposition of the doctrine.[4] Henry Sidgwick (1838–1900) is the third member of the trio of the great advocates of Utilitarianism in the nineteenth century.

Mill himself was privately educated by his father. He could read Plato in the original Greek with ease by the time he was ten. Much of his life was spent in England in the service of the East India Company. For a time he was a member of Parliament. In his earlier days he was a disciple of Bentham. But recent students of his work have found it difficult to classify his teaching with precision and even to harmonize it with his private life. Rather than attempt a brief critique of Mill, it will be more useful here to try to distinguish the main types of Utilitarian thinking.

It is customary to draw a basic distinction between *act* and *rule* Utilitarianism, although recent writers have suggested that the distinction is by no means as clear cut as the words imply. According to the former, the rightness or wrongness of each individual action is to be decided by its consequences.

---

[4] Mill's *Utilitarianism* first appeared in *Fraser's Magazine* in 1861. It is reprinted in a handy collection of *Mill's Ethical Writings*, edited by J. B. Schneewind (Collier-Macmillan, 1965).

According to the latter, we should consider the consequences, not of some particular act, but of adopting some general rule, such as 'Keep promises'. Bentham, Sidgwick and Mill are generally thought of as *act* Utilitarians, but there is some doubt about Mill.

Having drawn this broad distinction, we have then to ask, who is to benefit from the action under consideration? If we say that it is the person performing the act, we are then technically classified as *egoistic* Utilitarians. But if we say that we should take other people into consideration when judging the rightness or wrongness of an action, we are then classified as *universalistic* Utilitarians.

A further distinction which cuts across the previous ones is that between *hedonistic* and *ideal* Utilitarianism. A *hedonistic* Utilitarian like Bentham would say that the sole consideration is the *quantity* of pleasure (or lack of it) that an action produces. This approach draws no distinction in principle between an evening spent playing Bingo and one spent listening to Bach. It all depends upon the tastes of the person concerned. The *ideal* Utilitarian, on the other hand, tries to take other factors into consideration. He may hold that some things which people find pleasant (the taking of 'soft' drugs, for example) are in fact intrinsically bad, and that some things which people find unpleasant are intrinsically good.

Finally, Utilitarianism may be put forward as either *normative* or *descriptive*. In the former case it is a system of how we *ought* to think and behave. In the latter case it is an analysis of how we *do* in fact think and behave.

Utilitarianism has a certain superficial attractiveness. Although there is no longer a Utilitarian school of thinkers, Utilitarian considerations play an increasingly large part in public debate on matters like capital punishment, penal reform and abortion. For they seem to offer short cuts to difficult problems. To argue on the grounds of expediency seems easier than arguing on grounds of principle in a society where objective standards are called in question.

But as a complete ethical system, pure Utilitarianism has numerous snags. It does not explain *why* I should act so as to promote the greatest happiness of the greatest number. I might be able to see that my honesty is to the advantage of other people. But Utilitarianism does not explain *why* I should be honest.[5] It does not account for the fact that people do believe that some things are right and other things are wrong regardless of their consequences. The notion of promoting the greatest happiness of the greatest number is sometimes helpful. But sometimes it is impossible to decide which action will produce the greatest happiness, and often it is impossible to weigh the happiness of the individual against that of society at large. Like the teaching of Nietzsche, Utilitarianism is a stop-gap philosophy which has some claim to consideration on the assumption that God is dead. But even so, it is often helpless to decide which course of action is right, because the consequences are imponderable. And once Utilitarians start talking about obligations to promote happiness, they are in fact appealing to a metaphysical authority outside their particular system.

Peirce, James and Pragmatism

In this study we are concentrating attention on trends in European philosophy. But some mention must be made of a movement which originated in North America in the second half of the nineteenth century and continued to dominate American philosophy until the 1930s. The term Pragmatism derives from the Greek *pragmata* which means 'acts', 'affairs', 'business'. It has come to be associated with such slogans as 'Truth is what works', 'The true is the expedient' and 'Faith in a fact helps create the fact'.

As a technical, philosophical term, the word was coined by Charles Sanders Peirce (1839–1914).[6] It denoted an attempt to work out a theory of meaning, 'that a *conception*, that is, the rational purport of a word or other expression, lies exclusively in its conceivable bearing upon the conduct of life'.[7] This leads to the notion that the sole test of truth is its practical

[5] The idea that ethical principles can be deduced solely from matters of fact is sometimes referred to as the naturalistic fallacy.
[6] For a basic introduction see Charles S. Peirce, *Selected Writings* (*Values in a Universe of Chance*), edited by Philip P. Wiener (1958, Dover, New York, 1966).
[7] *Ibid.*, p. 183.

consequences. Truth is, therefore, relative. When applied to religion this means that a religion or any aspect of it is not to be valued for its own sake but for its psychological and moral effects.

Pragmatism was developed in different directions by William James (1842–1910), John Dewey (1859–1952) and others. It had some influence on liberal Catholics like G. Tyrrell and Baron von Hügel at the turn of the century. In *Pragmatism, A New Name for Some Old Ways of Thinking* (1907) William James argued that, 'If the hypothesis of God works satisfactorily in the widest sense of the word, it is true.' In *The Will to Believe* (1897) he advanced the doctrine of voluntarism, that under certain conditions truth can be found only by an act of the will. There are so many instances in life where the pros and cons of an issue cannot be weighed up on purely intellectual grounds. To refrain from a decision is in fact to make a decision. We must therefore choose, taking our lives into our own hands.

There are various elements of truth in all this. The Pragmatists were right when they drew attention to the fact that we cannot understand a concept without considering its consequences and relations with other concepts. It is not enough to note the dictionary meaning of a word. We must also study how it is used in any given context. In saying this the Pragmatists were anticipating the linguistic philosophers of the twentieth century. Moreover, James was drawing attention to an important aspect of religious belief when he stressed the element of choice. But the Christian faith is never a matter of blind choice. As we saw in discussing the Reformers, it is not a case of making an irrational choice in a situation where all the factors cancel each other out. Nor is the notion of God a mere working hypothesis (like that of Santa Claus) which in reality bears no relation to facts but which induces a certain euphoria. Christian faith depends upon an inner awareness of God which is there prior to any decision, but which deepens as one progresses in following Christ. And if experience, history or science were to show that the Christian account of existence was wrong (in the same way that growing up and finding out what really happens on Christmas Eve explodes the notion of Santa Claus), the whole Christian conception of God would have to go.[8]

Darwin and evolution

But by far the most potent single factor to undermine popular belief in the existence of God in modern times is the evolutionary theory of Charles Darwin. Darwin did not invent evolution. In *The Principles of Geology* (3 volumes, 1830–33) Sir Charles Lyell accounted for the present condition of the earth's surface by positing a gradual process of development. He argued that the chalk cliffs of Dover were the remains of marine creatures, deposited there at the rate of an inch or two a century, and then upheaved on to the shore. Fossils were the remains of creatures dating back to an almost incalculable antiquity. In 1844 an anonymous book *The Vestiges of the Natural History of Creation*[9] extended the idea of evolution from geology to the whole of animal life. There was no special once-and-for-all act of creation. Darwin's own grandfather, Erasmus Darwin, had held a doctrine of evolution.

Charles Darwin (1809–82) began his career as a medical student at Edinburgh, but his studies there ended in failure. He turned to theology at Cambridge, and barely scraped home in his final examinations. Already he knew that he could not go forward for ordination. From 1831 to 1836 he acted as a naturalist on a surveying expedition off the coast of South America in the Beagle. This furnished him with the basic material for his evolutionary theory. For long enough he toyed with the idea of writing a book. In the end his hand was forced, when he was sent a manuscript by A. R. Wallace which anticipated many of his own conclusions. In 1858 he and Wallace published a joint communication *On the Tendencies of Species to form Varieties*. It was followed a year later by his

---

[8] See below, pp. 176ff., 284.
[9] The book had an enormous sale, and by 1860 had gone through eleven editions. It later transpired that the author was Robert Chambers, the man who gave his name to *Chambers's Encyclopedia*. He was not a professional scientist but a prolific author and editor.

great work *The Origin of Species*.[1] The whole of the first edition was sold out on the day of publication.

On the whole the initial reception was lukewarm. Darwin's friend, T. H. Huxley, wrote an enthusiastic review in *The Times*, but the *Daily News* thought that it had all been said before in *The Vestiges*. The turning-point came at the Oxford meeting of the British Association the following year. The Bishop of Oxford, 'Soapy Sam' Wilberforce, had treated the audience to a fine display of rhetorical wit. But in reply Huxley demolished the bishop's speech as a piece of ignorant and 'aimless rhetoric'. Within a decade evolution became the accepted orthodoxy.

The reasons for this are interesting. For one thing, Darwin had argued his case well. He had amassed a great deal of data, and he drew attention to many genuine facts. But even so, Darwin himself had his doubts. As he read the reviews of his book, there were times when he wondered whether after all he had not made a colossal mistake. The experts of his day were by no means agreed. Yet Darwin's theories made more sense to reasonable people than the obscurantism of certain churchmen and the dogmatism of some of the older scientists. He drew attention to the apparent great waste and warfare in nature: the millions of acorns that never grew into trees, pollen that was never fertilized, animals that had to prey upon each other in order to survive.

There were two main parts to his theory. One which was not new was evolution, the suggestion that life as we know it has gradually developed over millions of years from a common ancestry and possibly from a single prototype being. What Darwin did here was to put it on a more scientific basis through the mass of material that he produced in its favour. But to this he added another idea, that of 'natural selection', or, as it is commonly described, the survival of the fittest. In order to exist, plants and animals have to prey upon each other. Those who develop new capacities and adapt themselves to their environment the quickest are those which survive. These

---

[1] The book is still in print in Everyman's Library. For its centenary edition a new introduction was written by W. R. Thompson, F.R.S., Director of the Commonwealth Institute of Biological Control, Ottawa.

new capacities are alleged to have become permanent features of such creatures in such a way that new species are evolved. Admittedly, the theory had to assume that this sometimes happened very suddenly, and it was not clear how birds descended from reptiles, mammals from earlier quadrupeds, quadrupeds from fishes, or vertebrates from invertebrates. Nevertheless, this became a kind of law, explaining the behaviour of the universe.[2] Moreover, although Darwin's closing passages make a couple of respectful references to the Creator,[3] the main thrust of his thinking was clear. Evolution removes the need for belief in God.

In later utterances Darwin's agnosticism came more into the open. In 1871 he published *The Descent of Man*. By that time his views were well established. He had able and vigorous advocates such as T. H. Huxley who also drew the same agnostic corollary. There were also those who climbed on the bandwaggon of evolution and made it the key to everything. Certainly, it chimed in with the optimistic, progressive spirit of the age.

It was largely through Herbert Spencer (1820–1903) that evolution reached the man in the street. Spencer saw the struggle for existence in every sphere of life. Evolution convinced him that nature ought not to be interfered with, and therefore that he ought to oppose state education, poor laws and housing reform. Both capitalist and socialist put evolution to good use. Business men such as Andrew Carnegie and J. D. Rockefeller told themselves that, though the individual might suffer in the dealings of big business, it was all part and parcel of the law of competition. Karl Marx found it equally useful. He read *The Origin of Species* in 1860, commenting that 'Darwin's book is very important and serves me as a basis in natural science for the struggle in history'.[4] Some years later he sought permission to dedicate his *Capital* to Darwin, but permission was refused. Nevertheless, evolution came to fulfil the role in Communist doctrine that Marx cast for it.

[2] See *The Origin of Species*, chapter IV on 'Natural Selection; or the Survival of the Fittest' (pp. 80–127). [3] *Ibid.*, pp. 462f.
[4] *Cf.* R. E. D. Clark, *Darwin: Before and After* (Paternoster Press, 1948), pp. 112f.

Churchmen were divided about evolution. Despite his agnosticism, Darwin was duly buried in Westminster Abbey. There were those like Dean Church and Archbishop Frederick Temple who believed that evolution was not incompatible with belief in the Creator. Evolution merely explained *how* the different species had come into being. As Temple said in his Bampton Lectures on *The Relations of Religion and Science* (1884), 'To the many partial designs which Paley's *Natural Theology* points out, and which still remain what they were, the doctrine of Evolution adds the design of perpetual progress . . . The doctrine of Evolution leaves the argument for an intelligent Creator and Governor of the earth stronger than it was before.'[5] But others, like C. H. Spurgeon, were frankly sceptical. More proof was needed. Darwin had yet to fish up the missing links.

Today the debate is still in progress. It is generally recognized that Genesis is not trying to give an exact, scientific account of creation, and that many of the features of its early chapters are intentionally symbolic.[6] On the other hand, although some form of evolution is widely accepted as scientific orthodoxy, acquiescence in it is by no means universal. In his introduction to the centenary edition of *The Origin of Species* W. R. Thompson confesses that he is 'not satisfied that Darwin proved his point or that his influence in scientific and public thinking has been beneficial'.[7] Thompson points out that 'Darwin did not show in the *Origin* that species had originated by natural selection; he merely showed, on the basis of certain facts and assumptions, how this might have happened, and as he had convinced himself he was able to convince others'.[8] He goes on to point out that the facts and interpretations on which Darwin had relied have ceased to be convincing. 'We now know that the variations determined by environmental changes – the individual differences regarded by Darwin as the material

[5] *The Relations of Religion and Science*, pp. 117, 122.
[6] *Cf.* N. H. Ridderbos, *Is there a Conflict between Genesis I and Natural Science?* (Eerdmans, Grand Rapids, 1957); Derek Kidner, *Genesis* (Tyndale Press, 1967).
[7] *The Origin of Species* (Everyman's Library, 1959), p. vii.
[8] *Ibid.*, p. xii.

on which natural selection acts – are not hereditary.'[9] Thompson admits that certain sudden variations or mutations are hereditary. But in general, 'they are useless, detrimental, or lethal'.[1]

On the other hand, Thompson thinks that *The Origin* sent many scientists on a false trail. A great deal of time and energy has been wasted trying to produce family trees showing the descent of vertebrates from invertebrates, but which involve a great deal of indemonstrable guess-work. 'A long-enduring and regrettable effect of the success of the *Origin* was the addiction of biologists to unverifiable speculation.'[2] Thompson concludes that Darwin's mixture of 'fact and fiction' satisfied a certain public appetite, but goes on to say, 'We are beginning to realize now that the method is unsound and the satisfaction illusory. But to understand our own thinking, to see what fallacies we must eradicate in order to establish general biology on a scientific basis, we can still return with profit to the source-book which is *The Origin of Species*.'[3]

V TRENDS IN THEOLOGY

The history of theological trends in modern times is a subject in its own right. It deserves much closer study than is possible within the scope of the present book. Nevertheless, it is impossible to understand the contemporary religious situation without some knowledge of what has happened in theology over the past two hundred years. In this final section of this chapter we shall attempt, therefore, to spotlight some of the important theological trends in the nineteenth century and note their connection with philosophy.

Liberal theology

The closing years of the eighteenth and the whole of the

---

[9] *Ibid.* 'For example, in a certain pure line of the house-fly, those with the longest wings may conceivably have an advantage – though I cannot see how this could be demonstrated. But we cannot, by choosing and mating these long-winged flies, produce a progressive increase in the proportion of long-winged flies, or a progressive increase in wing length.'
[1] *Ibid.*   [2] *Ibid.*, p. xxi.   [3] *Ibid.*, p. xxiv.

nineteenth century produced a continuous crop of rationalistic and fictitious lives of Jesus, written on the assumption that the miraculous and supernatural elements in the Bible are no longer worthy of credence. We have already noticed that the initial impulse in this enterprise was given by the English Deists,[4] and that it was taken up on the Continent by H. S. Reimarus and G. E. Lessing.[5] They were soon followed by lesser men like K. F. Bahrdt, K. H. Venturini, H. E. G. Paulus, K. A. Hase and Bruno Bauer whose musings lie embalmed in Albert Schweitzer's famous survey of *The Quest of the Historical Jesus* (1906).[6] But the most famous of all the nineteenth-century liberal 'lives of Jesus' were those of the German theologian, D. F. Strauss (1808–74), and the French orientalist, J. E. Renan (1823–92).

Strauss wrote more than once on the life of Jesus. But his *magnum opus* was his first and also the work which was to cost him his academic career. Strauss's *Life of Jesus* appeared in 1835–36.[7] It denied entirely the historical foundation of the supernatural elements in the Gospels. These were unintentionally created legends or myths which arose between the death of Jesus and the writing down of the Gospels in the second century. But this, Strauss averred, did not mean the end of all true religion. What was destroyed critically could still be salvaged with the aid of Hegel's Idealist philosophy. For what mattered were not the minor details of history, but the manifestation of the infinite Spirit in the finite. And this, Hegel had also maintained, was the central theme of history, philosophy and religion.

Renan's *Life of Jesus* (1863)[8] also set aside the supernatural elements in the Gospels. But the way he did it was rather different. Renan did not argue a case. Instead, he drew a very human picture of Jesus with a highly evocative background which made the reader feel the atmosphere of Galilee and Jerusalem. As Jesus roamed the length and breadth of

[4] See above, pp. 77f.   [5] See above, pp. 86ff.
[6] Eng. tr. by W. Montgomery (Black, (1910) 1954[3]).
[7] Eng. tr., 3 volumes, by George Eliot (1846).
[8] Eng. tr. with an introduction by Charles Gore (Everyman's Library, (1927) 1945).

Palestine preaching the 'sweet theology of love', he won the hearts of all and sundry. But after clashing with the rabbis at Jerusalem, he began to exchange his Jewish theology for revolutionary fervour. Towards the end he became obsessed with a strange longing for persecution and martyrdom. Before treachery and death put an end to his earthly career, he laid the foundations of a permanent body of followers. Although he made many mistakes, Jesus is assured of a permanent place without rival in his own sphere among the immortals of history. Renan's book passed through eight editions in three months and many more in the succeeding years. In a preface to the thirteenth edition he virtually admitted what many of his critics, orthodox and unorthodox, had been saying since the book first appeared. The book, he said, was not really scientific history at all. It was rather a picture of 'one of the ways in which things might have happened'.

The nearest English equivalent to Strauss and Renan was perhaps the anonymous *Ecce Homo* (1865),[9] written, it later transpired, by the future professor of modern history at Cambridge, Sir John Seeley. Strictly speaking, it was not a life of Jesus at all. It was more like an extended obituary. Seeley was more cagey than Strauss and Renan about denying the supernatural. He did not expressly reject it; he just wrote as if it were not there. He was not concerned with the miraculous healings of Jesus, but with Jesus as a moral marvel. Jesus had a passion for morality. He came not to teach it, but to infect men with it. The warmth of Jesus' personality had a wonderful power to transform men's lives.

In adopting this line of approach Seeley is typical of the mainstream of nineteenth-century liberalism. Its advocates felt unhappy about the supernatural elements in Christianity in the face of hostile attacks. They felt uncertain about the historicity of parts of the Bible. But at least they had the superb moral teaching of Jesus to hang on to. The historical Jesus of the mainstream liberals was a dynamic preacher of love and morality. He lived so close to God, that one might say that God was in him. Few went so far as Arthur Drews, in *The Christ Myth* (1910), who treated the whole gospel as a

[9] Available in Everyman's Library edition, (1908) 1932.

piece of fiction. But many were willing to concede that the divine Saviour of the Gospels was the product of the pious reflection of the early church. And the man who did more than anyone to foster this image of Christ was the apostle Paul, a man who had never known Jesus in the flesh. This was the picture painted by the foremost liberal church historian at the turn of the century, Adolf von Harnack (1851–1930), in his popular lectures, *What is Christianity?*[1] They were delivered to packed audiences at the University of Berlin in the winter of 1899–1900. Harnack had spoken extempore. He lived, of course, in the days before tape recorders. But an enterprising student took down the lectures in shorthand. After a few minor revisions they were then published and immediately became a theological best-seller. Harnack's portrait of Jesus was that of 'a man who has rest and peace for his soul, and is able to give life and strength to others'.[2] The gospel that he preached was not about himself but about the Father. It was concerned with the kingdom, the Fatherhood of God and the infinite value of the human soul, and the higher righteousness and the command to love.[3]

This type of approach, which stressed the humane and ethical elements in Christianity at the expense of the metaphysical and supernatural, was inherited from the leading systematic theologian in Germany in the second half of the nineteenth century, Albrecht Ritschl (1822–89). But ultimately it was part and parcel of the legacy of Kant and the Age of Enlightenment.[4] Kant had delivered a deadly onslaught upon metaphysics and the older natural theology. Belief in God was still admissible, but not on rational grounds. Traditional Christian theology must be scrapped. But religion could still be salvaged because of its close connections with morals.

Ritschl, who was professor of theology at Göttingen from 1864 until his death, followed Kant in rejecting metaphysics and in making ethics the heart of religion. He followed in the

---

[1] Eng. tr. by T. B. Saunders (Williams and Norgate, 1901, reprinted by Harper Torchbooks).
[2] *Ibid.*, p. 37.   [3] *Ibid.*, pp. 51, 144.
[4] See above, pp. 85f., 89f., 99–106.

footsteps of Schleiermacher,[5] in so far as he rejected both natural theology and revealed theology. Like Schleiermacher he tried to extract the essence of Christianity from Christian experience. But whereas Schleiermacher thought that he had found it in a *sense of absolute dependence*, Ritschl believed that he had discovered it in the realm of morals. It was Jesus' vocation to found the kingdom of God among men, and thus to be 'the Bearer of God's ethical lordship over men'.[6] His death, according to Ritschl, had nothing to do with atoning for sin. It was the supreme test of Christ's vocation.[7]

In later life Ritschl coined a pair of terms which have since passed into general theological vocabulary. He drew the distinction between *judgments of fact* and *judgments of value*.[8] The scientist makes judgments of fact on the basis of his precise observations, which he can test by controlled experiment. But in religion we are not able to make controlled experiments on God and on what happened in the past. Religious utterances, Ritschl argued, are value judgments – expressions of what this or that experience, event or person means to me. The distinction was perhaps a logical one on Ritschl's premises. But although it is important to distinguish the logical status of different types of assertions, it is important to notice that Ritschl's terms are themselves loaded (whether intentionally or not). They carry with them the suggestion that it is impossible to make valid, objective judgments in matters of religion, and that belief in an objective revelation of God (such as the Reformers believed in[9]) is out of the question for us today. Both points were taken for granted rather than proved in liberal, nineteenth-century theology.

The man who did most (at least in the eyes of the academic world) to discredit the moralistic Jesus of the nineteenth-century liberals was Albert Schweitzer (1875–1965). He did this partly in an essay on *The Mystery of the Kingdom of God:*

---

[5] See above, pp. 110f.
[6] *The Christian Doctrine of Justification and Reconciliation* (1874), Eng. tr. by H. R. Mackintosh and A. B. Macaulay (T. and T. Clark, Edinburgh, 1900), p. 451.
[7] *Ibid.*, p. 448.   [8] *Theologie und Metaphysik* (1881), pp. 9 and 34.
[9] See above, pp. 40–48.

The Secret of Jesus' Messiahship and Passion (1901)[1] and partly
in his doctorate thesis which we have already mentioned,
The Quest of the Historical Jesus (1906). The latter traced the
vicissitudes of critical theories from H. S. Reimarus in the
eighteenth century to his contemporary W. Wrede. Those who
have never dipped into Schweitzer will have their breath
taken away by his vivacity and style. The *Quest* is a *tour de force*
of theological journalism. It is possibly the most readable
and racy doctoral dissertation ever written. But its virtues are
apt to conceal its vices. Despite the vast number of authors
cited, Schweitzer appears to be almost totally unaware of
any theological work done outside the borders of France and
Germany. And even within his self-imposed limits, Schweitzer's
choice of material for discussion is often arbitrary. He certainly
leaves the reader in no doubt as to who are the heroes and
villains of the piece, but his skill as a role-caster depends upon
his own reconstruction of the historical Jesus. For it is by
this that everything else is judged.

At the end of his survey Schweitzer confronts the reader
with a choice between Wilhelm Wrede and himself. Wrede's
book on the messianic secret in the Gospels (*Das Messias-
geheimnis in den Evangelien*, 1901) was a thoroughgoing piece of
scepticism. It questioned the whole basis of the liberal reconstruction of Jesus. Schweitzer's own work was in many
ways complementary. It argued that the liberal, historical Jesus
could be constructed only at the expense of ignoring eschatology, the gospel teaching about the coming of the kingdom
and the approaching end of the age. The liberals had hung
on to the moral teaching of Jesus and closed their minds to his
teaching about the coming of the kingdom. Jesus, Schweitzer
argued, expected the kingdom to come shortly. When it came,
he would be revealed as the messianic son of man. With this
in view Jesus sent his disciples on a preparatory mission. He
did not even expect to see them back before the kingdom
came. When it did not come, Jesus changed his plans and
decided to force a show-down by sharing the messianic woes
himself and compelling the kingdom to come. The whole of
Jesus' moral teaching was an *interim ethic*, not designed to lay

[1] Eng. tr. (Black, (1914) 1956).

down principles for all time, but simply intended to fill the gap until the kingdom was finally established. But the whole plan misfired, and the net result was to cost Jesus his life.

Schweitzer helped to demolish the nineteenth-century 'historical' Jesus of the liberals by showing that they had ignored the eschatological element in Jesus' teaching. But the figure that he put in its place is scarcely better, for Jesus appears as a ranting, religious politician who blundered his way through life. If Schweitzer is right, then Jesus was wrong. What Schweitzer does is to substitute one rationalistic creation for another. The details are different, but the presuppositions are basically the same. Schweitzer is one with Strauss and Renan in eliminating the supernatural from history. He concludes, however, on an enigmatic note: after all that has been said about history, it is not history but life that shows us who Jesus really is.[2]

Schweitzer himself went on to study medicine (for which he earned another doctorate) and to go as a missionary to Lambaréné in French Equatorial Africa. But he was no ordinary missionary. Although Christ came into his teaching, his central theme was *respect for life*. His medical mission and his many subsequent writings bear eloquent testimony to his humane interests, although not all visitors to Lambaréné in his last years were impressed by his methods.[3]

Hand in hand with the many attempts made in the nineteenth century to reconstruct the life of Jesus on modern lines went the equally numerous attempts to investigate the biblical writings. One of the most notorious reconstructions of the New Testament was that of the so-called Tübingen School and its founder F. C. Baur (1792–1860). Baur saw the history of the early church as the outworking of a clash between two rival parties. On the one hand, there was the party of Jewish Christians led by Peter. And on the other hand, there was Paul who represented a newer, broader type of

[2] *The Quest of the Historical Jesus*, p. 401.
[3] For Schweitzer's own account see *My Life and Thought* (1931), Eng. tr. by C. T. Campion (Allen and Unwin, 1933 and subsequent editions). The best general study of Schweitzer is probably Werner Picht, *Albert Schweitzer: The Man and his Work*, Eng. tr. by E. Fitzgerald (Allen and Unwin, 1964).

Christianity, deeply influenced by the Greek world, which rejected the Jewish practice of circumcision and the narrower interpretation of the Law.[4] On this basis, Baur proceeded to evaluate the books of the New Testament. He would accept as genuine only those letters of Paul which bore traces of the conflict with the Judaizers. His list amounted to only four: Galatians, 1 and 2 Corinthians and Romans. Matthew, he held, was the earliest Gospel, for it seemed to him to be the most Jewish. John was the latest, because it bears little trace of the conflict which presumably means that it was by then patched up. Baur even detected in John traces of the second-century Gnostic and Montanist controversies. Naturally, on these premises, the Fourth Gospel was of little historical value.

Baur's thesis has often been represented as an attempt to read Hegelian philosophy into New Testament history. But Baur himself denied this.[5] Nevertheless, it was a classic, though by no means unique, case of an invention of an ingenious theory, accompanied by an equally ingenious manipulation of facts in order to prove it. At no point has Baur's thesis been vindicated by subsequent historical studies. Apart from the dubious attempt to reinterpret the history of the church around a single idea, it founders upon the dating of the New Testament books which can be deduced from the New Testament itself and from early Christian writings.

Before Baur, it was sometimes suggested that the Gospels, as we have them, are the results of independent oral traditions about Jesus being written down. As late as B. F. Westcott's *Introduction to the Study of the Gospels* (1851) this thesis was still argued. But in the meantime scholars began to entertain seriously the idea that the close similarities between Matthew, Mark and Luke might better be explained if they were in some way dependent upon each other or upon some common written sources. In 1835, the same year that Strauss's *Life of*

[4] Baur wrote voluminously. A select edition of his works, *Ausgewählte Werke,* edited by K. Scholder, is being published by Friedrich Frommann (Stuttgart, 1963–   ). Baur's *Paul, The Apostle of Jesus Christ*, was translated in 2 vols. (Williams and Norgate, 1876²). The latest study in English is that of Peter C. Hodgson, *The Formation of Historical Theology: A Study of Ferdinand Christian Baur* (Harper and Row, New York, 1966).

[5] *Cf.* Hodgson, *op. cit.*, pp. 1–4, 25f., 58f., 139f.

Jesus was published, there appeared a smaller, apparently insignificant work which nevertheless produced far greater repercussions in the long run. The reason for its temporary eclipse was partly that other theories and other books attracted greater attention, and partly that it was written in the decent obscurity of Latin. But Karl Lachmann's theory of the priority of Mark and the dependence on it of Matthew and Luke is perhaps the one theory of nineteenth-century Gospel criticism which is still generally accepted today.

The theory was championed in its early days by C. H. Weisse (1801–66) and C. G. Wilke (1786–1854). But it was not until after 1860 that it really established itself as critical orthodoxy. Its success was due in no small measure to H. J. Holtzmann (1832–1910), who added numerous refinements, not the least being the hypothesis of Q (an alleged collection of sayings of Jesus not used by Mark, who reports very little of Jesus' teaching, but used in different ways by Matthew and Luke).[6] On the Continent biblical criticism still tends to take the two-documentary hypothesis as its starting-point, even though it has further elaborated the study of the Gospels with form criticism.[7] In England the theory was further developed by B. H. Streeter in *The Four Gospels* (1924) in which he argued that there were originally four written sources (Mark, Q and documents behind Matthew and Luke). Today scholars do not talk as if they could go along to the British Museum and see Q there for themselves. They tend to talk about Q material. And some hold that the alleged Q passages are better explained by the mutual dependence of the Gospels upon each other and the strong possibility that Jesus (like all good teachers) repeated the same and similar lessons on numerous occasions. The Evangelists were thus not adapting the same material in different ways to suit their own ends, but were sometimes recording similar but different stories.

It would take us too far afield to trace the vicissitudes of

[6] Even today scholars are uncertain as to whether Q stands for the German *Quelle* (= 'source') or whether it was first chosen as being the next letter after P (P standing for the Petrine source, *i.e.* on the view that Mark's Gospel represents Peter's account).

[7] See below, pp. 186ff.; *cf.* pp. 281ff.

Old Testament criticism in the nineteenth century.[8] We have concentrated here on Gospel criticism as the crucial test case, trying to show how philosophical ideas impinged on biblical studies and also with the aim of showing how scepticism about the historicity of the Gospels, together with modern philosophical scepticism, has produced the prevailing climate of uncertainty about the truth of Christianity.

Catholic reactions

Liberal theology was by no means the only theology in the nineteenth century. Already in the 1830s there was grave concern in high Anglican circles at the rising tide of secularism and the growing influence of liberal ideas. Matters came to a head in 1833 when John Keble (1792–1866) preached his celebrated Assize Sermon. His text was 1 Samuel 12:23: 'As for me, God forbid that I should sin against the Lord in ceasing to pray for you.' His theme was national apostasy. In the same year John Henry Newman (1801–90) published the first of the *Tracts for the Times*. And so was born the Tractarian Movement. It was also called the Oxford Movement, because so many of its leading lights were Oxford dons. It was also the beginning of Anglo-Catholicism. For the Tractarian antidote to the irreligion of the times consisted in a return to the life and teaching of the primitive, catholic church.[9]

In its first phase from 1833 to 1845 it was largely concerned with vindicating the church as a divine institution and calling upon the Anglican clergy to fulfil their apostolic vocation. It was anti-ritual and anti-Rome. But as the years went by many of its adherents overcame their initial revulsion against Rome and abandoned their hopes of swinging round the Church of England to their Catholic ideals. In 1844 W. G. Ward's *Ideal of a Christian Church* frankly admitted that that

[8] For a history of critical theories see E. G. Kraeling, *The Old Testament since the Reformation* (Lutterworth Press, 1955). For a modern reassessment see K. A. Kitchen, *Ancient Orient and Old Testament* (Tyndale Press, 1966).
[9] For anthologies of Anglo-Catholic writings see O. Chadwick (ed.), *The Mind of the Oxford Movement* (Black, 1960); E. R. Fairweather (ed.), *The Oxford Movement* (OUP, New York, 1964).

ideal was to be found in the Church of Rome. By this time it had long been apparent that Newman's thoughts had already drifted in that direction. In 1841 he had published his notorious *Tract XC* which argued the improbable thesis that, although they set out to be Protestant, the compilers of the Thirty-Nine Articles of the Church of England had produced a thoroughly Catholic statement of doctrine. The argument was so specious and the intention so unpopular that the Tracts were terminated. For a time Newman lingered on in the Church of England. But in 1845 he made his submission to Rome.

The conversion of Newman, Ward and many of their disciples marked the end of the first phase of the Oxford Movement. Leadership now fell to the Regius Professor of Hebrew at Oxford, Edward Bouverie Pusey (1800–82). Apart from his Catholic teaching, Pusey produced a number of scholarly studies, defending the authenticity of the biblical writings against liberal attacks. Among them were his lectures on *Daniel the Prophet*.[1] Another leading Anglo-Catholic was H. P. Liddon who devoted his Bampton Lectures at Oxford for 1866 to the subject of *The Divinity of our Lord and Saviour Jesus Christ*. It was a massive and scholarly defence of orthodox Christian teaching against modern liberal views. It has never been refuted.

Although the original leaders of the Oxford Movement had been conservative in their approach to Christian teaching, the next generation felt that a somewhat more liberal approach was needed. In 1860 a group of broad churchmen had published *Essays and Reviews*, demanding the acceptance of modern critical views about the Bible. Today the book would be considered anaemic, but in the 1860s it created a tremendous stir. The bishops decided to prosecute, but in the end only two of the authors could be brought to court and they were eventually acquitted. Evangelicals and high churchmen were united in their opposition. Pusey's lectures on Daniel were part of the reply. But as time wore on, the second generation of Anglo-Catholics felt that radical critical views were not necessarily inconsistent with their position. In 1889 a number

[1] 1864, 9th edition with reply to critics, 1892.

F

of them joined together to produce *Lux Mundi: A Series of Studies in the Religion of the Incarnation*. In many ways they still conserved their old position. But in general they felt that so long as they could still hang on to the incarnation and the church, other doctrines (such as that of the verbal inspiration of Scripture) could be surrendered. Some of them made use of the idealism of T. H. Green. When the book appeared, Newman, now in the last year of his long life, pronounced that this was the end of Tractarianism. The movement did not at once fold up, but henceforth its character was changed. It continued to pervade large sections of the Anglican church. But over the years it became increasingly liberal, and in old age Charles Gore (1853–1932), the editor of *Lux Mundi*, felt that he was standing alone in Anglo-Catholic circles for the defence of the historic Christian faith.[2]

The Roman Catholic church was also keenly aware of the rising tide of secularism and the challenge of liberal ideas. But her methods of dealing with them were rather different. One way was to reassert the authority of the church in general and of the pope in particular. The second half of the nineteenth century witnessed a number of significant ventures in this direction under Popes Pius IX (1846–78) and Leo XIII (1878–1903).

In 1864 there was published the *Syllabus of Errors*.[3] It was a list of eighty ideas and doctrines, ranging from pantheism, naturalism and rationalism to socialism, Communism and Bible societies. It also listed errors concerning Christian marriage, the temporal power of the pope and contemporary liberalism. All were simply stated and condemned without reason or argument. Ten years earlier in 1854 Pius IX had

[2] On Gore and Anglo-Catholicism see the present writer's 'Charles Gore' in P. E. Hughes (ed.), *Creative Minds in Contemporary Theology* (Eerdmans, Grand Rapids, 1966), pp. 341–376.

[3] This document, together with all other important Catholic official pronouncements, is to be found in Latin in H. Denzinger, *Enchiridion Symbolorum* (Herder), a work which is constantly being brought up to date. An English translation of many of the documents in Denzinger appears in *The Church Teaches* (B. Herder Book Co.). Many important Catholic pronouncements also appear in English and Latin in P. Schaff, *The Creeds of Christendom*, II (New York, 1878).

defined the dogma of the Immaculate Conception (that the Blessed Virgin Mary had been preserved from all sin and guilt throughout her life from the moment of her conception by a special act of grace). In other words, Mary was deemed to be sinless. The dogma is interesting for many reasons, not least for the way in which this completely unfounded doctrine seems to be a step towards making Mary a sort of second redeemer alongside Christ.[4] But our interest here lies not so much in the dogma itself but in the way that it was promulgated. It was done so entirely on the authority of the pope himself. In other words, it was a kind of trial run for papal infallibility.

Papal infallibility was not defined until 1870. Up till then Catholics were deeply divided on the subject. It is no secret that many informed Catholics today wish that the dogma had never been defined. They are embarrassed by the fact that there are no grounds for it in Scripture and early church tradition. And the facts, both that Catholic theologians are uncertain which papal pronouncements are infallible, and that there has never been an official, infallible list of infallible pronouncements, are some indications of the vacuity of the dogma. Nevertheless, its advocates felt that the dogma was a logical development of Catholic teaching, and that they were striking a blow at modern secularism.

The dogma of papal infallibility was defined at the first Vatican Council. But this was not the only work of the Council. It produced two Constitutions. The dogma on infallibility appeared in the Constitution on the Church, but there was also the Constitution on the Faith. The latter committed the Catholic church to the Thomist view of faith and reason, and reaffirmed its belief in natural theology.[5] Chapter 2, canon 1 summed up its approach: 'If anyone says that the one true God, our creator and Lord, cannot be known with certainty by the natural light of human reason through those things which are made: let him be anathema.'[6]

---

[4] This trend seems to be confirmed by the practice of calling Mary *Co-redemptress* and crowned by the dogma of the assumption of Mary defined in 1950 (Denzinger, *op. cit.*, No. 2333; *cf.* 1978a).
[5] See above, pp. 26, 34ff.   [6] Denzinger, No. 1806.

Although no names were mentioned, Kant was an obvious opponent here, for Kant had denied this very thing.[7] Deists, materialists and pantheists were all singled out for attack. Faith and reason cannot contradict each other. Where reason disagrees with faith (*i.e.* the official teaching of the church), reason must give way.[8]

Nine years later further impetus was given to Thomism by the encyclical *Aeterni Patris* which asserted the permanent value of Aquinas's teaching, urging Catholic philosophers to draw their inspiration from it and adapt it to modern needs. Nevertheless, not all Catholic philosophers today are Thomists. And despite the *Syllabus of Errors* it was still necessary to issue a new syllabus, *Lamentabili,* reinforced by the encyclical letter *Pascendi,* in 1907. This was followed up by the Oath against Modernist Errors, *Sacrorum Antistitum* (1910). In the meantime, an official biblical commission was set up which reported from time to time on matters like the authorship of the Psalms and the historical character of the first chapters of Genesis and of the Gospels. As a matter of fact, Roman Catholic scholars have done a great deal of first-class work in the realm of biblical studies from this time onwards. Nevertheless, despite the numerous pronouncements, there are strong radical elements within the Catholic fold today.

Conservative scholarship

The word 'conservative' is perhaps an unfortunate one. It is a term which is loaded against itself. It conjures up the atmosphere of reaction for its own sake, of diehards making last-ditch efforts to thwart the honest intentions of the progressives. But in the sense that I am using it here, it denotes a wide variety of Christian scholars who believed that the historic Christian faith was still tenable despite modern philosophical and critical attacks. These scholars were not all Evangelicals, although they were agreed with the Evangelicals on essentials. We have already noted the work of Liddon and Pusey and how Evangelicals and Anglo-Catholics made common cause in their opposition to *Essays and Reviews.*

The Christian world owes an enormous debt to the Cam-

[7] See above, pp. 97–99.   [8] Denzinger, Nos. 1817f.

bridge trio of scholars B. F. Westcott (1825–1901), J. B. Lightfoot (1828–89) and F. J. A. Hort (1828–92). Westcott and Hort produced in 1881 the best Greek text of the New Testament of their time. Lightfoot edited *The Apostolic Fathers* (1885–90) and in so doing showed that the knowledge of the New Testament of these early second-century writers made untenable the theories of critics like Baur. The three scholars projected a series of commentaries on the whole of the New Testament. Unfortunately the project was never completed.[9] But the works that were finished became standard authorities, and did much to vindicate the historicity and authenticity of the New Testament. In this work they were by no means alone. Scholars such as Alfred Plummer, Sir William Ramsay, James Denney and H. B. Swete all made notable contributions. James Orr's *The Resurrection of Jesus* (1908) is still the best historical investigation of the New Testament data. Alfred Edersheim's *The Life and Times of Jesus the Messiah* (1883) combined a massive knowledge of rabbinics with careful scholarship and deep devotion.

On the Continent there were conservative scholars of great learning such as E. W. Hengstenberg (1802–69) and Theodor Zahn (1838–1933). In the United States the Princeton Theological Seminary was a centre of devout erudition. It was the home of such divines as Charles Hodge (1797–1878) and B. B. Warfield (1851—1921). The former's *Systematic Theology* (1871–72) and the latter's numerous writings on various subjects[1] still repay careful study. The leading preachers of the nineteenth century – men like C. H. Spurgeon (1834–92)

[9] Lightfoot was assigned the task of dealing with Paul. He wrote commentaries on *Galatians* (1865), *Philippians* (1868) and *Colossians and Philemon* (1875). Westcott wrote on *John* (1880), *The Epistles of St. John* (1883), *The Epistle to the Hebrews* (1889). His *Ephesians* was published posthumously in 1906. Hort produced only fragments on *1 Peter* (1898) and *James* (1909).
[1] After Warfield's death his numerous articles and studies were published in 10 volumes under various titles by OUP, New York (1927–). Of these *Christology and Criticism* (1929) is especially relevant to our discussion above. More recently the Presbyterian and Reformed Publishing Company of Philadelphia and other publishers have reissued certain selected extracts from the standard edition. These include *Biblical and Theological Studies* (1952) and *The Person and Work of Christ* (1950). For details of other works by Warfield see pp. 45, 72, 246, 306.

and J. C. Ryle (1816–1900) – were predominantly conservative in theology. While evangelical scholars were deeply concerned with theological and critical questions, it was the exception rather than the rule to take an interest in philosophy.[2]

Evangelicals rightly stressed men's personal relationship with God. Some of them could see that they must produce answers to liberal attacks on the Bible, otherwise their faith would be undermined. For them, scholarship had a purely negative value. It was a useful shield against the fiery darts of a Strauss or a Baur. Few paused to consider whether scholarship and philosophy might also enrich their faith and enlarge their understanding of God's works and divine truth. The disastrous results of the liberal espousal of Hegelianism or Kantianism were evident to the discerning. But the same discerning believers rarely asked whether their biblical faith might not also have philosophical implications which might profitably be developed in their own right.

The nineteenth century closed with a remarkable number of rival philosophies vying for the attention of modern man. Liberals tended to latch on to some form of Hegelianism or Kantianism. Both were in principle sub- and even anti-Christian. Roman Catholics were officially encouraged to espouse Thomism as the antidote to scepticism. Conservative Protestants did great work in the field of biblical scholarship, but few, if any, saw the need for a positive approach to philosophy relating it to their biblical faith. The history of philosophy in the twentieth century shows painfully in what way the Christian church has inherited the legacy of the nineteenth century.

[2] One such exception was James Orr who wrote a book on *David Hume and his Influence on Philosophy and Theology* (T. and T. Clark, Edinburgh, 1903). The same writer's *The Christian View of God and the World as Centring in the Incarnation* (Eliot, Edinburgh, 1893) compared biblical and philosophical ideas. Orr's wider view may well be due to his Scottish, Presbyterian background with its emphasis on the wholeness of truth.

4 PHILOSOPHY AND FAITH IN THE TWENTIETH CENTURY

Before the second World War the majority of British philosophers of religion were still trying to fend off the rising tide of scepticism by consolidating the bulwark of natural theology. Somehow or other one had to establish the validity of a religious interpretation of the world and of the idea of a Supreme Being as a necessary preliminary to introducing the Christian faith. Typical of the approach was a work which became a standard textbook, George Galloway's *The Philosophy of Religion* (1914). Galloway defined philosophy as 'reflexion on experience in order to apprehend its ultimate meaning'.[1] With this in mind he proceeded to take his readers on a conducted tour of human experience with a view to demonstrating that there was an ultimate Ground of things or Supreme Value or Good which gave meaning to experience.[2] A similar course was taken by Archbishop William Temple in various writings culminating in *Nature, Man and God* (1934).[3]

Both writers were consciously indebted to Idealism. To read both, one gets the feeling that, although natural theology is inadequate by itself, it is absolutely essential to Christian apologetics. To take one's stand simply upon the basis of the Christian religion would be unconvincing and inadequate, if not downright cheating. Christianity was to be vindicated by

[1] *The Philosophy of Religion* (T. and T. Clark, Edinburgh), p. 1.
[2] *Ibid.*, pp. 35ff.
[3] Temple's Gifford Lectures on natural theology, delivered in the University of Glasgow, 1932–33 and 1933–34 and published by Macmillan in 1934. Earlier philosophical writings included *Mens Creatrix* (1917) its and sequel, *Christus Veritas* (1924).

trying to find proof from outside. Such was the mood of pre-war British philosophical theology. Most professional philosophers seem blithely unaware of attempts made by such men as Karl Barth to work out an approach based upon the Christian revelation. And if they were not unaware, this view was patronizingly and peremptorily shrugged off.[4] Philosophers of religion seem to have been even more oblivious of two very different philosophical movements which sprang up on the Continent about the time of the first World War, Logical Positivism and Existentialism. The former began to hit British secular philosophy just before the second World War, and the latter made its main (though considerably less) impact after it. By the mid-1960s the issues raised by these two movements, coupled with a revival of nineteenth-century scepticism, had come to dominate discussions of philosophical theology. In some cases they had produced a mood of almost chronic despair which made writers like the Bishop of Woolwich plead for the abandonment of traditional Christian concepts of God.[5] Others went even further and have urged that the only salvation of religion lies in the death of God.

In this chapter we shall examine some of the more important trends. We shall begin with Logical Positivism and the linguistic analytic movement which followed in its wake. Then we shall turn to Existentialism and attempts to state theology in Existentialist terms. After this we shall look at the new radicalism of Bonhoeffer, *Honest to God* and the Death of God school. Finally we shall examine some of the views which do not fall into any of these categories, but which in some cases hold out more positive approaches to philosophy and the Christian faith.

I LOGICAL POSITIVISM AND LINGUISTIC ANALYSIS
Logical Positivism

Logical Positivism was an anti-metaphysical movement in philosophy. (The word *was* is used advisedly, for although the movement has made a deep impression upon modern philosophy, it no longer exists as such today.) It had two geogra-

---

[4] A notable exception to this was John Baillie's *Our Knowledge of God* (OUP, 1939).
[5] *Cf. Honest to God*, pp. 28–44.

phical roots,[6] the one English and the other Viennese. The English root was David Hume's empirical scepticism in the eighteenth century.[7] The other was considerably more recent. It grew out of a group of students and teachers of the University of Vienna which later was to acquire a certain fame as the Vienna Circle. Many of them were scientists, and all were sceptical of the Idealism which had established itself as philosophical orthodoxy in the German universities.[8] What was wanted was a modern, scientific philosophy which would sweep into oblivion the pseudo-problems of metaphysics. As early as 1907 members of the group began to meet in local cafés for informal meetings. But it was only when Moritz Schlick (1882–1936) became professor of philosophy at Vienna in 1922 that the group acquired anything like clear leadership and cohesion.[9] Another significant figure who, though an Austrian, was not directly associated with the group but who shared their same initial approach was Ludwig Wittgenstein (1889–1951). Wittgenstein spent much of his life in England, first as a research student in aeronautics at Manchester and then as a Cambridge philosopher. His *Tractatus Logico-Philosophicus* (1921)[1] is regarded as one of the great seminal works of modern philosophy.

The movement steadily gained ground, but it was not until A. J. Ayer published his *Language, Truth and Logic* (1936)[2] that an impact was made upon the wider philosophical public in this country. At one stroke Ayer spelt out the implications of Logical Positivism, declared open and total war upon metaphysics and theology, and made a name for himself as the

---

[6] *Cf.* Brand Blanshard, *Reason and Analysis* (Allen and Unwin, 1962), pp. 93–126. Blanshard's work is a massive critique of the movement.

[7] See above, pp. 66–73.   [8] See above, pp. 117–124.

[9] For a selection of their writings, including pieces by Moritz Schlick and Rudolf Carnap together with some by British writers, see *Logical Positivism*, edited by A. J. Ayer (Free Press, Glencoe, Illinois, and Allen and Unwin, London, 1959).

[1] It was published by Routledge and Kegan Paul in German with English translation (1922), new translation by D. F. Pears and B. F. McGuiness (1961).

[2] Published by Gollancz. It was revised and reset in a second edition in 1946, and has gone through many impressions. References here are to the second edition.

enfant terrible of Oxford philosophy. At the same time Ayer (who had spent some time at Vienna on postgraduate philosophical studies) felt obliged to soften the rigour of the original teaching of the Vienna Circle.

The chief weapon of the Logical Positivists was the Verification Principle. They used it in their endeavours to distinguish between genuine and pseudo statements. Now, the main purpose of language is to make statements about the world and to communicate experiences. In their quest for a scientific approach to knowledge the Logical Positivists believed that they had found in the Verification Principle an instrument for filtering out genuinely factual statements from those which appeared to be so, but were not in fact. The way to find out which is which is to ask how any given statement can be verified. The meaning and real nature of a statement is disclosed by its method of verification or lack of it.[3] The Logical Positivists claimed that statements were meaningful and genuine if they could be verified in a manner comparable to the way in which scientific hypotheses are tested by public experiment.

A. J. Ayer put it like this: 'We say that a sentence is factually significant to any given person, if, and only if, he knows how to verify the proposition which it purports to express – that is, if he knows what observations would lead him, under certain conditions, to accept the proposition as being true, or reject it as being false. If, on the other hand, the putative proposition is of such a character that the assumption of its truth, or falsehood, is consistent with any assumption whatsoever concerning the nature of his future experience, then, as far as he is concerned, it is, if not a tautology, a mere pseudo-proposition. The sentence expressing it may be emotionally significant to him; but it is not literally significant.'[4]

We shall return to the notions of tautology and emotional significance in a moment. But before doing so it is worth while stopping to note how Ayer envisaged the principle working. He admitted that a distinction had to be drawn between

---

[3] *Cf.* F. Waismann, 'The meaning of a statement is its method of verification' in *Erkenntnis*, I, 1930, p. 229.
[4] *Language, Truth and Logic*, p. 35.

'practical verifiability' and 'verifiability in principle'.[5] There were many things which were meaningful but which had not been absolutely verified. For example, at the time when Ayer was writing there were no means of knowing whether there were mountains on the other side of the moon. But the question whether or not there were any still made sense. One day means might be devised of finding out. So Ayer allowed that the idea was 'verifiable in principle', for one could say what sort of experiments might be relevant to ascertaining the truth of the statement.

There were also other types of statement which Ayer wanted to recognize as meaningful but which were not absolutely verifiable. Among these are scientific laws and such generalizations as 'Arsenic is poisonous'. A statement like this could not be said to have been verified in the strictest sense until every bit of arsenic in the world had been tested. Another type of statement which Ayer acknowledged to be meaningful but which did not pass the tests of the Vienna Circle are historical statements. One could not go back into the past and observe events for oneself. But to insist on this score that all statements about events in the past are meaningless is patently absurd. Accordingly, Ayer adopted what he called the 'weak' sense of verification.[6]

There was also another and quite different category of statements which were acknowledged to be meaningful. These were tautologies or analytic statements.[7] These were not statements of fact, however, but merely logical definitions. Their truth does not depend on whether there was anything observable which confirmed or denied the statement in question. It depends on whether the statement in question is self-consistent. Thus, to say that the same surface cannot be red all over and blue all over at the same time merely expresses a logical truth. It is a tautology. It merely repeats the same

---

[5] *Ibid.*, p. 36.

[6] 'A proposition is said to be verifiable, in the strong sense of the term, if, and only if, its truth could be conclusively established in experience. But it is verifiable, in the weak sense, if it is possible for experience to render it probable' (*ibid.*, p. 37).

[7] For Ayer's understanding of tautologies see *ibid.*, pp. 78ff.

idea in different words or states a definition without saying whether there is anything in reality corresponding to it. The statement we have instanced does not say anything about any particular surface. It is true only within the context of logical definition. It is purely hypothetical.

We now turn to the object of the whole exercise. This, it must be stressed, was not to test the *truth* of statements. That was, after all, the job of the appropriate academic discipline. Rather it was to test whether statements were *meaningful* or not. It was like a preliminary hearing to decide whether a case could be made out for a particular statement to go forward to the appropriate academic discipline as a subject for genuine investigation. In this way a distinction could be drawn between genuine questions worthy of investigation and pseudo-problems which had arisen entirely through a misuse of language. This brings us to the real crunch. For Ayer and his Viennese counterparts believed that the Verification Principle had not just disposed of a few odd theories and propositions. It had blown sky-high the whole of metaphysics[8] and theology and a good deal of ethics into the bargain.[9]

For to speak about anything over and above the physical world was, they claimed, ruled out by the Verification Principle. Admittedly, to talk about God existing looked on the face of it like a factual assertion. But God could not be seen, touched, or, for that matter, smelt. When people talk about God doing this or that, what in fact they observe is not God at all but some physical occurrence or event involving human beings. God is not a term of scientific explanation. One just cannot conduct scientific experiments on God. Grammatically, it might make good sense to say that God spoke to me, just as in fairy stories it makes good grammatical sense to say that a unicorn spoke to the princess. But whereas people recognize that the latter statement is obviously a kind of tautology which is true only within the context of make-belief, they have failed to realize that the former statement has no factual basis either. The whole of theology and metaphysical philosophy are

[8] *Cf.* Ayer's opening chapter on 'The Elimination of Metaphysics', *ibid.*, pp. 33–45.
[9] *Cf.* ch. VI on 'Critique of Ethics and Theology', *ibid.*, pp. 102–120.

gigantic category mistakes which have arisen through the misuse of language. People have fallen into the trap of thinking that, because words exist, there must be some reality corresponding to them. The Logical Positivists claimed that, because language about God, the soul and immortality could not be verified, it was either meaningless, or that it meant something rather different from what the speaker intended.

Many of what are commonly regarded as factual statements are really (on this theory) *emotive* utterances in disguise.[1] They do not say anything about anything that is objectively true; they are rather testimonies to the speaker's own private likes and dislikes (or those he would like to propagate) and to the conventions of society. Thus, a statement like 'Stealing is wrong' means (when duly processed) no more than 'I disapprove of stealing' or 'If everyone stole, society would be undermined'. Writing nearly twenty years after Ayer, R. B. Braithwaite has argued that 'the primary use of religious assertions is to announce allegiance to a set of moral principles'.[2] Thus, to say 'God is love' is not really to assert anything about a transcendent being. The essential meaning of these words is to announce the speaker's 'intention to follow an agapeistic way of life'.[3]

All this carries us a good way beyond old-fashioned empiricism, positivism and atheism. Whereas the latter argued that the Christian answers to the great theological and metaphysical questions were false, Logical Positivism argues that they are meaningless, because the questions are not real questions at all. If they have any meaning, it is not what they appear to have at face-value. When boiled down, theological pronouncements do not deal with transcendent realities at all. They are really veiled policy statements expressing our private attitudes and perhaps also announcing our intention to behave in this way or that.

[1] *Cf. ibid.*, p. 108.
[2] *An Empiricist's View of the Nature of Religious Belief*, Eddington Memorial Lecture for 1955, reprinted in *Christian Ethics and Contemporary Philosophy*, ed. I. T. Ramsey (SCM Press, 1966), p. 60. This volume also contains various replies to this view.
[3] *Ibid.*, p. 63.

Reaction

The bold, aggressive programme of the Positivists had obvious attractions for the modern mind. But the moment of triumph turned out to be the beginning of the downfall. Just as the Logical Positivists were poised to sweep all before them, they found that their own chief weapon was being turned against them. People began to ask whether the Verification Principle had itself been verified. Clearly it was not intended to be a tautology. Otherwise, it could not perform its exalted function of testing all factual statements. On the other hand, it was equally clear that it had not itself been verified by controlled experiment. Nor could it hardly be, for people found meaning in all kinds of outrageously metaphysical and theological utterances. In very few cases were believers willing to accept the kind of meaning that the young Ayer and (later on) the more elderly Braithwaite[4] wanted to assign to theological and moral statements. Regardless of whether they were true or not, it was still possible to claim that they meant something.

It is not without interest to note that Professor Ayer, writing in 1959, has acknowledged the validity of this objection.[5] He is unhappy with the suggestion prompted by Wittgenstein[6] that the criterion is a piece of metaphysics and useful *nonsense*. If it is nonsense, then it cannot be useful. He admits that 'The Vienna Circle tended to ignore this difficulty', but concludes, 'It seems to me fairly clear that what they were in fact doing was to adopt the verification principle as a convention.'[7]

To admit this is to move from the offensive to the defensive.

---

[4] It may be noted that Braithwaite preferred the Use Principle to the Verification Principle ('The meaning of any statement . . . will be taken as being given by the way that it is used', *ibid.*, p. 59). But his results were virtually the same and open to the same objections. E. L. Mascall has pointed out how his treatment fails to do justice to religious data and to his self-professed Use Principle (*Words and Images*, pp. 55–62). It treats all religions as if they were saying the same thing. It fails to distinguish between intentional stories (*e.g.* parables) and historical events. It forces an often alien interpretation on to religious utterances and makes God superfluous. Whether or not these points are true in themselves they cannot be deduced from an empirical examination of the way in which religious language is used.

[5] *Logical Positivism*, p. 15.   [6] *Cf. Tractatus*, No. 6. 54.
[7] *Ibid.*

The principle may work for certain kinds of *descriptive* factual statements, but it cannot be used as a Procrustean bed on to which everything else must be made to fit. All that it shows in fact is that there are various kinds of statements, including theological and metaphysical ones, which do not fall into the same category. The task, therefore, is not to dismiss them as nonsense without more ado, but to examine how they are used and what they mean.

Despite its defects, Logical Positivism set new trends in British philosophy. Since the war logical and linguistic analysis has been well-nigh its exclusive preoccupation. And until fairly recently Ayer's claim, that the task of philosophy was not to search for ultimate principles but to analyse the function and status of language,[8] has been accepted almost without question. For it was recognized that in the past many pseudo-problems had been generated through the misuse of language, and that clarification was an important function of philosophy.

One of the most eminent post-war Oxford philosophers (though he was not specially indebted to Wittgenstein or Ayer) was the late J. L. Austin, who was devoted to the analysis of language. He envisaged the task of philosophers as the compilation of a kind of catalogue of all possible functions of words. He devoted his labours to a relentless analysis of the way in which words are used. He himself published little during his lifetime, but his lectures on *Sense and Sensibilia*[9] give a good idea of what he considered to be the objectives and methods of philosophy. Although analytical concerns have dominated British philosophy, there are signs that some philosophers are restive at the almost exclusive preoccupation with it and that the time has now come for philosophers to take stock of its value and limitations. This appears, for example, in the symposium *Clarity is Not Enough: Essays in Criticism of Linguistic Philosophy*, edited by H. D. Lewis.[1] But we must leave off our account of contemporary philosophy

---

[8] *Language, Truth and Logic*, pp. 46–71.
[9] Reconstructed from Manuscript Notes by G. J. Warnock (OUP, 1962). Another posthumous work is his Harvard Lectures of 1955, *How to Do Things with Words*, edited by J. O. Urmson (OUP, 1962).
[1] Allen and Unwin, 1963.

and look now at some of the work that has been done on the status and function of religious language in response to the secular challenge.

Religious language
In recent years philosophers of religion have given a good deal of thought to religious language. Suggestive discussions have appeared in several books.[2] We shall not attempt to work out here a complete philosophy of language and the part that it plays in Christian experience. But it may be useful to notice some of the points that have been raised.

As we said earlier, when discussing Aquinas,[3] the truth of language about God is not a strict, literal truth. When we speak about God, we have to use words which apply in the first instance to finite things and people that exist in space and time. But God is not an object in space and time. Thus, when we call God our *Father*, we are using the word in a rather special sense. The word *father* normally denotes a man who has brought one or more children into the world by natural procreation. He can be seen and touched. But not so God. God is not a Father in the same physical sense.

All the language that we use about God presents similar difficulties. When we talk about him *loving, speaking* or *doing* this and that, we are using language in a special sense. For when we look more closely at these different activities, in none of them do we actually see God as an individual performing an action. What we see are human beings and events which for some reason we have chosen to describe in this rather odd way. What do we really mean when we use language in this way? And how can it be justified?

A frequent complaint of the agnostic philosopher is that religious people go on making utterances regardless of the facts. They still insist that God is love despite the countless tragedies we hear about every day on TV and in the newspapers. Does it really mean anything to say that God cares for the world? When the believer claims this, it looks as if he is making a factual assertion. But then we ask: Has anyone seen God? What

[2] For details see below, pp. 300f.
[3] See above, pp. 30–32.

about children dying from hunger and incurable diseases? A human father would be driven frantic to help his child in distress, but we cannot see any obvious supernatural efforts to do so. The believer might reply that God is spiritual and invisible; that God has entrusted the affairs of the world into the hands of men; and that heaven is more important than earth. But in the meantime his apparently factual assertion has considerably shrunk. He has so qualified his initial assertion that it looks as if it is about to die the death of a thousand qualifications.[4] The agnostic begins to wonder whether religious assertions are compatible with any state of affairs whatever. If so, they may be emotionally significant to the speaker, but they are not really factual statements at all.

One way of approaching this problem is to employ the technique of falsification. This is to ask whether there are any conceivable circumstances which would show the statement in question to be untrue. It is like a process of elimination. If someone says, 'Jane is a good cook',[5] and the roast beef she serves for Sunday lunch is tough, the cold version of it on Monday inedible and the offerings dished up during the rest of the week not much better, one might be tempted to think that the original statement was meaningless (or at least an indirect way of expressing devotion to Jane). If the speaker goes on making it, and yet admits that the particular dishes so far served do not substantiate the claim, the statement is well on the way to dying the death of a thousand qualifications. But if some test could be devised which would make the speaker withdraw his statement, if the test were failed, then at least it would show that the statement means something. It would help to pinpoint its meaning. Thus, if Jane finally succeeded in boiling an egg to everyone's satisfaction, it would show that the original statement has at least some meaning. And it would give some idea of how it must be understood, even if (in this case) its cash value is rather different from its face value.

To go back to our first example. When Christians say that

---

[4] *Cf.* Antony Flew in *New Essays in Philosophical Theology*, pp. 97f.
[5] I owe this illustration to F. Copleston, *Contemporary Philosophy* (Burns and Oates, 1956), p. 99.

God is love despite all that we see and hear around us, it might seem to the outsider that the statement is factually meaningless. It is apparently used regardless of what actually happens in the world. Could the statement be falsified? Can believers specify any conceivable circumstances which would make their assertion untrue? The answer is yes. It would be false if suffering never proved to be a blessing in disguise. It would be false if adversity was never a means of finding deeper meaning in life. It would be false if people had no experience of God working out a higher purpose in life. It would be false if adversity never offered others the opportunity of service and self-giving. It would be false if God had consigned all men to condemnation and had not sent his Son to redeem them. No doubt these answers raise other questions which in turn require explanation. But they also help to show not only how the statement could be shown to be false; they help to pin-point its meaning.

A scholar who has done a good deal of work on the use and meaning of religious language is Ian T. Ramsey. He has suggested that one of the ways in which language functions is like a working *model*. A model is a representation of something else which enables us to grasp the thing that it stands for. In the context of religious language a *model* is 'a situation with which we are all familiar, and which can be used for reaching another situation with which we are not so familiar; one which, without the model, we should not recognize so easily'.[6] Such *models* are often accompanied by what Bishop Ramsey calls *qualifiers*. The latter is 'a directive which prescribes a special way of developing those "model" situations'.[7]

Thus, when we say that God is 'infinitely wise', the word *wise* names the model situation. The qualifier *infinitely* points the way in which it is to be understood. We have some idea of what wisdom means. The third-form boy is 'scarcely wise'; the sixth-form prefect 'rather wise'; the undergraduate 'definitely wise'; the lecturer (one hopes) 'very wise'. But the qualifier

[6] *Religious Language* (SCM Press, 1957), p. 61. In a later volume of lectures, *Christian Discourse: Some Logical Explorations* (OUP, 1965), Ramsey extended his approach to biblical language and *Honest to God*.
[7] *Ibid.*, p. 62.

infinitely does not merely indicate that God's wisdom is a scaled-up version of man's. It 'presides over, gathers together and completes the sequence'.[8] We might not be able to conceive precisely what is involved in the statement that God is 'infinitely wise'. In the nature of the case we cannot see God as he is in himself. But the *model* puts us on to a clue towards understanding its meaning, and the *qualifier* reminds us that we are not to take the clue in a strictly literal way.

Various writers have drawn attention to the symbolic character of language.[9] Words, statements and the mental images that they conjure up are like symbols which stand for something else and through which the mind encounters that thing, event or person. Basically, symbols have two aspects. There is the symbolic material, the word, picture, image or sign and that to which it points. To treat the symbolic material on its own, apart from what it stands for, is to miss the whole point. Genuine symbols are not simply bare images. They present a medium through which we may participate in the reality that they represent. When John the Baptist said, 'Behold, the Lamb of God, who takes away the sin of the world!'[1] he was employing symbolism. Neither the original hearers nor readers of the Bible today imagine that he was talking about a four-legged, woolly animal. But those who know something about the Old Testament thought world and have had Christian experience know that the symbol co-ordinates and gives meaning to their experience. In the nature of the case, it is impossible to describe it in direct, literal terms. Nor is the symbol to be used to the exclusion of others. It needs to be complemented by many others such as the Good Shepherd, the Light of the World, the Bread of Life, the true Vine. But, each in its own way, these symbols shed light and meaning upon the experience of those who seek to know their meaning.

---

[8] *Ibid.*, p. 66.
[9] *Cf.* Austin Farrer, *The Glass of Vision* (Dacre Press, 1948); E. L. Mascall, *Words and Images* and *Theology and Images* (Mowbray, 1963); Sidney Hook (ed.), *Religious Experience and Truth*, which includes important statements by Tillich and replies by various scholars; F. W. Dillistone, *Christianity and Symbolism* (Collins, 1955) and the symposium edited by him, *Myth and Symbol* (SPCK, 1966).
[1] John 1:29.

Through them the mind grasps an element of reality which is otherwise inaccessible.

In saying this, it is important to notice two further points. One concerns the material of theological discourse; the other concerns those who use it.

From what has been said so far it should be apparent that religious language is never literally true. It is always figurative. It is like a parable in the sense that it has a double meaning. Something is related in earthly terms, but its real significance lies beyond them. If it is meaningful at all, it must, as Aquinas pointed out, be analogical.[2] Religious statements are neither wholly like nor wholly unlike their point of reference. If they are true at all, there must be some genuine similarity.

To this the objection has been raised that we can never step outside the analogical discourse and compare our symbolic statements with the reality they claim to represent. Even when we try to describe one analogy, we have to use another to do it. But this objection is far less damning than it might appear at first sight. For it is one thing to say that we never see the reference point of the analogy as it is in itself. It is something else to say that we never see it at all. The former is true, so far as this life is concerned; but the latter is not. For the believer the analogies which he uses can be vindicated because they have brought his experience of God into focus. They are valid because they throw light upon life, not only his own but upon those of his fellow believers.

This brings us to our second point. It is that the meaningfulness or otherwise of any religious symbol or utterance does not depend entirely upon the utterance itself. It also depends upon the speaker and the hearer. The speaker may or may not be using language in a precise or generally understandable way. The fault here does not lie with theological discourse as such but with the individual speaker. But unless the hearer's experience is also sufficiently wide and attuned to what is being said, he is bound to miss the point. His mind will inevitably stick at some aspect of the symbolic material and not press on to the reality which it represents. In other words, he will have made a category mistake no less serious than that into

[2] See above, pp. 30–32.

which agnostic analysts accuse believers of falling. The fault will not lie in the inadequacy of the discourse but with the paucity of the critic's own experience.

It is impossible within the scope of this study to pursue this question further. It remains to be said that the different approaches to religious language mentioned here are not necessarily mutually exclusive alternatives. Still less do they necessarily undermine the authority of the Bible. Rather, they help in their different ways towards a deeper understanding of the rich and complex phenomenon of language and thus also of the nature of our experience of God. It is an ill wind that blows no-one any good. And like many another heresy and attack on the Christian faith, Logical Positivism and modern philosophy may yet turn out to be the means of pointing Christians to a deeper understanding of the ways of God.

II EXISTENTIALISM
Background and character

For the past quarter century and more British philosophy has been dominated by Logical Positivism and its aftermath, linguistic analysis. Existentialism is still – despite translations of Existentialist philosophers and an interest in certain theological circles[3] – a characteristically continental movement. But perhaps it would be nearer the mark to say that Existentialism is one of those –isms which is not so much a movement with a more-or-less common programme as a tendency or attitude. There are Existentialists who are atheists, and there are Existentialists who are professing Christians. There are Existentialists who deny that it is possible to work out a philosophical system, and there are those who do the opposite. Existentialism sprang up in Germany after the first World War; it flourished in France immediately after the second.[4]

Existentialism has been defined as an attempt to philosophize from the standpoint of the actor rather than, as was

[3] *Cf.* John Macquarrie, *An Existentialist Theology* (SCM Press, 1955); *Studies in Christian Existentialism* (SCM Press, 1965).
[4] A useful selection of Existentialist writings is contained in *Existentialism from Dostoevsky to Sartre* edited by Walter Kaufmann (World Publishing Company, Cleveland and New York, 1956).

traditional, from that of the detached spectator.[5] Or again: 'A proposition or truth is said to be *existential* when I cannot apprehend or assent to it from the standpoint of a mere spectator but only on the ground of my total existence.'[6] The term Existentialism derives from the German *Existenz-philosophie*. In everyday speech we talk about people and things existing. But in the context of Existentialism the word *existence* has acquired a more specialized meaning. It is not so much concerned with the fact that this or that person or thing is there, as with the fact that as human beings we have lives to be lived.

Professor H. B. Acton's summary is well worth repeating: 'The word is then used to emphasize the claim that each individual person is unique in terms of any metaphysical or scientific system; that he is a being who chooses as well as a being who thinks or contemplates; that he is free and that, because he is free, he suffers; and that since his future depends in part upon his free choices it is not altogether predictable. There are also suggestions, in this special usage, that existence is something genuine or authentic by contrast with insincerity, that a man who merely contemplates the world is failing to make the acts of choice which his situation demands. Running through all these different though connected suggestions is the fundamental idea that each person exists and chooses in time and has only a limited amount of it at his disposal in which to make decisions which matter so much to him. Time is short; there are urgent decisions to take; we are free to take them, but the thought of how much depends upon our decision makes our freedom a source of anguish, for we cannot know with any certainty what will become of us.'[7]

The pedigree of contemporary Existentialism is often (and rightly) traced back to the nineteenth-century Danish writer

[5] E. L. Allen, *Existentialism from Within* (Routledge and Kegan Paul, 1953); *cf.* F. Copleston, *Contemporary Philosophy*, pp. 127f.

[6] Karl Heim quoted by Alec R. Vidler, *The Church in an Age of Revolution* (Pelican, 1961), p. 211.

[7] *Encyclopaedia Britannica*, VIII, p. 968A. The article on 'Existentialism' here quoted, and that by Alasdair MacIntyre in *The Encyclopedia of Philosophy*, III, 147–154, are the best brief surveys of Existentialism known to the present writer.

Søren Kierkegaard,[8] who spent his life attacking grandiose philosophical systems and wrestling with problems of human existence. Another writer who may justly be numbered among the patriarchs of Existentialism was the Russian novelist Feodor Dostoievsky (1821–81), whose writings reveal his personal disenchantment with rationalistic Humanism. For him the universe did not make sense; its apparent order was deceptive. The individual is thrown into this inhospitable world in which he is fighting a losing battle for survival. Similar themes were also sounded by the German philosopher Nietzsche,[9] whose writings were concerned with the problems of human existence that were inevitably raised by the assumption that God was dead.

Existentialism, as we shall see in a few moments, has found its way into the writings of certain theologians. But it has also produced a militant atheistic progeny. One the best-known atheistic Existentialists is the French novelist, dramatist and philosopher Jean-Paul Sartre (b. 1905). Like Kierkegaard, Sartre is protesting against systems. He also believes that there are no external authorities given to us objectively. But whereas Kierkegaard was concerned with Christian existence, Sartre is concerned with the full implications of atheism for personal existence. Unlike the French secular thinkers of the late nineteenth century who scrapped the idea of God but wished to retain Christian morality, Sartre insists that the true atheist cannot cheat in this way. He must be consistent to the bitter end. Dostoievsky once wrote: 'If God did not exist, everything would be permitted.' This, Sartre insists, is the starting-point of Existentialism.[1] Man is dumped into the world. Whether he likes it or not, he must fend for himself. He must work out his own values. He cannot avoid making choices. Even when he tries to put off a choice, that in itself is an act of choice. And what he chooses all contributes towards making him the kind of person that he is becoming. Man's nature is never fixed at any time. It is always the product of what he does, thinks

---

[8] See above, pp. 125–132.   [9] See above, pp. 137–141.
[1] *Existentialism and Humanism* (1946), Eng. tr. by Philip Mairet (Methuen, 1948), p. 33. The book is based upon a lecture in which Sartre gives a kind of personal confession of faith. It is an excellent introduction to his views.

and chooses. And all the time hanging over him is the prospect of death and the anxieties which are part and parcel of his lonely existence. Man is right to pursue high ideals, but death mocks everything and in the end brings everything to nothing.

A good deal of Sartre's writing is devoted to describing and analysing human reactions. But he has also written a massive treatise *Being and Nothingness: An Essay on Phenomenological Ontology* (1943).[2] It is a kind of metaphysical edifice erected upon Existentialist foundations. Another Existentialist philosopher who has gone in for system-building is the German thinker Martin Heidegger (b. 1889), whose *magnum opus* is entitled *Being and Time* (1927).[3] Here he sees man caught up in the processes of history and society, determined yet free, and free yet enslaved. So much of everyday life is really a flight from man's authentic existence. Heidegger calls upon men to realize their destiny, to recognize their freedom in the face of the inevitability of death.

Existentialism is in part a protest movement against modern, mass society. The organization of industry, technology, politics and bureaucracy tend to stifle individual thought and action and cultivate conformist mediocrity. But different Existentialists have reacted in different ways to the problems of society. Some favour a revival of Humanism. For a time in the early thirties Heidegger backed the National Socialists. Sartre has long been a Marxist fellow-traveller. But his stress on individual freedom stops short of rigid Marxist determination.

In some ways the continental Existentialists make their contemporary British philosophical counterparts look rather trivial. Their concern for life is much more impressive than the minutiae of linguistic analysis. But when we try to read the more speculative treatises of Sartre and Heidegger it is not difficult to see the point of the analysts' accusation that they are playing about with words. When they talk about Being and Nothingness as if they were substantial entities, it looks very much as if they are guilty (as A. J. Ayer has suggested) of a systematic misuse of the verb 'to be'. Existentialist analyses

[2] Eng. tr. by Hazel E. Barnes (Methuen, 1957).
[3] Eng. tr. by John Macquarrie and Edward Robinson (SCM Press, 1962).

of people's reactions often give revealing insights into human behaviour. But the metaphysical systems of the Existentialists seem no more solid and enduring than those of the Idealists which they are designed to replace.

To one who does not subscribe to Existentialist premises, the distinction between *authentic* and *inauthentic* existence seems rather curious. If the world is irrational, and if there are no objective values, how can playing bingo be described as less authentic than listening to Beethoven? To prefer one rather than the other is purely a matter of personal taste. To talk about transcending one's existence by realizing one's finitude may be all right for some people. But it is no more authentic than spending every evening in the pub. Life is equally pointless either way. Atheistic Existentialism is a heroic attempt to philosophize about life on the assumption that there is no God. If we remove this premise and believe that God exists and that he makes himself known to men, then so much of it becomes an exercise in futility. What remains is a number of insights and attitudes which may or may not be acute and relevant.

There are several theologians who in their different ways have been classed as Existentialists. Among them is the Russian Nicolai Berdyaev (1874–1948), who began as a sceptic with Marxist leanings but returned to the Orthodox Church and from 1922 onwards lived as an *émigré* in Paris. Berdyaev was a profuse writer, but lack of space prevents detailed examination of his thought here. Those who are interested cannot do better than begin with *Christian Existentialism: A Berdyaev Anthology*.[4] In the meantime, we must turn to two writers who have exerted considerably more influence on Western thought, Rudolf Bultmann and Paul Tillich.

Bultmann

Whether one agrees with him or not, no-one can deny the enormous influence that Rudolf Bultmann has had upon New Testament studies over the past fifty years, especially on the Continent. Perhaps he could be described as the twentieth-

[4] Selected and translated by Donald A. Lowrie (Allen and Unwin, 1965).

century equivalent to F. C. Baur.[5] In his own way he is no less sceptical of the historical value of the biblical writings. But the place occupied by Idealism in Baur's thought is filled in Bultmann's by Existentialism.

Bultmann was born in 1884. He studied and taught at several German universities before becoming professor of New Testament studies at Marburg in 1921, a post he occupied until his retirement in 1951. In the course of his career Bultmann has written a great deal. It is possible to detect certain phases in his outlook. But with Bultmann it is not a case of one stage beginning where another ends, but of a cumulative development.

Already about the time of the first World War Bultmann was one of the pioneers of form criticism. Perhaps the German term *Formgeschichte* (literally *form history*) expresses better the techniques and outlook that are involved here. The form critics endorsed the documentary criticism of the nineteenth century,[6] but they held that it was not enough. They believed that the Gospels must be further analysed into the various forms which the early church gave them before they were put into writing. These forms, Bultmann believes, tell us not so much what Jesus actually said and did, but rather what the early church believed about him. Many of them were consciously or unconsciously invented by Christians of different outlooks to suit their own didactic or polemical needs. When Bultmann has duly carried out his analysis the result is that we know next to nothing about the historical Jesus but an awful lot about the beliefs of the primitive church. Bultmann worked out his approach in a work which has gone through numerous editions since it was first published, *The History of the Synoptic Tradition* (1921).[7]

In 1926 Bultmann published a little book entitled *Jesus*.[8] Already he interprets the gospel in existential terms. What

[5] See above, pp. 157f.   [6] See above, pp. 158f.
[7] Eng. tr. by John Marsh of the 3rd German edition, 1958 (Blackwell, Oxford, 1963). For a briefer statement of his approach see *Form Criticism: Two Essays on New Testament Research* by Rudolf Bultmann and Karl Kundsin, Eng. tr. by F. C. Grant (1934; Harper Torchbook, New York, 1966³).
[8] Eng. tr. by L. P. Smith and E. Huntress, *Jesus and the Word* (Nicolson and Watson, 1935).

matters is not something that Jesus did objectively outside us and for us. Nor is there such a thing as an objective word of God. Jesus is a preacher of the Word, summoning men to decision, and thus enabling us 'to interpret our own existence'.[9] Truth emerges in this subjective response.

In 1941 New Testament studies took a new turn when Bultmann circulated on duplicated sheets amongst a small group of friends his essay on 'New Testament and Mythology'.[1] Earlier liberal theologians had claimed that certain events in the New Testament, such as the virgin birth, the empty tomb, the resurrection and ascension of Jesus, were mythical. Bultmann's point was that mythology was not confined simply to isolated items; the whole ethos and thought forms of the New Testament were mythological. The whole pre-scientific idea of a three-decker universe of heaven, earth and hell, peopled with spiritual powers, of man's need of atonement, of the supernatural breaking into this world was myth derived from pre-Christian Gnosticism on the one hand and Judaism on the other. Bultmann contended that these ideas were unacceptable to modern man, and presented a needless barrier to the gospel. But he added, 'The real purpose of myth is not to present an objective picture of the world as it is, but to express man's understanding of himself in the world in which he lives.'[2] What is required is the demythologization of the Christian message, the removal and reinterpretation of the offending myths so that the gospel may be presented in its purity. When this has been done, the result is that the Fall has nothing to do with Adam. It is essentially a picture of man's 'self-assertion'.[3] The atonement spoken of in passages like 1 John 4:10; Romans 8:32; John 3:16 and Galatians 1:4; 2:19f. is not to be thought of as an objective event performed by Christ. It is an 'act of God through which man becomes capable of self-commitment, capable of faith and love, of his authentic life'.[4]

[9] *Ibid.*, p. 11; *cf.* pp. 218f.
[1] Eng. tr. by R. H. Fuller in the symposium *Kerygma and Myth: a Theological Debate*, I, edited by H. W. Bartsch (SPCK, 1957). Bultmann himself gave a more popular statement of his position in 1951 in *Jesus Christ and Mythology* (SCM Press, 1960).
[2] *Kerygma and Myth*, I, p. 10.   [3] *Ibid.*, p. 30.   [4] *Ibid.*, p. 33.

Bultmann's teaching combines a radical scepticism with
scarcely undiluted Existentialism. The positions outlined
here were worked out more fully in a series of larger works.[5]
But they remain essentially the same. We cannot know *what*
Jesus was like; we only know *that* he lived and died.[6] But
this does not matter. 'The resurrection itself is not an event
of past history . . . But the historical problem is scarcely relevant to Christian belief in the resurrection. For the historical
event of the rise of Easter faith means for us what it meant for
the first disciples – namely, the self-manifestation of the
risen Lord, the act of God in which the redemptive event of
the cross is completed.'[7] But when we ask what is the redemptive event of which Bultmann speaks, the answer seems to be
that it is 'an opportunity of understanding ourselves'. Faith
is that which 'alone can illuminate our understanding of ourselves'.[8] It is the means of realizing our 'authentic life' of 'self-
commitment'.[9] Bultmann is not at all abashed by his critics'
claim that he is restating the gospel in terms of Heidegger's
Existentialism. Instead, he tries to turn the tables by claiming
that the critics 'are blinding their eyes to the real problem,
which is that the philosophers are saying the same thing as the
New Testament and saying it quite independently'.[1]

All this raises numerous questions into which it is impossible
to go in any detail in the present study. But this much may be
said. While Bultmann is still enjoying considerable vogue both
on the Continent and in Anglo-American radical circles,
there are those of his own students who think that he has gone
too far both in his scepticism and in his espousal of Existentialism. Some of them have embarked upon what has come to be

---

[5] *The Gospel of John* (1941); *Theology of the New Testament*, 2 volumes, translated by K. Grobel (SCM Press, 1952, 1955); *Primitive Christianity*, Eng. tr.
by R. H. Fuller (Fontana, 1956).
[6] *Cf.* his essay on 'The Primitive Christian Kerygma and the Historical
Jesus' in *The Historical Jesus and the Kerygmatic Christ*, edited by Carl E.
Braaten and Roy A. Harrisville (Abingdon, New York and Nashville,
1964).
[7] *Kerygma and Myth*, I, p. 42.   [8] *Ibid.*, pp. 41f.   [9] *Ibid.*, p. 31.
[1] *Ibid.*, p. 25. For a short time in 1927–28 Bultmann and Heidegger were
colleagues at Marburg. It was in this period that Heidegger published
Being and Time. Paul Tillich was also at Marburg in 1924–25.

called the new quest of the historical Jesus.[2] There are also those who question the validity of form criticism as a technique for understanding the New Testament.[3] Bultmann's claim that the early Christians were so preoccupied with their resurrection experiences that they were utterly uninterested in Jesus' acts and words is incredible. But it is no less so than the further claim that later on they felt free to invent episodes and compose sayings by means of which they constructed a fictitious life of Jesus. All this sets great question marks against their intelligence and integrity which Bultmann brushes all too lightly aside. No serious scholar today would question the influence of a historian's own outlook, aims and background upon his choice of material and the way in which he uses it. But this is very different from saying that the Evangelists' choice and presentation of their material bears no relation to what in fact took place. Bultmann's own techniques as a historian in *The History of the Synoptic Tradition* have to be studied at first hand to be believed. If it is possible to construe an event or a saying as unauthentic, no matter how far-fetched the explanation may be, Bultmann is sure to hit upon it.

Bultmann's handling of myth is equally open to question.[4]

[2] For discussions of this movement from various standpoints see James M. Robinson, *A New Quest of the Historical Jesus* (SCM Press, 1959); Hugh Anderson, *Jesus and Christian Origins: A Commentary on Modern Viewpoints* (OUP, New York, 1964); Carl F. H. Henry (ed.), *Jesus of Nazareth: Saviour and Lord* (Tyndale Press, 1966); and more briefly F. F. Bruce, 'History and the Gospel' in *Faith and Thought*, Vol. 93, No. 3, 1964, for appraisals of the question.

[3] *Cf.* T. W. Manson, 'The Life of Jesus: Some Tendencies in Present-day Research' in W. D. Davies and D. Daube (eds.), *The Background of the New Testament and its Eschatology* (CUP, 1954). Form criticism has been attacked by Scandinavian critics, notably by B. Gerhardsson, *Memory and Manuscript* (Uppsala, 1961), for its lack of attention to Jewish teaching methods and failure to appreciate the way in which the disciples would have preserved their Master's teaching. For a general assessment of the position see D. Guthrie, *New Testament Introduction: The Gospels and Acts* (Tyndale Press, 1965), pp. 178–194.

[4] For brief discussions see F. F. Bruce, 'Myth and the New Testament' in *TSF Bulletin*, No. 44, 1966, and Karl Barth, 'Rudolf Bultmann – An Attempt to Understand Him' in *Kerygma and Myth*, II, 1962, pp. 83–132. An important study of myth which takes a very different line from Bultmann is the article on *mythos* by G. Stählin in *Theological Dictionary of the Bible*, ed.

He lays great store by the claim that the New Testament view of Christ was borrowed from Gnostic mythology. But all the evidence for Gnostic redeemer myths comes from post-Christian sources. In fact, it points to the probability that the Gnostics derived their teaching from Christianity. Moreover, it is far from clear that the biblical writers thought of a literal three-decker universe. Their thought may have been pre-Copernican and pictorial. But this is not necessarily the same as being literal and mythological. Nor is it evident that the gospel can be reduced without remainder to Existentialist terms. It is true that there are many passages in the Bible which suddenly bring the reader face to face with himself and ask about the meaning of existence. And there are times when Bultmann speaks with eloquence and insight on the choices before man and his need to commit himself. But it is never really clear to what Bultmann is inviting us to commit ourselves. So often it seems to be blind trust in a message which Bultmann himself has been at pains to show to be untrustworthy. For Bultmann, the resurrection of Christ 'is utterly inconceivable' as a historical fact. He speaks of 'the resuscitation of a corpse' as an incredible 'mythical event'.[5] Yet from the very first Christianity was based upon this event. As Paul wrote to the church at Corinth: 'If Christ has not been raised, then our preaching is in vain and your faith is in vain.'[6] It is only by a most curious piece of double-think that Bultmann can make the preaching of the cross and resurrection of Christ the means of our self-understanding and the way to authentic existence. And yet, however much the Bible may need interpretation and restatement in modern terms, it is impossible to reduce what it says about heaven, hell, judgment, atonement and salvation to a mere matter of human self-understanding and a new openness to life. Moreover, the Existentialist way of speaking and the ideas that they are trying to put over are often far more difficult for even the intelligent and educated than the text of the Bible itself.

All this raises the vital question of method of approach and

G. Kittel, Eng. tr. by G. W. Bromiley (Eerdmans, Grand Rapids), IV, pp. 762–795.
[5] *Kerygma and Myth*, I, p. 39.   [6] 1 Corinthians 15:14.

with it that of the relationship of philosophy to faith. Put in its simplest and starkest terms, Bultmann argues that we must approach the Christian faith in the light of our general understanding of the world, and interpret it according to our basic philosophy of life. This means that in practice Bultmann forces the New Testament into the mould of rationalistic scepticism, tempered by Existentialism. Anything that fails to fit is either removed or reinterpreted in such a way as to harmonize, however far-fetched the result may be.

Now it cannot be denied that we bring to every new experience our existing experiences and general attitudes to life. The question arises whether, when we encounter anything new and different, we should modify our existing views or explain away the new thing in terms of our preconceived philosophy. Bultmann has opted for the latter alternative. In doing so, he gives the appearance of wanting to be up to date with all his talk about restating the Christian message in terms that will meet the demands of modern science and philosophy. In fact, his work is a remarkable exhibition of a closed mind and persistent refusal to examine empirically the data of the New Testament. This is not to deny that Bultmann has done a great deal of work analysing biblical teaching. But all along the line his preconceived ideas force him to read into the New Testament interpretations which he had already derived from his rationalism and Existentialism, instead of listening to the interpretation that the data themselves bring.

At the outset we compared Bultmann with F. C. Baur. Perhaps in a hundred years Bultmann, too, will be just as much an academic curiosity as Baur is today. But the issues that Bultmann raises are issues that are far wider than the work of a particular man. In the last analysis, it is a question of theological and philosophical method. And this raises questions which scholars have begun to take seriously only in the last couple of decades.

Tillich

Another thinker whose name is associated with Existentialism (though in a quite different way) is Paul Tillich. His is one of those names which seem to have a built-in intellectual aura.

Nor is this entirely without justification, for Tillich, who was born in 1886 and who died in 1965, has had two long and distinguished academic careers.

He was born in East Prussia and spent his early years on the boundary between town and country life. In later years this prompted Tillich to think of his life as being spent in boundary situations, where different cultures and outlooks meet. He interprets his thought as the product of such perpetual cultural, social and intellectual clashes.[7] After a Ph.D. at Breslau in 1911, Licentiate at Halle the following year, and service as a chaplain in World War I, Tillich embarked upon a teaching career which took him to the universities of Berlin, Marburg, Dresden, Leipzig and Frankfurt. It was a period marked by a deep interest in philosophy, particularly German Idealism.[8] But these years also saw Tillich becoming increasingly concerned with religious socialism and Existentialism. This first career was abruptly terminated by the advent of Adolf Hitler.

The year 1933 saw Tillich (now forty-seven) launch out upon his second career. Thanks to Reinhold Niebuhr, he obtained a post at the Union Theological Seminary, New York. Eventually he became a full professor there, teaching philosophical theology. In 1940 he became an American citizen, and on retiring from his post at the Union Seminary in 1954 he became a University Professor at Harvard. It was a distinction accorded only to outstanding academic figures, which enabled him to lecture on any subject he chose without being responsible for administration and examination courses.

Over the years Tillich collected some fifteen doctorates, and a steady stream of books flowed from his pen. These range from collections of sermons like *The Shaking of the Foundations*,[9] *The New Being*[1] and *The Eternal Now*[2] to essays and lectures like

---

[7] *Cf.* Tillich's autobiographical essay *On the Boundary* (Collins, 1967). This first appeared as part of his *Interpretation of History* (1936). An introduction by J. Heywood Thomas brings it up to date. Further 'Autobiographical Reflections' appear in the symposium *The Theology of Paul Tillich*, edited by Charles W. Kegley and Robert W. Bretall (Macmillan, New York, 1961).
[8] See above, pp. 117–123. *Cf. On the Boundary*, pp. 46ff. Tillich wrote his doctorate and licentiate on Schelling.
[9] SCM Press, 1949; Pelican, 1962.
[1] SCM Press, 1956.   [2] SCM Press, 1963.

The Protestant Era,[3] The Courage to Be[4] and Love, Power and Justice.[5] Posthumous works based upon tape-recordings include Ultimate Concern: Tillich in Dialogue[6] and Perspectives on 19th and 20th Century Protestant Theology.[7] But the great work of Tillich's life which often overlaps with these smaller ones is his three-volumed Systematic Theology.[8]

To pick up Tillich's Systematic Theology after studying traditional textbooks is like straying into a room full of Picassos. Everywhere the perspectives are strange. While some features are oddly familiar, others are conspicuously absent. There are next to no biblical texts. There are few references to classical theologians and fewer still to contemporary scholars. But there is a lot of talk about ontology, structures and concrete. The whole thing is more like philosophy than theology. And in fact, this is intentional. For the difference between the two, according to Tillich, is largely one of perspective. Both are concerned with being.[9]

In their attempts to grapple with the problems presented by being, the ways of the philosopher and the theologian tend to part at three points. (1) Whereas the philosopher tries to be detached as he looks at the structure of being, the theologian is 'existential'. He looks at being as one who is desperately involved – 'with the whole of his existence, with his finitude and his anxiety, with his self-contradictions and his despair, with the healing forces in him and his social situation'.[1] (2) There is also a difference of sources. The philosopher is concerned with the structure of reality as a whole; he seeks to grasp the logos or reason which permeates all being. The theologian looks not at logos in general, but at the Logos[2] who became flesh and is manifested in the life of the church. (3) Whereas the philosopher deals with the structure of being in general (time and space,

---

[3] Chicago University Press, 1948; abridged 1962.
[4] Fontana, 1962.   [5] OUP, 1954.
[6] Edited by D. Mackenzie Brown, based upon seminars in the University of California, 1963 (SCM Press, 1965).
[7] Edited by Carl E. Braaten (SCM Press, 1967).
[8] Nisbet, I, 1953; II, 1957; III, 1964.
[9] Systematic Theology, I, pp. 25–32.   [1] Ibid., I, p. 26.
[2] The Greek word logos means 'reason' or 'word'. It figures in John 1: 1ff.: 'In the beginning was the Word . . .'

G

etc.), the theologian is concerned with the human aspect of *being*, the personal problems of life. Above all, he is concerned with what Tillich calls *the quest for a 'new being'*.

Later on we shall have occasion to look more closely at some of these terms. In the meantime, it is important to underline the fact that for Tillich theology is never a matter simply of piling up biblical texts. The gospel has to be stripped of its non-essentials and transposed into terms which mean something to modern man. Thus Tillich finds it more significant to speak in terms of *being* than of the words and deed of God who exists over and above the world but who breaks into the world. He defines the object of theology as 'what concerns us ultimately'.[3] By way of clarification he adds: 'Our ultimate concern is that which determines our being or non-being. Only those statements are theological which deal with their object in so far as it can become a matter of being or non-being for us.'[4]

The notion of God as *what concerns us ultimately* has acquired a certain fame at second-hand through *Honest to God*.[5] In fact, it recurs throughout Tillich's *Systematic Theology*. But perhaps it receives its most striking exposition in *The Shaking of the Foundations*.[6] If we do not know what the word God means, or what Tillich means when he speaks of God as the 'infinite and inexhaustible depth and ground of all being', he advises us to translate it and think of God in terms of our *ultimate concern* or what we take seriously without reservation. No matter if this contradicts our previous notions of God. No matter if we claim to be atheists. Those who know about *ultimate concern* know about the depths of being, and those who know about this cannot really be atheists. For *being* is what we are talking about when we speak about God.

Other terms which Tillich uses for God are *being itself, the power of being* and *the ground of being*.[7] Basic to Tillich's view is the conviction that God is neither *a thing* nor *a being*. God is beyond things and beings; he is *being itself*. If he were a thing or a being, he would be finite. Even to regard God as the

---

[3] *Systematic Theology*, I, p. 15.   [4] *Ibid.*, I, p. 17.
[5] *Honest to God*, pp. 21f.   [6] *The Shaking of the Foundations*, pp. 63f.
[7] *Systematic Theology*, I, pp. 261ff. and often.

highest being would reduce him to the level of a creature. Tillich holds that God is beyond the limitations of existence and beyond the range of conceptual thought, for both existence and conceptual thought belong to the realm of the finite and are limited in time and space. On the other hand, every finite being participates in *being itself*. Otherwise, it would not have the power of being. It would simply be swallowed up by non-being, or indeed it would never have emerged out of non-being.[8]

It is as atheistic, Tillich insists, to affirm the existence of God as to deny it. For *being itself* transcends existence. For the same reason it is wrong to attempt to prove God's existence. For existence with all the limitations of time and space which the term itself implies belongs only to beings and things, not to *being itself*. It is this which underlies Tillich's rejection of the traditional arguments for the existence of God.[9] The attempt to find a first cause leads at best to a cause adequate to produce the universe, but still of the same order as the universe. In the last analysis, such a cause is still finite, whereas for Tillich God is beyond all finite causes. But though logically and theologically defective, the traditional arguments have at least this to say for them: they sense both a distinction and a relationship between finite and infinite being.

When Tillich turns to the subject of man and his sin, he sees them in terms of *being* and *estrangement from being*. Although related to being, we live in a state of estrangement from it. 'Man is estranged from the ground of his being, from other beings, and from himself.'[1] In other ages men were concerned about eternal life and justification. Today these ideas are obsolete for most people. But the same thing can be expressed in terms of estrangement from the ground of our being. And this, Tillich contends, means more to twentieth-century man. It is estrangement which is responsible for the tensions of modern life. We try to conceal it from ourselves by enterprises like the space race, enthusiasm for technical progress and materialism. But in the end it is a matter of alienation from the *ground of our being*.

[8] *Ibid.*, I, p. 263.   [9] *Ibid.*, I, pp. 227–233.   [1] *Ibid.*, II, p. 51.

Being and *estrangement from being* turn up again as the twin keys to the person and work of Christ. For Christ is the one in whom estrangement is overcome, and through whom those who confess him are once more rightly related to the *ground of their being*. Or, to use Tillich's often-repeated phrase, *Jesus as the Christ is the bearer of the New Being*.

All this is elaborately worked out in the second half of the second volume of *Systematic Theology*. Here we can only note some of the more important facets of Tillich's thought. For Tillich 'the central story of the Gospel' is Peter's confession of Christ (Mark 8:27-33).[2] On the one hand, it points to Jesus as the Christ, the one in whom estrangement is overcome. On the other hand, Jesus' warning about suffering and death indicates how estrangement is to be overcome. Suffering and death are an expression of the New Being in Christ. As Tillich goes on to explain, they are 'a consequence of the inescapable conflict between the forces of existential estrangement and the bearer of that by which existence is conquered. Only by taking suffering and death upon himself could Jesus be the Christ, because only in this way could he participate completely in existence and conquer every force of estrangement which tried to dissolve his unity with God'.[3]

Tillich's exposition of how man shares in this conquest of estrangement appears in Volume III of *Systematic Theology*, but his general approach is outlined at the close of Volume II.[4] Regeneration has little in common with evangelistic attempts to create emotional reactions in the individual. Basically, it is 'the state of having been drawn into the new reality manifest in Jesus as the Christ'.[5] Justification involves being accepted in spite of ourselves. There is nothing in man which enables God to accept him. 'He must accept that he is accepted; he must accept acceptance.'[6] Sanctification is the process by which the power of the New Being transforms personality and community both inside and outside the church.

This radical reinterpretation of Christ's person and work is in fact the other side of the coin of Tillich's equally radical

---

[2] *Ibid.*, II, pp. 112ff.; *cf. The Shaking of the Foundations*, pp. 143-150.
[3] *Ibid.*, II, p. 141.   [4] *Ibid.*, II, pp. 203-208.   [5] *Ibid.*, II, p. 204.
[6] *Ibid.*, II, p. 206; *cf. The Shaking of the Foundations*, pp. 155-165.

rejection of orthodox interpretations and the historicity of the Gospels. For Tillich there can be no tension between divine love and justice. The atonement is in no sense a penal satisfaction, putting away the wrath of God. Men receive forgiveness in spite of Christ's death, not because of it.[7] The assertion that 'God has become man' is 'not a paradoxical but a nonsensical statement'.[8] The biblical accounts of the crucifixion are 'often contradictory legendary reports'.[9] While the resurrection is more than 'the manifestation of a bodiless "spirit" ' or 'an intensification of the memory of Jesus', to ask about the molecules of the physical body of Jesus is to compound absurdity with blasphemy.[1] The view which Tillich deems most adequate to the facts is what he terms the *restitution theory*: Jesus is restored 'to the dignity of the Christ in the minds of the disciples'.[2]

Such scepticism is only symptomatic of Tillich's contention that 'the attempt to give a foundation to Christian faith and theology through historical research is a failure'.[3] This attitude, he acknowledges, he has derived from Schweitzer's *Quest of the Historical Jesus* and Bultmann's *History of the Synoptic Tradition*.[4] We cannot penetrate through the faith of the early church to the Jesus of history. This may be cold comfort to the plain man who wants to know whether what is reported in the Bible actually happened. But neither historical research nor Christian faith avail for Tillich. 'Faith cannot guarantee the name "Jesus" in respect of him who was the Christ. It must leave that to the incertitudes of our historical knowledge. But faith does guarantee the factual transformation of reality in that personal life which the New Testament expresses in its picture of Jesus as the Christ.'[5] In other words, what the Christian faith offers is not hard facts, but certain symbols through which we may participate in the New Being. Jesus himself is such a symbol. Of himself he is nothing. The significant thing is that 'He remained transparent to the divine

[7] *Ibid.*, II, pp. 196–203. [8] *Ibid.*, II, p. 109.
[9] *Ibid.*, II, p. 178. [1] *Ibid.*, II, p. 180.
[2] *Ibid.*, II, p. 182. [3] *Ibid.*, II, p. 123.
[4] *On the Boundary*, p. 49. *Cf.* above, pp. 156f. and 186.
[5] *Systematic Theology*, II, p. 123.

mystery until his death, which was the final manifestation of his transparency'.[6] As such, Jesus was neither God nor the New Being itself, but the Bearer of the New Being. As a religion Christianity is 'neither final nor universal'. Rather, it is a witness to that which is final and universal.[7]

The past few years have seen a spate of books on Tillich. Some are favourable, others hostile. Several works have been written by Roman Catholics and one at least by a Jewish rabbi.[8] Tillich's work on symbolism has already been alluded to.[9] It contains some valuable observations. But his use of it in conjunction with Christology leaves much to be desired. For Tillich's Christ is little more than a symbolic figure with no real roots in history. We are left with what the Catholic theologian G. H. Tavard describes as 'a diluted Christology which might be acceptable to a Hindu or a Buddhist: they can accept everything in Tillich's exposition, except precisely the fact that Jesus himself and no other was, and is, and ever shall be, the Christ'.[1]

Part of the reason for this is the fact that Tillich takes over almost lock, stock and barrel the critical views of Albert Schweitzer and Rudolf Bultmann. These writers do not set much store by the historical trustworthiness of the New Testament. But part of the reason is Tillich's system, of which another recent writer, Kenneth Hamilton, has said: 'To see Tillich's system as a whole is to see that it is incompatible with the Christian gospel.'[2]

Sweeping as it may be, there is a good deal of justice in this verdict. For Tillich starts with his notion of *being*, and then forces the gospel to lie on a Procrustean bed of preconceived ideas, lopping off any item which does not quite fit. The disastrous consequences of this method are far-reaching.

On the one hand, it saddles Christianity with a dubious philosophy of uncertain worth and questionable foundation. Tillich is repeatedly taken to task by his critics for his loose-

---

[6] *Ibid.*, I, pp. 149f.   [7] *Ibid.*
[8] See below, pp. 299, 302.   [9] See above, p. 179.
[1] *Paul Tillich and the Christian Message* (Burns and Oates, 1962), p. 167.
[2] *The System and the Gospel: A Critique of Paul Tillich* (SCM Press, 1963), p. 227.

ness in handling terms. The *Systematic Theology* never adequately demonstrates that his concept of *being* is a valid one. The mere fact that the English language contains the word does not mean to say that we can add up the sum of everything that exists and then call it *being*, as if *being* were a meaningful description of the sum total or a tangible abstractable common characteristic. Still less does it give us leave to talk about the *ground of being*, the *power of being* and *alienation from being* without more ado. These ideas upon which the whole edifice is erected are not demonstrated but taken for granted. The result is something which is often barely distinguishable from Pantheism. It is certainly difficult to see with what propriety Tillich uses the word *God* in any Christian sense. It is hardly Trinitarian. His idea is not personal in any familiar or traditional sense. It is more an all-pervading, rational power, but not a person who communicates and with whom man can enter into communion. Tillich's view of *being* most often seems to be an aspect of the world rather than a God who exists over and above it and who is independent of it. We have included Tillich under the general heading of Existentialism, for so much of his work deals with questions of existence. But so much of it also harks back to nineteenth-century concepts of the Absolute Spirit. Tillich is not an Existentialist pure and simple. It would be nearer the mark to describe him as an Idealist in Existentialist clothing.

Apart from being vulnerable as philosophy, Tillich's system does less than justice to the evidence of the New Testament. He rides rough-shod over the biblical witness to the incarnation, atonement and resurrection of Jesus. The extent of this can be appreciated only by comparing Tillich's teaching point by point with Scripture.

Tillich's teaching is sometimes represented as a bridge between the Christian message and the modern mind. But if these criticisms are valid, it is not so much a thoroughfare as a dead end. It misrepresents the modern mind by foisting upon it a philosophy of *being* to which few secular thinkers today would subscribe, and it mutilates the gospel. The root difficulty lies with Tillich's faulty method. For theology the primary datum is God's revelation of himself in Christ, as witnessed to by the primary documents, Scripture. This is demanded by the very nature of the Christian faith.[3] Theological truth is not general truth, capable of being discovered by reflecting upon life in general. While it illuminates life in general, it can only be discovered from the Word of God. Tillich, however, reverses the process, and makes his version of general truth the test of revelation. In so doing, he commits a serious error on two levels. On the scientific level he misconceives the object of his study, and consequently employs defective techniques throughout. On the religious level he turns Christian Theism into a variety of Pantheism, and consequently substitutes an amorphous idea for the living God.

This verdict may sound strange to those who know Tillich only through his sermons. For in some of them there are many passages of great insight which throw fresh illumination upon familiar themes. Here Tillich often talks as if he believes that the events recounted in Scripture really happened. At bottom there seem to be two Tillichs. There is Tillich the preacher, who seems to believe the biblical passages that he is expounding. And there is Tillich the system-builder, who empties them of their original content in order to fill them with something else. As Fr. Tavard remarks, 'While recognizing the many misconceptions in his theology, one must also acknowledge the unmistakable ring of self-commitment in his sermons. Tillich as a preacher is infinitely more faithful to the Word than Tillich the system-builder.'[4]

III THE NEW RADICALISM
The revival of radicalism
To speak of a revival of radicalism may be misleading. The older radicalism of the nineteenth century may have been moribund for the past thirty years and more, but it was never quite dead. After the first World War it was eclipsed by a renewed interest in biblical theology. This was in part due to the reaction on the Continent of such men as Karl Barth and Emil

---

[3] Cf. (e.g.) Matthew 5:17ff.; 16:17; Luke 24:27; John 5:39–47; 1 Corinthians 1:15–31; 2 Corinthians 3:12 – 4:6; 1 Thessalonians 2:13f.; Hebrews 1:1f.; 1 Peter 1:25.
[4] Paul Tillich and the Christian Message, p. 139.

Brunner to the inadequacies of liberalism. It was also in part due to a growing interest in biblical studies in both Protestant and Catholic circles. By the 1950s there were those who were already delivering funeral orations over the corpse of liberal theology. But there were also more cautious observers who pointed out that an interest in biblical studies was not quite the same as embracing biblical religion. It was by no means a foregone conclusion that it was only a matter of time before the two would coincide.

The 1960s have seen a partial revival of radicalism in Britain and North America. The term partial is used advisedly, because it is far from clear how the movement will develop, or even whether it could be described as a coherent movement at all. What has happened is that a number of books have been published, demanding a restatement of Christianity in terms that the authors feel will meet the requirements of secular thought. The authors disagree amongst themselves as to what precisely these terms are. But they all in some degree acknowledge a debt to continental thinkers. And they all express dissatisfaction with more traditional forms of Christianity. The books include the Cambridge symposium *Soundings*[5] which its authors saw as a kind of twentieth-century equivalent to *Essays and Reviews*.[6] In the United States there was Paul van Buren's *The Secular Meaning of the Gospel*[7] and the various publications of what may be called the Death of God school. In Britain Professor Ronald Gregor Smith has assessed the situation in *Secular Christianity*.[8] But the book which hit the most headlines was the Bishop of Woolwich's *Honest to God*.[9] It was followed by various sequels, implementing and correcting the original thesis.[1] But it was hardly to be expected that these should provoke the same degree of excitement.

Like most forms of radicalism, the new religious radicalism

[5] Edited by A. R. Vidler (CUP, 1962).
[6] *Soundings*, p. xi; *cf.* above, p. 161.
[7] SCM Press, 1963.   [8] Collins, 1966.   [9] SCM Press, 1963.
[1] *Christian Morals Today* (1964); *The Honest to God Debate: Some Reactions to the Book 'Honest to God'* edited by David L. Edwards, with a new chapter by its author John A. T. Robinson (1963); *The New Reformation?* (1965) (all SCM Press); *But That I Can't Believe* (Fontana, 1967); *Exploration into God* (SCM Press, 1967).

is a movement of protest. Although individuals have put forward suggestions, it has no accepted positive programme for either theology, evangelism or the running of the church. Rather, it attempts to register a series of protests against others who have. To that extent it is a parasitic movement. Use of such a term is not part of a smear campaign which would substitute calumny for careful thought. But it is difficult to find another which analyses equally accurately the character of the movement. For it is first and foremost a movement of dissatisfaction, owing its existence to that which it attacks most. But as with most things, there is no smoke without fire, and before we can judge the value of the remedy prescribed by the new radicals, it is important to diagnose the situation correctly.

Speaking as one who has had to make his own spiritual pilgrimage from hostility and doubt to Christian faith, I can only say that I have a good deal of sympathy with several of the starting-points of the new radicalism. Orthodoxy is all too often guilty of presenting the gospel in terms which make it seem utterly remote from modern life. Church worship and evangelistic meetings are steeped in a sweet syrup of Victoriana that make acceptance or rejection of the gospel depend not so much on the gospel itself but upon its trappings. All too often acceptance of the gospel is identified with complete withdrawal from the world. Or rather, it is identified with non-participation and lack of interest in so much of real life and withdrawal into a kind of limbo existence of private pietism. In the face of this situation the radicals have rightly called for a re-thinking of the nature and implications of the Christian message.

But the new radicals have gone a good deal further than this in both their diagnosis and cure. The failure of the churches to make any serious impact upon the vast majority of the population has led them to ask whether the substance of the gospel and even our ideas of God do not need changing. Secular science leaves no room for God, and therefore some of them urge that God himself must go in the interests of evangelism. Many of the radicals are deeply impressed by Bultmann's pleas for demythologization.[2] And therefore the gospel must be

[2] See above, pp. 188ff.

stripped of the supernatural and restated in secular terms. When this has been done, the results sometimes bear marked resemblances to Tillich's theory of *being* and reconciliation with the *ground of our being*.[3] It is fairly easy to see what the radicals are attacking. It is not always easy to see what they are putting in its place.

Bonhoeffer

One of the most enigmatic figures in the whole movement is Dietrich Bonhoeffer, who has become almost a kind of oracle. Bonhoeffer was born in 1906. His father was professor of psychiatry at Berlin, and the young Bonhoeffer seemed set for a distinguished career in any profession that he chose. At twenty-one he submitted a doctorate thesis on the doctrine of the church, *Sanctorum Communio*.[4] This was followed up by a further thesis on *Act and Being* (1931)[5] which was submitted for his 'habilitation' as a university teacher at Berlin. But Bonhoeffer did not pursue a narrowly academic career. He took on several pastoral engagements including one in England, ministering to Lutheran communities. The outbreak of war saw him in the United States on a lecture tour. Although a professed opponent of Hitler, he chose to return to Germany. For a time he enjoyed a limited freedom, but he was forbidden to lecture in Berlin, to publish or to preach. He soon became heavily committed to the resistance and was associated with the group which made an abortive attempt on Hitler's life in July 1944. Bonhoeffer himself had already been arrested in April 1943. He was imprisoned for two years and hanged in April 1945.

Before the second World War Bonhoeffer published *The Cost of Discipleship*,[6] and delivered numerous unpublished lectures.[7] But his most provocative work was written in prison in

[3] See above, pp. 193–196.
[4] Collins, 1964. [5] Eng. tr. by Bernard Noble (Collins, 1962).
[6] Munich, 1937. Eng. tr. by R. H. Fuller (1948; revised and unabridged edition, 1959, SCM Press).
[7] These are in process of being edited. Among those so far published are *Christology*, Eng. tr. by John Bowden (Collins, 1966) and *No Rusty Swords: Letters, Lectures and Notes 1928–1936*, I, *The Way to Freedom: Letters, Lectures and Notes, 1935–1939*, II, edited by E. H. Robertson (Collins, 1965–66).

note form and was only later put together by friends and admirers. Among these writings are his *Ethics*[8] and the famous *Letters and Papers from Prison*.[9] What Bonhoeffer would have done, had he survived the war, is impossible to say. Nevertheless, it is his random thoughts, jotted down in prison, that have been his main contribution to post-war radicalism.

Two of the most striking of Bonhoeffer's ideas are those of the world coming of age and of religionless Christianity. The former was not new. Kant believed himself to be standing on the threshold of such a world,[1] though as a matter of fact, despite his efforts, men continued to assume the existence of God, even if they did not pay much attention to him. Doubtless Bonhoeffer was well aware of Kant's pronouncement. But he believed that the modern world had now reached that state of affairs. He did not mean to say that modern man was behaving in any more mature a way than his predecessors. But unlike the latter, he was throwing off all forms of divine parental restraint and was taking no notice of any authority outside himself. This process has been going on since the Renaissance. It is time that the church faced up to it, and recognized that modern man lives *as if God were not there*.

On the one hand we have the deism of Descartes who holds that the world is a mechanism which runs on its own without any intervention of God. On the other hand there is the pantheism of Spinoza, with its identification of God with nature. In the last resort Kant is a deist, Fichte and Hegel pantheists. All along the line there is a growing tendency to assert the autonomy of man and the world . . . There is no longer any need for God as a working hypothesis, whether in morals, politics or science. Nor is there any need for such a God in religion or philosophy (Feuerbach). In the name of intellectual honesty these working hypotheses should be dropped or dispensed with as far as possible. A scientist or a physician who seeks to provide edification is a hybrid.[2]

[8] Edited by Eberhard Bethge, Eng. tr. by Neville Horton Smith (SCM Press, 1955; Fontana, 1964).
[9] Edited by Eberhard Bethge (SCM Press, 1953; Fontana, 1959).
[1] See above, pp. 91f.   [2] *Letters and Papers from Prison*, p. 121.

Hitherto the church has tried to win people to repentance and faith in Christ on the assumption that they accepted the existence of God and knew something of what religion involved. This can no longer be taken for granted. On Bonhoeffer's mind weighed the question: Where does the church go from here?

Our whole nineteen-hundred-year-old Christian preaching and theology rests upon the 'religious premise' of man. What we call Christianity has always been a pattern – perhaps a true pattern – of religion. But if one day it becomes apparent that this *a priori* 'premise' simply does not exist, but was a historical and temporary form of human self-expression, i.e. if we reach the stage of being radically without religion – and I think this is more or less the case already, else how is it, that this war, unlike any of those before it, is not calling forth any 'religious' reaction? – what does this mean for 'Christianity'?[3]

Bonhoeffer believed that we must rethink our notions of God.

Man's religiosity makes him look in his distress to the power of God in the world; he uses God as a *Deus ex machina*. The Bible however directs him to the powerlessness and suffering of God; only a suffering God can help. To this extent we may say that the process we have described by which the world came of age was an abandonment of a false conception of God, and a clearing of the decks for the God of the Bible, who conquers power and space in the world by his weakness. This must be the starting point for our 'worldly' interpretation.[4]

For Bonhoeffer the Christian life meant not withdrawal from the world but total involvement in it. He explains what he means a day or two later on (18 July 1944). The Christian, he writes, 'is challenged to participate in the sufferings of God at the hands of a godless world'.[5]

He must therefore plunge himself into the life of a godless world, without attempting to gloss over its ungodliness with

[3] *Ibid.*, p. 91.   [4] *Ibid.*, p. 122.   [5] *Ibid.*, p. 122.

a veneer of religion or trying to transfigure it. He must live a 'worldly' life and so participate in the suffering of God. He *may* live a worldly life as one emancipated from all false religions and obligations. To be a Christian does not mean to be religious in a particular way, to cultivate some particular form of asceticism (as a sinner, a penitent or a saint), but to be a man. It is not some religious act which makes a Christian what he is, but participation in the suffering of God in the life of the world.[6]

This re-echoes a pre-war theme of Bonhoeffer's that there can be no *cheap grace* for the Christian.[7] Although free, grace is not freedom from all obligations. It is just the opposite. 'Cheap grace means the justification of sin without the justification of the sinner.' But costly grace is '*costly* because it calls us to follow, and it is *grace* because it calls us to follow *Jesus Christ*. It is costly because it costs a man his life, and it is grace because it gives a man the only true life. It is costly because it condemns sin, and grace because it justifies the sinner. Above all, it is *costly* because it cost God the life of his Son'.[8] Such grace has to be acted upon in the world. It led to a new conception of the church which Bonhoeffer hoped to work out one day in a book but which never got beyond an outline sketch. Its concluding theme was: 'The Church is her true self only when she exists for humanity.'[9]

It would be easy to go on multiplying quotable pronouncements from Bonhoeffer's pen. Those reproduced here give some idea of the enigmatic, oracular quality which have made them such useful ammunition for the radicals. On one occasion (in the same Spring of 1944 when most of his more radical conjectures were put to paper) Bonhoeffer said that he did not think that Bultmann's demythologizing went far enough.[1] But the reasons he gave are interesting. Bultmann was preoccupied with mythological conceptions and was at bottom an old-fashioned liberal wanting to separate God and miracles. Bonhoeffer, on the other hand, wants to interpret them in his *non-religious sense.*

---

[6] *Ibid.*, p. 123.
[8] *Ibid.*, pp. 35–37.
[1] *Ibid.*, p. 94.

[7] *The Cost of Discipleship*, pp. 35–47.
[9] *Letters and Papers from Prison*, p. 166.

Was Bonhoeffer a radical? To answer this question would take more time and space than we have available here. But on the whole, I am inclined to think that Bonhoeffer's radicalism has been exaggerated. It is true that his view of the helpless suffering God suggests a new kind of Deism. Like old-fashioned Deism God does not actually do anything positive. The difference lies in the fact that God comes to take part in affairs and suffers like the rest of us. It is also true that Bishop Robinson has claimed him as an ally, and *Honest to God* tries to give substance to the notion of religionless Christianity.[2] But some of those who knew Bonhoeffer best are convinced that this idea has been wrested out of the context of Bonhoeffer's life and thought.[3] It is far from clear that Bonhoeffer wanted to abolish organized Christianity. What he said was that the church can no longer take certain things for granted. He stressed what is stressed on every page of the Gospels and the Old Testament prophets, that Christianity is a life to be lived. Faith has to be translated into action, not in a narrowly pietistic sense but in a way that touches every department of life. What that way was he left unexplained. But it is clear that he did not want to abolish God. Still less did he want to identify God with nature, the world or life. Rather he wanted to clear 'the decks for the God of the Bible'. His faith in this God is deeply engraved in many of his utterances, prayers and meditations in prison.

In the past decade Bonhoeffer has been made into an apostle of radicalism and a modish theologian. Whether he would have relished either is dubious. It may be indelicate but not illegitimate to ask, with Gerhard Ebeling, whether Bonhoeffer would have made the same mark had he survived Buchenwald and Flossenburg.[4] But perhaps Karl Barth's open verdict is the fairest. In the Bonhoeffer symposium *World Come of Age*[5] he describes him (he knew him personally) as 'an impulsive,

[2] *Honest to God*, pp. 36–39 and *passim*.
[3] *Cf.* Julius Rieger, *Dietrich Bonhoeffer in England* (Lettner-Verlag, Berlin, 1966). Rieger has also contributed to the symposium *I Knew Dietrich Bonhoeffer* (Collins, 1967).
[4] *Word and Faith*, Eng. tr. by James W. Leitch (SCM Press, 1963), p. 102.
[5] Edited by Ronald Gregor Smith (Collins, 1967).

visionary thinker who was suddenly seized by an idea to which
he gave lively form, and then after a time he called a halt
(one never knew whether it was final or temporary) with some
provisional last point or other'.[6] Nevertheless, he could also
say: 'What an open and rich and at the same time deep and
disturbed man stands before us – somehow shaming and com-
forting us at the same time.'[7]

Honest to God

If Bonhoeffer's radicalism is a trifle suspect, there can be no
doubt about that of the Bishop of Woolwich. Even so it was a
radicalism that came fully into the open only relatively late
in Dr. Robinson's career. After the war John Robinson made a
steady reputation for himself as an independent-minded,
biblical theologian with such works as *The Body: A Study in
Pauline Theology* (1952) and *Jesus and his Coming* (1957).
As Dean of Clare College, Cambridge, he had engaged in
liturgical experiments. Although some of his ideas were on
the liberal side, it is only in retrospect that the radicalism of
Honest to God can be seen evolving.[8] Its ideas first hit the public
at large in a Sunday newspaper article in *The Observer* for 17
March 1963 to which the publishers gave the headline 'Our
Image of God Must Go'. The article was designed to herald a
small paperback of less than 150 pages. Even then no-one
could have guessed that it would have turned out to be one of
the best-selling theological works (apart from the Bible itself)
of all time. World sales have now topped the million mark.

Part of the reason for this was its readability. It spelt out in a
forceful way for the general reader what had hitherto been
accessible only to a more narrow theological public. Admittedly, the bishop did not say much that was new. Much of it
was straightforward nineteenth-century radicalism, brought
up to date by the language of Bultmann, Tillich and Bonhoeffer who are treated as the three wise men of twentieth-

[6] *World Come of Age*, pp. 89f.   [7] *Ibid.*, p. 89.
[8] In 1966 a Roman Catholic scholar, Richard P. McBrien, published his
doctorate thesis on *The Church in the Thought of Bishop John Robinson* (SCM
Press) with a commendatory foreword by Bishop Robinson himself. In it he
attempted to show how *Honest to God* fitted into Dr. Robinson's other writings.

century theology. The novelty lay partly in the fact that here was someone bringing the three together for the first time and trying to make a synthesis out of them,[9] but more especially in the fact that that person happened to be a bishop of the established church whose office appeared to lend semi-official weight to the whole undertaking.

Robinson starts with the conviction that the idea of God 'up there' (whether physically, metaphysically or metaphorically) is outdated, meaningless and wrong.[1] A good deal of time is spent caricaturing the idea and asking such rhetorical questions as: 'But suppose such a super-Being "out there" is really only a sophisticated version of the Old Man in the sky? Suppose belief in God does not, indeed cannot, mean being persuaded of the "existence" of some entity, even a supreme entity, which might or might not be there, like life on Mars.'[2] He then adds that devotionally and practically this conception of God leaves him cold.[3] But all this is intended to pave the way for the question, 'The End of Theism?'[4] and for answering it with ideas lifted out of Tillich, Bultmann and Bonhoeffer.

From Tillich he gets the idea of God, not as 'a projection "out there", an Other beyond the skies, of whose existence we have to convince ourselves, but the Ground of our very being'.[5] The simple reader might feel that he needed to convince himself just as much of the existence of *the* Ground of his being. But Dr. Robinson hastened to reassure him by quoting a paragraph from a sermon by Tillich which explained that this means 'your ultimate concern', 'what you take seriously without any reservation ... For if you know that God means depth, you know much about him. You cannot then call yourself an atheist or unbeliever. For you cannot think or say: Life has no depth! Life is shallow. Being itself is surface only. If you could say this in complete seriousness, you would be an atheist; but otherwise you are not. He who knows about depth knows about

[9] In a newspaper interview with Ved Mehta, subsequently published in *The New Theologian* (Weidenfeld and Nicolson, 1966, pp. 79f.), Dr. Robinson agreed with this suggestion.
[1] *Honest to God*, pp. 11ff.   [2] *Ibid.*, p. 17.
[3] *Ibid.*, p. 19.   [4] *Ibid.*, pp. 29-44.   [5] *Ibid.*, p. 22.

God.'[6] The pronouncement proved to be one of the storm-centres of the book. We shall return to it in a few moments.

From Bultmann Dr. Robinson got the idea of demythologizing.[7] But, like Bonhoeffer, he felt that Bultmann did not go far enough.[8] What is needed is recognition of the world's coming of age, a determination to reject the idea of God hovering over the world like a *deus ex machina*, and to live as if he were not there. We must work out a 'worldly', religionless Christianity. For 'If Christianity is to survive, let alone to recapture "secular"man, there is no time to lose in detaching it from this scheme of thought, from this particular theology or *logos* about *theos*, and thinking hard about what we should put in its place'.[9]

The scheme of thought referred to here is that of Theism which the bishop defines as belief in 'a supreme Person, a self-existent subject of infinite goodness and power, who enters into a relationship with us comparable with that of one human personality with another'.[1] In place of this traditional Christian idea of God who is other than and over and above the universe, the bishop wants to say that ' "reality at its very deepest level is personal", that personality is of *ultimate* significance in the constitution of the universe, that in personal relationships we touch the final meaning of existence as nowhere else'.[2] Whether these different clauses are intended to be complementary or to say the same thing in different words is not clear. It may be that the latter two are designed to provide escape-routes from the apparent Pantheism of the first. But it is the pantheistic interpretation which receives the strongest emphasis in the ensuing elaboration. Feuerbach is quoted with approval when he says that 'To predicate personality of God is nothing else than to declare personality as the absolute essence'.[3] Belief in God is redefined as 'the trust, the well-nigh incredible trust, that to give ourselves to the utter-

---

[6] *Ibid.; cf.* above on Tillich, pp. 194f.

[7] *Ibid.*, pp. 23ff.; 32ff.; *cf.* above, pp. 187ff.

[8] *Ibid.*, p. 35; *cf.* above, p. 206.   [9] *Ibid.*, p. 43.

[1] *Ibid.*, p. 48.   [2] *Ibid.*, pp. 48f.

[3] *Ibid.*, p. 49, quoting *The Essence of Christianity*, p. 97. (On Feuerbach see above, pp. 133f.)

most in love is not to be confounded but to be "accepted",
that Love is the ground of our being, to which ultimately we
"come home" '.[4] And consequently, theological statements
are said to be 'not a description of "the highest Being" but an
analysis of the depths of personal relationships – or, rather, an
analysis of the depths of *all* experience "interpreted by love".
Theology, as Tillich insists, is about "that which concerns us
ultimately". A statement is "theological" not because it relates to a particular Being called "God", but because it asks
ultimate questions about the meaning of existence . . . it is
saying that *God*, the final truth and reality "deep down
things", *is* love'.[5]

This new conception of God is the basis for the bishop's programme for a New Reformation. In the book of that title he
proceeds to apply it to various matters of church politics and
practice. But consideration of such matters falls outside our
present scope. Nevertheless, it is worth while pausing to see
how the bishop proceeds in *Honest to God* to apply it to three
further aspects of Christian belief: the person of Christ, worship, and ethics. A whole chapter is devoted to each.

In approaching the person of Christ Dr. Robinson adopts
the same tactic of softening up the ground by ridicule, caricature and rhetorical questions. He takes the precaution of safe-
guarding himself by conceding that the orthodox view that
Christ was fully divine and fully human 'is within its own terms
unexceptionable – except that properly speaking it is not a
solution but a statement of the problem'.[6] But caution is soon
thrown to the winds, and it is at once apparent that the view
being advocated does not simply bring orthodoxy up to
date, but condemns it root and branch. Or, to be more precise, the view argued by Dr. Robinson is really a modern form
of views rejected by the early church because they did not fit
the facts of Scripture.

But this does not daunt the bishop from claiming: 'The
supranaturalist view of the incarnation can never really rid
itself of the idea of the prince who appears in the guise of a
beggar. However genuinely destitute the beggar may be, he *is*
a prince; and that in the end is what matters. But suppose the

[4] *Ibid.*, p. 49.   [5] *Ibid.*, p. 49.   [6] *Ibid.*, p. 65.

whole notion of "a God" who "visits" the earth in the person of "his Son" is as mythical as the prince in the fairy story? Suppose there is no realm "out there" from which the "Man from heaven" arrives? Suppose the Christmas myth (the invasion of "this side" by "the other side") – as opposed to the Christmas history (the birth of the man Jesus of Nazareth) – has to go? Are we prepared for that?"[7]

The option that we are left with is really a modification of the old-fashioned liberal view of Jesus as the perfect man who lived close to God,[8] which in turn revived the old Ebionite and Adoptionist heresies of the early centuries. Having ruled out the possibility that Jesus was God, we are left with the alternative that Jesus was a perfect man who walked closely with God. But whereas the early heretics believed that the man Jesus was somehow adopted into the Godhead, and the liberals believed that Jesus was just a very good man, Dr. Robinson describes him as 'a window into God at work'.[9] 'Jesus . . . reveals God by being utterly transparent to him, precisely as he is nothing "in himself".'[1] This, moreover, is the key to the atonement. It has nothing to do with the 'mythological' idea of bearing man's punishment for sin.[2] Rather, it is 'in his utter self-surrender to others in love, that he discloses and lays bare the Ground of man's being as Love'.[3]

When he turns to the subject of prayer and ethics, Bishop Robinson pronounces them to be 'simply the inside and outside of the same thing. Indeed, they could both be defined, from the Christian point of view, as meeting the unconditional in the conditioned in unconditional personal relationship'.[4] Prayer is not withdrawal from this world to give oneself and one's concerns to One who is beyond it.[5] Intercession 'may consist simply in listening, when we take the otherness of the other person most seriously'.[6] Similarly, ethics (which are expounded under the heading of 'The New Morality') are not to be based upon laws and principles 'derived "at second hand" from God'.[7] We are not even to think of them as being

[7] Ibid., p. 67.   [8] See above, pp. 151–157.
[9] Honest to God, p. 71.   [1] Ibid., p. 73.   [2] Ibid., pp. 78f.
[3] Ibid., p. 75.   [4] Ibid., p. 105.   [5] Ibid., pp. 91ff.
[6] Ibid., p. 99.   [7] Ibid., p. 106.

'objectively and immutably' given and 'written into the universe'.[8] There is 'nothing prescribed – except love'.[9] The 'only intrinsic evil is lack of love'.[1]

All this leads up to a view of behaviour which has been called situation ethics.[2] There are no objective rules for conduct which are always valid. There is no coherent system. You can never say (as the bishop goes on to do) that divorce is always wrong. In the same way you can never say (although the bishop refrains from saying so) that stealing, or, for that matter, murder and adultery are always wrong. Everything is relative to the situation. The rightness or wrongness of an action depends upon the amount one cares in the context of the situation.

This view of moral questions is, in fact, of a piece with his view of God. Ostensibly it is trying to dig down to basic principles. In practice, it is decided by the apparent needs of the passing moment. It is not without justice that J. Stafford Wright has called the bishop's teaching as a whole 'situation doctrine'. For the form it takes is not decided by what God has revealed of himself. It is shaped by what the bishop takes to be views acceptable to certain modern-minded people in the situation that he finds them.

Few books in modern times have provoked such a barrage of comment and criticism as *Honest to God*. Some of them were short and sharp like J. I. Packer's *Keep Yourselves from Idols*.[3] A lengthier reply from a Church of Scotland scholar was J. M. Morrison's *Honesty and God*.[4] Many of the reviews and articles were compiled by David Edwards into a book on *The Honest to God Debate*. An Anglo-Catholic reply came from O. Fielding Clarke in *For Christ's Sake*.[5] The Archbishop of Canterbury himself had a go in *Image Old and New*.[6] While he rebuked some of the bishop's charges, his work gave the general ap-

---

[8] *Ibid.*, p. 107.   [9] *Ibid.*, p. 116.   [1] *Ibid.*, p. 118.
[2] In developing this idea the bishop appeals to the work of the American scholar Joseph Fletcher. Since then Professor Fletcher has further expanded his views in *Situation Ethics: The New Morality* (SCM Press, 1966) and *Moral Responsibility: Situation Ethics at Work* (SCM Press, 1967).
[3] Church Book Room Press, 1963.
[4] Saint Andrew Press, Edinburgh, 1966.
[5] Religious Education Press, 1963.   [6] SPCK, 1963.

pearance of trying to pour oil upon troubled waters. But the most important of all the critiques came from the pen of the Anglo-Catholic philosopher and theologian, Professor E. L. Mascall, in *The Secularisation of Christianity*[7] which dealt not merely with Bishop Robinson but with the revival of radicalism in general.

When all due allowances have been made for Bishop Robinson's swashbuckling enthusiasm and his valid complaint that orthodoxy can become sterile and meaningless, it has to be said that so much of his own argument has the appearance of a conjuring trick – or at least of desiring to have his cake and eat it. This comes out, for example, in his treatment of the 'New Morality'. We leave aside the charges that it is really the old immorality in disguise. There is much in the bishop's discussion which brings back into focus Jesus' pronouncement that the second great commandment is to love one's neighbour as oneself.[8] He rightly sees the need to get clear the real reasons for doing (or not doing) things. The real difficulty about his exposition of the new morality is his attempt to reduce ethics to the single idea of love and abolish the idea of responsibility to an authority over and above the people concerned. For in practice he does neither. When he says that there is 'nothing prescribed – except love', he is in fact smuggling back into his scheme the very notion of obligation to an external authority of the type that he has just denounced. The idea of love does not necessarily carry with it that of obligation to love. The mere fact that other people are there does not mean that we should love them, unless there is some authority over and above us which tells us that we should do so. In practice people recognize such an authority when they say that stealing, adultery and murder are wrong and caring for others is right. But this in turn raises the whole question of the nature and *otherness* of this authority which the book so assiduously tries to sweep under the carpet. Nor may we turn a blind eye to the fact (however strenuously denied in some quarters) that people are aware of their responsibility before the one who is the author of their existence and whose

[7] Darton, Longman and Todd, 1965.
[8] Matthew 22:39; Mark 12:31; Luke 10:27.

service, according to Jesus, constitutes the first commandment.[9]

We must leave aside here the details of the question of the biblical basis of the orthodox view of the person of Christ.[1] Enough has already been said to show that (whether true or false) the bishop's view is not a restatement of orthodoxy but a flat denial of it. For further discussion the reader is advised to turn to the books already referred to.

In the last analysis Bishop Robinson's position stands or falls by his view of God and the methods he uses to obtain it. His book is not the result of a careful analysis of the grounds on which people have asserted Christian belief. Nor is it even a thorough examination of objections. At no point does he attempt to get to grips with the biblical view of revelation and the witness to God of the writers of Scripture. Instead, he begins with a caricature of the idea of God 'up there', although he admits that the expression is merely symbolical. In its place he proposes to substitute the notions of depth, ultimate concern and Ground of being. Now there is nothing wrong with these terms as such. It all depends upon the use to which they are put. Depth is a good biblical metaphor, complementing that of height. The other two terms are equally good, their value depends on how they are used. It is here that Dr. Robinson's philosophical sleight of hand (or muddled thinking) makes itself felt again. If he means to say that we know God in the depths of our experiences and in the things that we are most concerned about, he is saying no more and no less than the orthodox Theist whom he is at pains to ridicule. God is still outside and other than nature. But if he really means (as he apparently does) that God is to be identified with depth and these concerns, that God does not exist over and above them, and that 'the final truth and reality – "deep down things" *is* love' (whatever this may mean) – then he is either a pantheistic atheist or an atheistic pantheist. The word God seems to mean that the universe as a whole is personal.

Whether such an idea can do the job of rescuing Christianity for popular consumption is very doubtful. Even more

<hr/>

[9] Matthew 22:37f.; Mark 12:30; Luke 10:27.
[1] I have attempted a brief summary of this in *Karl Barth and the Christian Message* (Tyndale Press, 1967), pp. 67–76.

dubious are the grounds on which it is asserted. It is open to the same objections as Tillich and old-fashioned Idealism.[2] But there are indications that this is no longer the bishop's present view. In *The Honest to God Debate* he has admitted that the equation of depth and ultimate concern with God 'is false. A depth-experience by itself brings, at best, only an unconscious knowledge of God'.[3] He also goes on to admit that in practice he cannot pray to the Ground of his being. 'I would say at once that I do not pray to the ground of my being. I pray to God as Father.'[4] But if this is so, what becomes of the original bold hypothesis? It might seem that the bishop is fighting a discreet rearguard action, withdrawing under as much cover as possible from the advanced positions of *Honest to God*. But if this is so, he has given the whole game away. The need for realism and relevance remains, but, like the proverbial cake, the bishop cannot have his Theism and eat it. The whole episode appears to have been a hectic exercise in spring-cleaning. But now that the dust is settling, everything seems to be where it was before. It remains for the bishop to say whether he honestly

---

[2] See above, pp. 199 and 124, 127.
[3] *The Honest to God Debate*, p. 261. The phrase is that of Dr. D. D. Evans, but Dr. Robinson accepts it as a valid criticism.
[4] *Ibid.*, pp. 261ff.

In *Exploration into God* (1967) Dr Robinson professes surprise at the failure of his critics not to see that, 'Above all, I was presupposing a fundamental conviction and commitment to the heart of the Christian faith – summed up in "the grace of our Lord Jesus Christ and the love of God and the fellowship of [*sic*] Holy Spirit" – which I scarcely thought it necessary to state' (p. 14). But this is precisely the difficulty which is not resolved either by this protestation or by the new book as a whole. Does the bishop believe in the triune God of the biblical revelation, or is this merely a figurative way of expressing a profoundly mysterious aspect of human experience, which could be equally or better expressed in other ways?

We are again treated to the same cavalier dismissals of Theism, and told that it makes religion harder for some people. Tillich is again said to offer a third option between Theism and atheism. It is symptomatic of the whole undertaking that, in a book ostensibly concerned with Christian belief in God, the Trinity is mentioned only three times (and that in passing). The final inconclusive chapter is devoted to exploring 'Beyond the God of Theism'. And the closing words tell us that 'the most appropriate model – perhaps the only appropriate model today – for a satisfactory theology of the Incarnation is a panentheistic one' (p. 145).

wants to go the whole way with *Honest to God* and part company with Christianity, or to go back. In his collection of semi-popular utterances entitled *But That I Can't Believe* he spends a good deal of time airing his personal grievances. What he actually believes about God is hidden behind the smoke-screen. He appears to be pressing on regardless. But it is difficult to see that he can go on honestly behaving as if the positions he was fighting for in *Honest to God* had been established.

The Death of God school

After the fireworks of *Honest to God*, anything that followed it was bound to seem an anticlimax, even if it was still more radical. But while the Bishop of Woolwich was producing his *succès de scandale*, there were several scholars in the United States – apparently working independently of each other – enlarging on the theme of the death of God. Among these were Paul van Buren, who set out his ideas in *The Secular Meaning of the Gospel*[5]; William Hamilton, who was one of the first in the field with *The New Essence of Christianity*[6] (a title which brought

[5] SCM Press, 1963. Van Buren has expanded his ideas in *Theological Explorations* (SCM Press, 1968), but this book appeared too late to be taken into account in the present study.

[6] 1961 (British edition published by Darton, Longman and Todd, 1966). Since then Hamilton has travelled much further in the direction of atheism. In the symposium *Frontline Theology* (edited by Dean Peerman, SCM Press, 1967) he confesses that about the age of forty he suddenly realized that he had been talking a lot of platitudes. At the same time he began to feel that the 'death of God' theology best fitted his attitude. The phrase expresses the sense of irretrievable loss after taking God for granted for so long. Nevertheless, he still believes in Jesus as 'the one to whom I repair, the one before whom I stand, the one whose way with others is also to be my way because there is something there, in his words, his life, his way with others, his death, that I do not find elsewhere' (p. 75).

The dividing-line between this opting for Jesus and the person who comes out in the appeal at an evangelistic crusade without really knowing why is barely perceptible. To say this is not to condemn either outright. It is merely to say that a person cannot stop there for ever. For the only Jesus we know of is that of the New Testament, whose message was concerned with the kingdom of *God* and whose life was devoted to doing the will of his *heavenly Father*. In whatever strata of the New Testament we look we cannot find Jesus without Theism.

back memories of Feuerbach's militant atheism of over a
century ago); and Gabriel Vahanian with *The Death of God:
The Culture of Our Post-Christian Era*[7] and *Wait without Idols.*[8]
Harvey Cox touched upon the subject in *The Secular City.*[9]
These have now been joined by the prior of a Dutch Roman
Catholic order, Robert Adolfs, whose book *The Grave of God*[1]
has been condemned by the General of his order. But the most
crusading member of the school is Thomas J. J. Altizer, who
has expounded his paradoxical views in *The Gospel of Christian
Atheism.*[2]

In the United States the movement has been dubbed with
the creed: 'God is dead and Jesus is his Son.' In fact, the titles
listed above represent a wide variety of views and a correspondingly wide variety of routes by which they have been attained.
Hamilton's is an original probing, tentative essay. Vahanian is
concerned with the decline of belief in the western world and
the need for new concepts to replace the outworn traditional
ones. Van Buren's work is ostensibly a piece of linguistic
analysis.

For a time van Buren was a disciple of Barth,[3] but he
changed his views in the light of the discussions of the British
linguistic analysts. He contends that 'Today, we cannot even
understand the Nietzschian cry that "God is dead!" for if it
were so, how could we know? No, the problem now is that
the *word* "God" is dead.'[4] But it is questionable whether this
itself is a meaningful assertion. There are certainly millions of
people for whom the word *God* is not dead and for whom there
are areas of life which could not otherwise be described without introducing the idea of God. All that it shows is that van
Buren has capitulated before the false antitheses presented by
certain analytic philosophers who profess to find the word
meaningless. The limitations of his thinking and reading are
shown up all too clearly by his previous discussion. Nevertheless,

[7] Braziller, New York, 1961.   [8] Braziller, New York, 1964.
[9] SCM Press, 1965.   [1] Burns and Oates, 1967.
[2] Collins, 1967.
[3] He wrote a doctorate thesis under Barth on *Christ in Our Place: The Sub-
stitutionary Character of Calvin's Doctrine of Reconciliation* (Oliver and Boyd,
1957).
[4] *The Secular Meaning of the Gospel*, p. 103.

it is sufficient to compel van Buren to attempt to reduce the gospel to purely secular terms. Thus the doctrine of creation is said to express 'an affirmative view of the world of men and things'[5] (whatever that may mean). The mission of the church is not to make others into Christians or even for a man to tell his neighbour why he is 'for' him. It is the way of practising liberty and the way of love upon which a man finds himself.[6]

While it is possible to see some very faint resemblances with certain aspects of Christianity, it is difficult to see what gospel is left when van Buren has finished with it. What has happened (as Professor Mascall has pointed out[7]) is something that has happened over and over again in the history of the church. The Christian faith has been tied to a particular philosophy. It happened in the past with Platonism, Aristotelianism and Idealism. But seldom has it been done in so naïve a fashion or with such forlorn results.

Altizer's British publishers make the claim that *The Gospel of Christian Atheism* makes *Honest to God* look orthodox. No doubt they are right. But this is not the same as saying that its thesis is true or the thinking behind it profound. It is a hotch-potch of nineteenth-century ideas made indigestible by the author's esoteric jargon and lack of careful reasoning. Instead of careful investigation the reader is treated to an endless stream of unsubstantiated claims and references to the por-tentous pronouncements of Nietzsche, Blake and Hegel. Lest the reader think that the present writer is being too hard on the author, he may care to test his skill in deciphering a sentence like: 'Insofar as an eschatological epiphany of Christ can occur only in conjunction with a realization in total experience of the kenotic process of self-negation, we should expect that epiphany to occur in the heart of darkness, for only the univer-sal triumph of the Antichrist can provide an arena for the total manifestation of Christ.'[8] And when he has done that there are plenty more on any page he cares to choose.

'Epiphany' (like 'sacrality', 'primordial', 'every alien other' and 'incarnation') is one of the key-words left unex-

---

[5] *Ibid.*, p. 177.   [6] *Ibid.*, pp. 191f.
[7] *The Secularisation of Christianity*, pp. 103f.
[8] *The Gospel of Christian Atheism*, p. 120.

plained and unjustified.[9] Another is the term *Word*. Of this
Altizer writes that 'the Christian must always be open to the
transfiguring power of the Incarnate Word, knowing that the
Word is in process of renewing all things, not by recalling
them to their pristine form in the Beginning, but rather by
making them new so that they can pass into the End'.[1] Theology is then said to be 'a thinking response to the Word that is
present upon the horizon of faith'. But what is this Word? It is
apparently not the Second Person of the Trinity, whom Altizer
does not believe in. Could it be Altizer's version of Hegel's
Geist?[2] But upon what grounds could the existence of such a
Word be asserted, and how is it connected with Jesus in whom
Altizer apparently professes some faith? The difficulty is increased by the assertion that theology 'must accept the principle
that the Word can be and is indeed present, even though it is
not possible to discern any traditional signs of its activity, and
despite the fact that the life and movement of our time would
appear to be so irrevocably anti-Christian'.[3]

All this looks suspiciously as if, having pronounced a funeral
oration for God on the housetops, Altizer is trying to smuggle
him back in under the guise of the Word, however un-Chris-
tian, incoherent and groundless the attempt may be. But the
death of God did not take place (as with Nietzsche) when
people stopped believing in him. 'The radical Christian knows
that God has truly died in Jesus and that his death has liber-
ated humanity from the oppressive presence of the primordial
Being.'[4] But this is soon counteracted by the claim that 'Jesus
is the name of the love of God, a love that eternally dies for

---

[9] 'Incarnation' is said to reach its consummation 'when God finally appears
in human experience as the contradiction of life and the deification of
nothingness' (*ibid.*, p. 95).

[1] *Ibid.*, p. 18.

[2] 'The death of God in Christ is an inevitable consequence of the movement
of God into the world, of Spirit into flesh, and the actualization of the death
of God in the totality of experience is a decisive sign of the continuing and
forward movement of the divine process, as it continues to negate its
particular given expressions, by moving ever more fully into the depths of
the profane' (*ibid.*, p. 110; *cf.* Hegel, *Phenomenology of Mind*, Eng. tr.,
pp. 780ff.; see above, pp. 119–123, and p. 139, n. 5).

[3] *Ibid.*, p. 19.   [4] *Ibid.*, p. 71.

man. Truly to pronounce his name – and for the radical Christian the names of Jesus and God are ultimately one – is to participate in God's death in Jesus and thereby to know the God who *is* Jesus as the expanding or forward-moving process who is becoming "One Man" '.[5] Is this a cryptic way of saying what the atheistic Humanists are saying more effectively about loving each other, or is it an admission that all the talk about the death of God is just a stunt? Perhaps Altizer will explain in a sequel. But if he does, it is to be hoped that he will take a good dose of linguistic analysis in the meantime.

Has, then, the new radicalism anything of importance to say? In substance it says little that has not been said already. Its distinctive theses are clearly incapable of standing up to close scrutiny. But at least it indicates a hunger and a fear. The hunger is for a restatement of Christianity in terms that will stand up in the light of modern thought and which can be translated into terms which are relevant to the twentieth century. The fear is that orthodox Christianity is incapable of meeting these needs. It is up to orthodoxy to show that it can.

IV THE BROADER SPECTRUM

As in everything, philosophy has its fads and fashions which change as regularly as the seasons. For a time one particular thinker or movement will be in vogue, and then he will disappear as quickly as he came. At the present time various brands of the new radicalism are being energetically canvassed in certain circles. Bultmann's shadow still lies over continental theology. Questions of logical analysis occupy the attentions of most British secular philosophers. But these are by no means the only important trends in philosophy today. If our picture of the twentieth-century scene is to be anything like fair, we must consider certain other figures and movements. Some we have touched on already. Others were more popular twenty years ago than they are now. One at least – Teilhard de Chardin – has acquired more fame posthumously than he did in his lifetime. And some will doubtless come into their own again when the dust has settled on the novelties of the moment.

[5] *Ibid.*, p. 75.

Secular British philosophy
We have already seen how in the second quarter of the twentieth century British philosophy was dominated by linguistic
analysis. Even when it passed out of the initial phases of
Logical Positivism it was preoccupied with problems of language, meaning and knowledge.

Wittgenstein. In some ways the movement is typified by the
solitary figure of Wittgenstein at Cambridge, restlessly analysing
the structure of thought, for ever questioning.[6] He was constantly dogged by the fear that his ideas might be distorted by
disciples and critics alike. Yet he was reluctant to publish
because of his dissatisfaction with his own inadequacies.[7] Of
all the twentieth-century philosophers Wittgenstein comes
nearest to the popular image of the eccentric recluse. He was
invariably casually dressed. His rooms at Cambridge were
sparsely furnished, equipped with only a bed, table and canvas
chairs. When students came for tutorials they had to bring
their own seating. With Wittgenstein philosophy was a highly
specialist discipline devoted to the analysis of language and
thought. But it was also a kind of mind-loosening exercise.
As he once said in a lecture,

> What I give is the morphology of the use of an expression.
> I show that it has kinds of uses of which you had not
> dreamed. In philosophy one feels *forced* to look at a concept
> in a certain way. What I do is to suggest, or even invent,
> other ways of looking at it. I suggest possibilities of which
> you had not previously thought. You thought that there was
> one possibility, or only two at most. But I made you think
> of others. Furthermore, I made you see that it was absurd
> to expect the concept to conform to those narrow possibili-

[6] See above, pp. 169, 174.
[7] Wittgenstein usually wrote in German which was then translated into
English. His last major work which is regarded by many as the most important contribution to philosophy in the twentieth century was the posthumous *Philosophical Investigations* (Blackwell, Oxford, 1953, 1958²). It
contains the German original and the Eng. tr. of G.E.M. Anscombe on
facing pages. Other notes and drafts which have also been posthumously
published include his *Preliminary Studies for 'The Philosophical Investigations'*,
Generally known as The Blue and Brown Books (Blackwell, Oxford, 1958),
and *Zettel* (Blackwell, Oxford, 1967).

ties. Thus your mental cramp is relieved, and you are free to look around the field of use of the expression and to describe the different kinds of uses of it.[8]

This is a far cry from the old conception of philosophy as a kind of master-key which would unlock all the secrets of the universe. But it has the virtue of cutting down the subject to life-size. It hinders it from poaching on the proper preserve of other academic disciplines, and thereby frees it to perform the salutary task of making us aware of the scope and limitations of language and thought.

Moore. Other leading philosophers are not so easily type-cast. Most of them have one foot in the analytic camp. But neither G. E. Moore nor Bertrand Russell (who were also Cambridge philosophers) were analysts pure and simple. The name of George Edward Moore (1873–1958) has come up already in connection with the ontological argument[9] and Idealism[1] (both of which he rejects). In his lectures delivered in 1910–1911, which were subsequently published some forty years later under the title *Some Main Problems of Philosophy*,[2] Moore claimed that there were three main topics in philosophy.[3]

[8] Quoted from Norman Malcolm, *Ludwig Wittgenstein: A Memoir* (OUP, 1958, revised 1966), p. 50. In the *Philosophical Investigations* Wittgenstein speaks of 'language games'. Instead of trying to restrict meaning to preconceived ideas of what is meaningful, he compares language to a number of games which are being played more or less simultaneously. In order to understand what a particular utterance means, we have to understand what the 'game' is and what the 'rules' are. 'Doesn't the analogy between language and games throw light here? We can easily imagine people amusing themselves in a field by playing with a ball so as to start various existing games, but playing many without finishing them and in between throwing the ball aimlessly into the air, chasing one another with the ball and bombarding one another for a joke and so on. And now someone says: The whole time they are playing a ball-game and following definite rules at every throw.

'And is there not also the case where we play and – make up the rules as we go along? And there is even one where we alter them – as we go along' (*op. cit.*, § 83, p. 39°).

[9] See above, p. 21.   [1] See above, p. 124.   [2] Allen and Unwin, 1953.
[3] This was somewhat modified in 'A Reply to My Critics' in P. A. Schilpp, *The Philosophy of G. E. Moore* (Evanston, 1942), in which he prefers to speak of method rather than metaphysics.

The first and primary aim of philosophy is to provide a metaphysical inventory of the universe, that is, 'a general description of the *whole* of this universe, mentioning all the most important kinds of things that we *know* to be in it, considering how far it is likely that there are in it important kinds of things which we do not absolutely *know* to be in it'. The second concerned knowledge. It was to classify the ways in which we know things. The third topic was ethics.[4]

Moore is remembered as a defender of common sense in philosophy. In an essay on 'A Defence of Common Sense' (1925)[5] he drew a distinction between the meaning and truth of what is said on the one hand, and the analysis of that meaning on the other. In many cases the former is clear and comprehensible. It is the latter which is obscure and difficult. In the realm of ethics he attacked what he termed 'the naturalistic fallacy', that is, the attempt to explain away the notion of 'good' as if it were nothing more than (for example) the pleasure which it gives.[6] We may recognize goodness when we come across it. But in the last analysis it cannot be broken down into constituent elements. Goodness is simply goodness.

As a schoolboy Moore was converted to 'ultra-evangelicalism', and for a period of about two years he felt obliged to witness and distribute tracts. The experience proved very painful, and before he left school he was won back to 'complete agnosticism'. He does not seem to have deviated from this in later life, holding that there was no evidence to support belief in God and almost as little against it.

[4] Moore dealt with the subject in *Principia Ethica* (CUP, 1903; paperback 1959) and *Ethics* (1912; paperback 1966).
[5] Reprinted in *Philosophical Papers* (1959).
[6] 'When they say "Pleasure is good", we cannot believe that they merely mean "Pleasure is pleasure" and nothing more than that. . . . We may be able to say how it is related to other things: that, for example, it is in the mind, that it causes desire, that we are conscious of it, etc., etc. We can, I say, describe its relations to other things, but define it we can *not*. And if anybody tried to define pleasure for us as being any other natural object; if anybody were to say, that pleasure *means* the sensation of red, and were to proceed to deduce from that that pleasure is a colour, we should be entitled to laugh at him and to distrust his future statements about pleasure. Well, that would be the same fallacy which I have called the naturalistic fallacy' (*Principia Ethica*, pp. 12f.).

Russell. A thinker about whose hostility to religion no doubt can be entertained is Bertrand Russell. Recently he has been feted by a volume of essays entitled *Bertrand Russell: Philosopher of the Century*[7] which includes among other things contributions from A. J. Ayer, C. D. Broad and Aldous Huxley. But if this accolade is merited at all, it must be for his contributions to matters other than religion, despite the energy and wit that he has lavished upon this subject.

Bertrand Arthur William, third Earl Russell, was born in 1872. He became a Fellow of Trinity College, Cambridge, in 1895, and from 1910 to 1916 he was a college lecturer. He began as an Idealist, but soon rejected it. An early work was on *The Philosophy of Leibniz* (1900). But his reputation as a thinker of the first rank was established by his *Principia Mathematica* (3 volumes, 1910–13), a work which he wrote in collaboration with A. N. Whitehead.

Unlike Moore, Russell began by having little sympathy with defending common sense. 'The point of philosophy', he once remarked, 'is to start with something so simple as not to seem worth stating, and to end with something so paradoxical that no one will believe it.'[8] In his middle period he developed a doctrine similar to that of the Logical Positivists which he termed Logical Atomism.[9] Through rigorous use of logical analysis Russell came to the conclusion that we can arrive at ultimate 'atomic facts' which are logically independent of each other and of being known. But he later came to admit that there might be necessary connections between distinct events.

Although Russell has written a good deal on the question of knowledge,[1] he has failed (as his admirer and biographer,

---

[7] Edited by Ralph Schoenman (Allan and Unwin, 1967).
[8] *Logic and Knowledge*, edited by R. C. Marsh (Allen and Unwin, 1956), p. 193.
[9] Papers dealing with this are reprinted in *Logic and Knowledge* and also in *Logical Positivism*, edited by A. J. Ayer. Russell's views deeply influenced his pupil Ludwig Wittgenstein.
[1] Later writings include *An Inquiry into Meaning and Truth* (Allen and Unwin, 1940; Pelican, 1962) and *Human Knowledge: Its Scope and Limits* (Allen and Unwin, 1948.)

H

Alan Wood, has pointed out[2]) to work a thoroughly satisfactory and coherent approach. In his later writings he has fallen back more on the value of common sense, and also attacked the Logical Positivists for their narrowly linguistic preoccupations. Lord Russell has never been exclusively concerned with philosophical puzzles. And in the last few years his energies have been devoted to humanitarian questions. A passionate advocate of nuclear disarmament, he queried in an interview with the Indian journalist Ved Mehta the latter's interest in philosophy. Why waste time on philosophy when mankind is in danger of destroying itself? 'I have to read at least one detective book a day', he added, 'to drug myself against the nuclear threat.'[3]

In the course of his long life Bertrand Russell has been a man of many parts. He was a candidate for Parliament on three occasions but was defeated each time. He has been twice jailed in connection with his pacifist activities. He has been awarded a Nobel prize and the Order of Merit. He has been divorced three times and married four. His literary output reveals him to be not only one of the most prolific but perhaps also the most lucid and witty philosophic writer of modern times. His *History of Western Philosophy*[4] is perhaps the only treatment of the subject which can be read in bed.

His treatment of religion is in similar vein. The reader of books like *Religion and Science*[5] and *Why I am Not a Christian*[6] is treated to lengthy catalogues of the follies that have been committed in the name of religion, which lose nothing in the telling. Russell's razor-sharp mind has no difficulty in slicing through the old-fashioned arguments of natural theology.

[2] *Bertrand Russell: The Passionate Sceptic* (Allen and Unwin, 1957), p. 196.
[3] *Fly and the Fly-Bottle*, p. 41.
[4] Allen and Unwin, 1946 and several reprints.
[5] OUP, 1935.
[6] *Why I am Not a Christian and Other Essays on Related Subjects*, edited by Paul Edwards (Allen and Unwin, 1957 and several reprints). It includes the transcript of his debate with Fr. F. C. Copleston on 'The Existence of God' broadcast by the BBC in 1948. The title is taken from a lecture given at Battersea Town Hall in 1927. It is interesting to compare it with H. G. Wood, *Why Mr. Bertrand Russell is Not a Christian: An Essay in Controversy* (SCM Press, 1928).

Perhaps the casual reader will be impressed by the cocksure confidence of his generalizations and even dazzled by his parodies of certain aspects of religion. But when it comes to the point he conspicuously avoids coming to grips with biblical religion. He rips a few sayings of Christ out of context. But for the most part he contents himself with shying at Aunt Sallies. The serious reader who wants a balanced statement of the pros and cons is best advised to look elsewhere. Nevertheless, anyone who wants to test his reflexes in argument will find Russell a good sparring-partner.

Humanism

Bertrand Russell is a professed Humanist. But even the brief interview with Ved Mehta is sufficient to show that he is by no means confident in human progress. There was a time earlier on in the century when Humanists could present a reasonably united front. As a more-or-less coherent body of beliefs and disbeliefs which almost amounted to a creed:

(1) man is not natively depraved; (2) the end of life is life itself, the good life on earth instead of the beatific life after death; (3) man is capable, guided solely by the light of reason and experience, of perfecting the good life on earth; and (4) the first and essential condition of the good life on earth is the freeing of men's minds from the bonds of ignorance and superstition, and of their bodies from the arbitrary oppression of the constituted social authorities.[7]

If this definition has a touch of parody about it, it is not all that wide of the mark. It could very well stand as a paraphrase of how many in the rationalist, Humanist tradition understood Pope's line: 'The proper study of mankind is man.'

But as the twentieth century has worn on the Humanist creed has been shaken. Like the church, the Humanist camp is divided against itself. The point is underlined by a short but significant symposium on *Objections to Humanism* which

[7] Carl Becker, *The Heavenly City of the Eighteenth-Century Philosophers* (Yale, 1932), p. 102.

appeared under the editorship of H. J. Blackham,[8] Director
of the British Humanist Association.

Of the four contributors, Kingsley Martin (the former editor of *The New Statesman*) takes the most orthodox Humanist
line. He grants that Humanist hopes have received severe
setbacks in the first half of the twentieth century. People are not
as rational as they might be; the church and other irrational
institutions still have a considerable pull over the masses.
Science is not quite the panacea it was once thought to be.
The two World Wars have put a damper on belief in the
inevitability of progress. But once having rid himself of these
admissions, Mr. Martin soon finds himself in familiar country.
Indeed, the reader may find himself wondering whether the
author has really understood his original brief. For what began
as objections to Humanism soon turns out to be objections
to everything else but Humanism. After having had a good
go at (*inter alia*) Fascism, Rome, the Church of England and
the doctrine of the Trinity, Mr. Martin concludes: 'The
humanist faith is that reason can play a decisive role and that
religious doctrines are for the most part obstructive . . . The
future depends on ourselves, not on any doctrine. We may
believe that men progress, not towards Utopia or perfectibility,
but towards a happier and more reasonable society.'[9]

The other contributors are decidedly less optimistic. Indeed,
they soon give the lie to Mr. Martin's contention that 'The
concern of thinking people is with the health, wealth and happiness of mankind'.[1] The poetess, novelist and critic Kathleen
Nott pleads with her fellow Humanists to come to terms with
the non-rational side of life. Her essay is a passionate protest
against shallow materialism. Rationalism is sterile, she argues,
when it becomes preoccupied with reason and proof and not
with life. All too often, philosophers from Descartes down to
the contemporary empiricists have got bogged down with
problems of verification.

Ronald Hepburn (then professor of philosophy at Notting-

---

[8] Constable, 1963. H. J. Blackham has written a larger book which seeks to
set contemporary humanism in historical perspective and contrast it with
Christianity, *The Human Tradition* (Routledge, 1953).
[9] *Objections to Humanism*, pp. 102f.   [1] *Ibid.*, p. 102.

ham and now at Edinburgh) is even more sympathetic to religion. He tries to see what the Humanist can make of mystical and religious experiences. His essay is a penetrating, if tentative, critique of natural theology. Far from relegating religion to the scrapheap of muddle-headed and even perverse thinking, Professor Hepburn pleads for a careful sifting of the evidence. He is even prepared to admit that when this has been done, 'There may survive . . . moral concepts of a richness that shows up the meagreness of the humanist's own. And there may survive ways of seeing humanity, transfigurations of the supposedly familiar world, which – even when we are quite unable to assimilate or domesticate them – can haunt and trouble and goad the imagination.'[2]

But perhaps most significant of all are the editor's own two essays. In his introduction he insists that any similarity between Christian and Humanist ethics is purely accidental. The former are based upon Christian beliefs; the latter should be grounded entirely upon social considerations. For the Humanist there can be no single ultimate good. There are no absolute moral standards. Everything hinges upon the demands of this life. But it is in his final contribution on 'The Pointlessness of it All' that we are brought face to face with the implications of Humanism.

Humanism is a kind of religion in so far as it has a kind of creed. But it is a religion without God. If there is a God, he is unknowable, and cannot be taken into account. Man must live for man alone. For, whether he likes it or not, man has been dumped into the world and has to fend for himself. In a very real sense, he is his own creator. He has to create his own standards. He has to create his own goals. And he has to make his own way towards them.

The only sure thing in life is death. It is as if we are all living on a gigantic conveyor belt moving relentlessly towards the crematorium. What, then, is the point of it all? Does not this make the previous essays sound rather shallow? Mr. Blackham has an answer. If this is really so, then at least we can recognize it and make the best of a bad job. What to some might seem the big weakness of Humanism, becomes in Mr.

[2] *Ibid.*, p. 54.

Blackham's hands the strongest plank in his platform. 'I am the author of my own experience. That experience may be but a sorry or trivial tale of what happens to me. Or I may take it in hand and create an experience that is worth sharing, not for its moral but for itself.'[3]

The gospel of Humanism invites men to make the best of a bad job. The world is ultimately pointless. All we can do is to try to give it a few temporary points before we pass into the abyss of nothingness. The ancients said: Eat, drink, and be merry, for tomorrow we die. The Humanism of the sixties has become more sophisticated. It allows man to be serious in his merry-making. The image is new, but the basic idea is the same. Life has no other meaning than that which we give it ourselves, and no other end but death.

This in itself is not an objection to Humanism. For this view of life is perhaps the best we can do, if we assume that God does not exist and that he does not care for the world. It is better to face the facts and recognize that this is the only valid alternative to Christianity than to pretend that there are various intermediate options open to us. But does the Humanist really face facts? Mr. Blackham is aware of the charge that modern secular man makes up his mind against Christianity without giving it a serious hearing. He admits that it is serious. For him the crucial question is the biblical one: 'What think ye of Christ?' which is to be supplemented by the further question 'How do you respond to the community of believers?'[4] In the last analysis the validity of Humanism, no less than that of Christianity, turns upon the answers that we give to these questions.

Three independent thinkers

No account of the twentieth-century scene would be complete without some mention of Rudolf Otto, Martin Buber and Teilhard de Chardin. All three have continental origins; but in their approach to religion they take independent lines. This is the sole reason for grouping them together here.

Otto. Rudolf Otto (1869–1937) was born at Peine, Hanover.

[3] *Ibid.*, pp. 126f.   [4] *Ibid.*, p. 15.

He taught at the universities of Göttingen and Breslau before taking up a chair of theology at Marburg (becoming Professor Emeritus in 1929). In the English-speaking world he is largely remembered for two books. *The Kingdom of God and the Son of Man* (1934)[5] is an attempt to understand the New Testament against the background of history. But our main interest here lies in his earlier work in philosophical theology, *The Idea of the Holy* (1917).[6]

In a sense Otto stands in the main stream of German philosophical theology since Kant. Like all its leading representatives, he was trying to survey religion and extract from it its essence which would enable modern man to distinguish what was vital and important from the secondary and peripheral. But whereas Kant and Ritschl saw this essence in morality, and Schleiermacher in the religious man's sense of absolute dependence, Otto found it in what he termed the *Numinous*.

Otto argued that, since the Reformation, theologians and philosophers alike have been preoccupied with doctrines, dogmas and arguments, in other words, with the rational and moral elements in religion. But for Otto the quintessence of religion did not reside in these. It lay rather in what is denoted by the word *holy*. But this latter term has become so overlaid with doctrinal and moral associations that Otto preferred to coin his own term based upon the Latin word for divinity, *numen*. It is something which is quite different from moral perfection.[7] It is something which is 'Wholly Other' from the natural world.[8] The numinous state of mind 'is perfectly *sui generis* and irreducible to any other; and therefore, like every absolutely primary and elementary datum, while it admits of being discussed, it cannot be strictly defined'.[9] The term numinous is really an ideogram. It does not describe what it stands for. It is like a symbolic unknown X which stands for something, but the thing itself has to be experienced before we know what the X stands for. Otto himself puts it this way: 'This X of ours is not precisely *this* experience, but akin

[5] Eng. tr. by Floyd V. Filson and Bertram Lee Woolf (Lutterworth, 1938).
[6] Eng. tr. by John W. Harvey (OUP, 1923; Pelican, 1959). Quotations here are from the latter edition.
[7] *The Idea of the Holy*, pp. 19f.   [8] *Ibid.*, p. 39.   [9] *Ibid.*, p. 21.

to this one and the opposite of that other. Cannot you now realize for yourself what it is? In other words our X cannot, strictly speaking, be taught, it can only be evoked, awakened in the mind; as everything that comes "of the spirit" must be awakened.'[1]

When Otto tries to pinpoint his meaning further, he describes the numinous as a *Mysterium Tremendum*,[2] a mystery which fills one with awe and dread. On the lowest level we experience something of it in ghost stories.[3] On a deeper level it is the sense of daunting majesty which Isaiah had in the Temple.[4] Rationally it is inexplicable. Otto quotes as a kind of text for his theme the line of Tersteegen: 'A God comprehended is no God.'[5] But alongside its daunting, awe-inspiring quality, the numinous has an element of attraction. Otto feels that Jonathan Edwards caught something of this when he wrote: 'The conceptions which the saints have of the loveliness of God and that kind of delight which they experience in it are quite peculiar and entirely different from anything which a natural man can possess or of which he can form any proper notion.'[6]

In some ways Otto has performed a valuable service in drawing attention to a basic element in religion which others had overlooked. He shows that religion is more than morality in disguise and that its central concern is with that which is other than the world of nature and matter. But the very nature of his undertaking has led him to overstate his case. As with all attempts to reduce religion to a single essential idea he is obliged to stretch his material where it does not quite fit and lop pieces off which overlap. This compels him to explain away or treat as non-essential a good deal of the evidence. Nowhere is this more blatant than in his handling of the biblical view of holiness where he finds himself obliged to expunge from it the notion of God's moral perfection.[7] But a central theme of biblical religion, beginning with the Law and the Prophets and running right through the New Testament, is the moral per-

---

[1] *Ibid.*, p. 21.   [2] *Ibid.*, pp. 26–55.   [3] *Ibid.*, p. 29.
[4] Isaiah 6 (*cf. ibid.*, p. 65).   [5] *Ibid.*, p. 39.
[6] *Ibid.*, p. 52, quoting an extract from Jonathan Edwards in William James, *The Varieties of Religious Experience*, p. 229.   [7] *Cf. ibid.*, pp. 99ff.

fection of God and the consequent moral holiness required of men. Otto's theory as it stands puts an impersonal idea at the heart of religion instead of the living personal God. In the last analysis his numinous is not the living God of the Bible who is supremely rational and utterly righteous as well as utterly loving. His deity is not one who takes the initiative in his dealing with men.

The great weakness with Otto is his method. He tries to be empirical. The difficulty is that he is not empirical enough. He takes sample specimens of different religions and then constructs a theory. There are at least two major defects here. One is the assumption that religion can be handled in this way – that they have all a common, abstractable characteristic, and that once this has been abstracted the rest is non-essential. It may be that most religions have certain common outward forms. But this does not entitle us to say that their essential content is identical. This could be done only if it could be demonstrated on the basis of exhaustive inquiry. But Otto does not give such a detailed investigation. Moreover, it is far from clear that the advocates of the different religions would agree that the content of their religion was the same. In the case of Christianity the samples that Otto takes are neither wide enough nor are they examined carefully enough. His treatment of them leaves the impression that his major concern is not to let the texts speak for themselves but to read into them a preconceived theory. From that point of view his thesis is a forlorn undertaking. But at least it is a reminder of an element in religion which others have missed or closed their eyes to.

Buber. Martin Buber (1878–1965) is unique among western philosophers. He was born a Jew in central Europe and was brought up in the Jewish faith. Before he left school he came under the influence of Kant and Nietzsche, and while at university – he studied at Vienna, Leipzig, Berlin and Zürich – he read many of the fashionable writers and thinkers of the day. But for all that, he remained loyal to Judaism. On graduating he plunged into publishing. The literature he was concerned with had distinctly Jewish nationalistic themes. In 1923 he was appointed Professor of Jewish History of Religion and Ethics at Frankfurt, but was deprived of his post by the Nazis ten years later. In 1938 he left Germany for Palestine to accept the chair of sociology at the Hebrew University of Jerusalem. Though already sixty, he now embarked upon the period of his greatest intellectual activity. He retired in 1951. His published works in German fill three massive volumes. His major writings in English are all pre-war. They include *The Kingship of God*,[8] *Between Man and Man*,[9] and, best known of all, *I and Thou*.[1]

Buber's thought has ranged widely over sociology, psychology, education, biblical criticism and theology. Perhaps he could be called a Humanist, but his Humanism is deeply tinged with religion. He once summed up the Jewish mystical faith to which he himself subscribed as: 'God is to be seen in every thing, and reached by every pure deed.'[2] Curiously enough, Buber's approach to religion is the opposite of Otto's. The latter's concern is with the impersonal experience of the 'wholly other', the numinous. Buber's is with personal relationships and with that which underlies them.

In *I and Thou* Buber argues that there are two basic kinds of relationship, the I-It and the I-Thou. The former belongs to superficial experience, when we see things and people as merely phenomena. But when we probe deeper, it is possible to enter into personal relationships not only with other people but also with things. It is here that we encounter a Thou over against our I. And this is the realm also where we encounter God. 'In every sphere in its own way, through each process of becoming that is present to us we look out toward the fringe of the eternal *Thou*; in each we are aware of a breath from the eternal *Thou*; in each *Thou* we address the eternal *Thou*.'[3]

---

[8] 1932. Eng. tr. by R. Scheimann (Allen and Unwin, 1967).

[9] A collection of various writings dating from between 1928 and 1938, translated and introduced by Ronald Gregor Smith (Kegan Paul, 1947; Fontana, 1961).

[1] Translated by Ronald Gregor Smith (T. and T. Clark, Edinburgh, 1937; revised edition, 1958).

[2] *Mein Weg zum Chassidismus*, in *Werke*, III, p. 962, quoted by R. Gregor Smith in *Martin Buber* (Carey Kingsgate Press, 1966), p. 7.

[3] *I and Thou* (1st edition), p. 6; *cf.* the conclusion of *Between Man and Man*, p. 247.

It would be wrong to think of Buber as a Pantheist. Nor is it his intention to ascribe personality to inanimate objects.[4] It would be nearer the mark to describe him as a panentheist, that is, one who believes that God is in all things but who is not necessarily identical with them.[5] Buber's thought is a mixture of many things. There can be no doubt that the Jewish Old Testament awareness of God's omnipresence and the significance of every human action has left a deep mark on his thinking. It is less clear that his mind has been affected by the biblical view of divine transcendence. Like much Jewish thinking, not least that which was popular at the time of Christ, Buber's thought seems to be restricted to earthly expectations. This has prompted the comment from a learned Catholic commentator that Buber's 'view of the Jewish conception of prophecy is wanting in the transcendent element implied by its fulfilment; it never rises above itself, and because it remains imprisoned within the scheme of its own thought, it is finally precipitated into the paradox . . . of social Utopianism'.[6]

Buber interprets the personality of Jesus in terms of his I-Thou concept. 'How powerful, even to being overpowering, and how legitimate, even to being self-evident, is the saying of *I* by Jesus! For it is the *I* of unconditional relation in which the man calls his *Thou* Father in such a way that he himself is simply Son, and nothing else but Son. Whenever he says *I* he can only mean the *I* of the holy primary word that has been raised for him into unconditional being. If separation ever touches him, his solidarity of relation is greater; he speaks to others only out of this solidarity. It is useless to seek to limit this *I* to a power in itself or this *Thou* to something dwelling in ourselves, and once again to empty the real, the present relation, of reality. *I* and *Thou* abide; every man can say *Thou*

---

[4] Although he speaks of being able to enter into personal relationship with a tree, he also says that he has no experience of consciousness in the tree. 'I encounter no soul or dryad of the tree, but the tree itself' (*I and Thou*, p. 8).
[5] When questioned about proof of the 'eternal Thou' in all relational events, Buber retorted to Gregor Smith, 'Proved? You know that it is so.' From this the latter deduced that Buber's world view was a matter of faith rather than demonstrative proof (*Martin Buber*, pp. 21f.).
[6] Hans Urs von Balthasar, *Martin Buber and Christianity*, Eng. tr. by Alexander Dru (Harvill Press, 1961), p. 77.

and is then *I*, every man can say Father and is then Son: reality abides.'[7]

To say this is to come so near and yet so far from the Christ of the New Testament and of Christian experience. In the last analysis, Buber's Jesus is no more than a vivid example of what we all can be. Again we are bound to say that here is a view of man which has genuine insights. But, as with so many ostensibly empirical approaches to religion, it has to be asked whether Buber is really empirical enough. He has reminded philosophers of the personal dimension of human existence and of the way God encounters us through other people. His I-Thou concept has been a liberating influence on philosophy. But it can also be a strait-jacket which prevents him from getting to grips with things outside its scope. Christians believe that the figure of Christ is one of those things.

Teilhard de Chardin. One of the most interesting religious phenomena of the late 1950s and the mid-1960s has been the posthumous popularity of the Jesuit scientist and mystic Fr. Teilhard de Chardin. There is now a Pierre Teilhard de Chardin Association of Great Britain and Ireland which publishes its own *Teilhard Review*. Comparable associations have already been founded in France, Germany, Belgium, the U.S.A. and other countries. Teilhard has found champions in the most unlikely places. Sir Julian Huxley wrote an introduction to Teilhard's most important scientific work, *The Phenomenon of Man*.[8] But although this has been followed by a stream of other writings (accompanied by an almost equal spate of commentaries, biographies and studies), it has to be remembered that the former were suppressed during his lifetime and that most of his days were spent in semi-obscurity.

Pierre Teilhard de Chardin (1881–1955) was one of eleven children, the son of a small landowner in central France. At the age of ten he was sent as a boarder to a Jesuit College. Even as a schoolboy he was fascinated by geology and minera-

---

[7] *I and Thou*, pp. 66f.
[8] Collins, 1959, and numerous reprints including a Fontana paperback edition.

logy. He was ordained priest in 1912. In the years leading up to this he had studied not only the customary theology and philosophy but evolutionary theory, and had already acquired considerable competence in geology and palaeontology. For a time he worked under Marcellin Boule in Paris at the Institute of Human Palaeontology at the Museum of Natural History. Here his thoughts were directed to what was to become the main interest of his life – the evolution of man.

During the first World War he served as a stretcher-bearer at the front. He was decorated three times as well as being mentioned in dispatches. His impressions of the war and thoughts on God's purposes appear in *The Making of a Mind: Letters from a Soldier-Priest, 1914–1919*.[9] After the war he resumed his scientific studies. His great aim was to reconcile Christian theology with evolutionary theory, in order to achieve a scientific view of the divine purpose and man's place in the universe.

In 1922 Teilhard took his doctorate at the Sorbonne and was already lecturing on geology. The following year he went on a palaeontological mission to China. His experiences are recorded in his *Letters of a Traveller*.[1] They also inspired the mystical meditation on the cosmic significance of the eucharist which he called *The Mass on the World*. In English it appears in a collection of essays, stories and meditations, entitled *Hymn of the Universe*.[2] On his return to France allegations were made to his religious superiors complaining about his unorthodoxy and he was removed from his teaching post. He was subsequently forbidden to publish anything relating to his evolutionary theories. This did not prevent him from writing. But Teilhard remained loyal to his order, and none of his major writings was published during his lifetime.

Teilhard returned to China in 1926 where, apart from brief visits to several countries, he was to remain for the next twenty years. He took part in numerous expeditions including one which unearthed the skull of Peking man. The years of enforced exile proved to be a period of incubation for Teilhard's speculative ideas. *The Phenomenon of Man* was written in

[9] Collins, 1965.   [1] Collins, 1962.   [2] Collins, 1965.

1938. *Le Milieu Divin: An Essay on the Interior Life*[3] was written a decade earlier. His numerous other works written at this time are in process of being edited and published in French and English editions.[4] As recently as 1962 the Vatican Holy Office issued a *Monitum* decree warning bishops and heads of Catholic seminaries against the dangers of his writings. But this has not prevented Catholics and others from eagerly devouring his ideas.

On returning to France after the second World War Teilhard received numerous honours, and he took part in debates with leading French scholars. Permission to publish anything but the most technical studies was still withheld by the authorities of his church, who also prevented his name from going forward for a teaching chair at the College de France. Teilhard spent the last four years of his life at the Wenner-Gren Foundation in New York. He died suddenly on Easter Day 1955.

We have sketched Teilhard's career in some detail because it is so interwoven with his thought. Perhaps the simplest statement of his philosophy is that contained in a letter addressed to the General of the Society of Jesus in which he explained his view of 'The unique significance of Man as the spear-head of Life; the position of Catholicism as the central axis in the convergent bundle of human activities; and finally the essential function as consummator assumed by the risen Christ at the centre and peak of Creation: these three elements have driven (and continue to drive) roots so deep and so entangled in the whole fabric of my intellectual and religious perception that I could now tear them out only at the cost of destroying everything'.[5]

While the goal here is clear, it is not easy for the general reader to follow Teilhard's thought along the many devious

[3] Collins, 1960, and numerous reprints including a Fontana paperback. This edition includes an interesting memoir by his friend and fellow Jesuit, Pierre Leroy, and also a letter dated 1951 in which Teilhard protests his loyalty to the General of his order but also claiming the integrity of his thought.
[4] Other works include *The Future of Man*, *The Appearance of Man* and *Man's Place in Nature*. They are being published by Collins under the general editorship of Bernard Wall.
[5] *Cf. Le Milieu Divin*, p. 38 (see above, n. 3).

paths he follows along the way. Part of the difficulty arises from the fact that Teilhard was a palaeontologist, and few readers have the necessary knowledge of biology, geology and fossils to understand, let alone assess, what he is talking about. This difficulty is accentuated, not only by the fact that Teilhard is trying to develop his science in a special way, but also by the fact that he coins his own terms in the process.

Teilhard's thought has two starting-points: evolution and the Catholic faith. His originality lies in the way that he endeavours to combine the two. For him 'Evolution is a light illuminating all facts, a curve that all lines must follow'.[6] But evolution is not simply a way of understanding the past; it is our guide towards understanding man's future development. Even after Darwin many people have continued to think of the universe in general and of man in particular as something static, fixed and finished. What distinguishes a really 'modern' man is his ability to think in terms of 'biological space-time' and man's future developments.[7] For Teilhard as a Catholic this means thinking about man's future in relation to God. We are to think of God not simply as 'God on high', transcendent and outside the world (as in traditional theology), nor as purely immanent, 'God within' (as in liberal and radical theology), but as 'God ahead' in living union with man.

Teilhard holds that the earth was formed not less than five and probably not more than ten thousand million years ago. He also holds that scientific contemplation of its history leads to the conclusion that it is moving in a discernible direction according to what he calls the Law of Complexity Consciousness,[8] and what others refer to as Teilhard's Law. On the one hand, there has been a tendency in evolution for matter to become increasingly complex. And on the other hand, there is a corresponding rise in the consciousness of matter. Teilhard describes this process in terms of spheres. The idea is borrowed from the pictorial way of describing the different layers of the

[6] *The Phenomenon of Man*, p. 241. (Reference is here made to the paperback edition which is different from the original hardback version.)
[7] *Ibid.*, p. 241.
[8] *Ibid.*, pp. 328–330 and *passim.*

earth as barysphere (its molten interior), lithosphere (its hard crust), hydrosphere (the water in the sea and air) and atmosphere (the gaseous envelope surrounding the earth). At the turn of the century the word biosphere was coined to denote the living layer of creatures which had evolved out of the other layers. In 1920 Teilhard and E. Le Roy coined the word *noosphere*.[9] It is used to denote the next stage in evolution, the formation of a 'mind layer' on the earth. With the appearance of thinking man on the earth the entire state of the planet is transformed.

It is at this point that Teilhard peers into the future. By projecting the lines of evolution so far posited and by linking them with his Catholic faith, Teilhard looks towards the 'Omega point' of the universe. It is the stage when God will be 'all in all'.[1] It may be described as 'a superior form of pantheism', for it is 'the expectation of perfect unity, steeped in which each element will reach its consummation at the same time as the universe'.[2] In all this science and theology are complementary. They both look at the same thing in different ways. Science looks at the upward progress of phenomena. Theology is concerned with their inner principle, Christ. 'Christ, principle of universal vitality because sprung up as man among men, put himself in the position (maintained ever since) to subdue under himself, to purify, to direct and superanimate the general ascent of consciousness into which he inserted himself. By a perennial act of communion and sublimation, he aggregates to himself the total psychism of the earth. And when he has gathered everything together and transformed everything, he will close in upon himself and his conquests, thereby rejoining, in a final gesture, the divine focus he has never left.'[3]

Teilhard's work has been compared with the process philosophy of A. N. Whitehead (1861–1947) and revived by a number of contemporary American radicals such as Charles

[9] *Ibid.*, pp. 200–204 and *passim*. Literally, it means the *mind-sphere*. It derives from the Greek word *nous* (= mind).
[1] *Ibid.*, p. 322; *cf.* 1 Corinthians 15:28.
[2] *Ibid.*, p. 322; *cf. Hymn of the Universe*, pp. 53f.
[3] *Ibid.*, p. 322; *cf. Hymn of the Universe*, pp. 41–55, 144.

Hartshorne, Norman Pittenger, D. D. Williams, Schubert Ogden and John Cobb. The comparison has been welcomed on their part. Like Teilhard they believe that evolution must be taken with utmost seriousness. They reject the theistic idea of God as a being over and above the universe and prefer the idea of panentheism – that all things occur 'within God'. To some God is not so much a being as the dynamic behind evolution, emerging all the time in everything in history and nature. Against this background Christ is seen as a symbol of divine activity in the world rather than as an 'intervention'. He is a man in whom God worked rather than God incarnate. Sin is more a failure of achievement and deviation of aim than radical evil.[4] Whether Teilhard would have felt himself at home in such company is questionable. However *avant garde* may have been his ideas on God and evolution, he always protested that he was a loyal son of the Catholic Church. He does not appear to have been interested in radicalism as such. What he wanted to do was to restate his Catholic faith in terms of a vast evolutionary time-scale. How far was he successful?

Some feel that Teilhard's vision meets the great spiritual need of our time. Others find themselves repelled by his unintelligibility. The authorities of the Church of Rome felt that his work minimized original sin and compromised the nature of God. Nor are the scientists agreed about the validity of its methods and conclusions. Sir Julian Huxley sees resemblances between Teilhard's approach and his own. But other scientists feel less confident about the scientific character of such works as *The Phenomenon of Man*.[5] It is by no means clear that scientific

[4] For a brief popular statement of process theology see Norman Pittenger, *God in Process* (SCM Press, 1967). A British restatement appears in Peter Hamilton, *The Living God and the Modern World* (Hodder, 1967).

In so far as process philosophers say that God is active in all nature and history they are saying no more than orthodox Christian Theism. But in so far that they say that the universe is an *aspect* or *manifestation* of God they are rejecting Christianity. If there is one thing that the Bible, secular science and common sense are agreed upon it is that nature is *not* God either in its sum total or its particular parts.

Process philosophy is further characterized by a fairly radical attitude to the Bible and the store it sets by Existentialism and the depth-psychology of Freud and Jung for guidance in the realm of personal relationships.

[5] *Cf.* the study by the late J. J. Duyvené de Wit, Professor of Zoology in the

data on their own would warrant Teilhard's conclusions. In discussing Darwin and evolution we noted the unease that has been felt in some scientific circles recently with evolutionary theory. From a theological point of view Teilhard's work requires closer definition and precision than he gave it. His main concern was with the cosmic significance of Christ in the sphere of creation. The rest of Christian teaching seems to have been pushed to the periphery of his thought. Teilhard seems to arrive at his Omega Point at the expense of ignoring a good deal of Christ's teaching along the way. There is much in his writings that suggests that mankind will get there regardless. The biblical theme of judgment hardly enters into it. His works hardly suggest that our response to God in this life affects eternity.

Perhaps it is best to treat Teilhard's work not so much as a closely argued case (which it certainly is not). His thought often seems loose and lacking in proof. Rather it is like a piece of thinking aloud, sometimes highly technical, often meandering. The mystical may be wrapped up in scientific jargon but that does not make it any more scientific. Perhaps his work is best described as stating a problem rather than offering a definitive solution. This at least is how the author himself thought of it. 'In this arrangement of values I may have gone astray at many points. It is up to others to try to do better. My one hope is that I have made the reader feel both the reality, difficulty, and urgency of the problem and, at the same time, the scale and the form which the solution cannot escape.'[6] And about this there can be no debate.

Neo-Thomism
In the Middle Ages Thomas Aquinas endeavoured to produce a synthesis of classical philosophy and the teaching of the church. For some time after his death Aquinas was regarded with grave suspicion as an innovator. But over the centuries

University of the Orange Free State, in *Creative Minds in Contemporary Theology*, edited by P. E. Hughes (Eerdmans, Grand Rapids, 1966), pp. 407-450.
[6] *The Phenomenon of Man*, p. 318.

Thomism has established itself as *the* (though never quite exclusively so) philosophy of the Roman Catholic Church.[7]

In achieving this position Thomism has seen many vicissitudes. But in modern times there has been a revival of Thomism in both the Church of Rome and the Anglican communion. Perhaps it would be too much to speak of a Neo-Thomist school within the Church of England. It would be more accurate to say that certain distinguished thinkers, such as E. L. Mascall, Professor of Historical Theology in the University of London, and A. M. Farrer (1904–68), of Keble College, Oxford, are keeping the Thomist tradition alive. In the Roman Catholic Church there are vigorous centres of Thomist thought such as the Medieval Institute at Toronto. Among the leading representatives of Thomism in the Catholic Church today are Jacques Maritain (b. 1882) and Etienne Gilson (b. 1884).

The modern Neo-Thomists are not slavishly tied to the texts of Aquinas. But, like Thomas, they endeavour to reassert the validity of natural theology in some form or other. In *He Who Is*[8] and its sequel, *Existence and Analogy*,[9] Mascall has attempted to restate rational arguments for the existence of God and the Thomist doctrine of analogy.[1] In *The Degrees of Knowledge* Maritain seeks to show that 'Thomistic realism, in preserving, according to a truly critical method, the value of the knowledge of things, opens the way to an exploration of the world of reflection in its very inwardness and to the establishment of its metaphysical topology, so to speak; thus, "philosophy of being" is at once, and *par excellence*, "philosophy of mind".'[2] Austin Farrer feels that it is illegitimate and un-

---

[7] See above, pp. 36, 163f. For an example of a contemporary Non-Thomist approach see Dom Illtyd Trethowan, *An Essay in Christian Philosophy* (Longmans, 1954).

[8] Longmans, 1943, and several reprints.

[9] Longmans, 1949, and reprints.

[1] See above, pp. 26–32.

[2] *Distinguish to Unite or The Degrees of Knowledge*, new Eng. tr. by Gerald B. Phelan (Bles, 1959), p. ix. At the age of 85 Maritain wrote a kind of philosophical testament *The Peasant of the Garonne: An Old Layman Questions Himself about the Present Time* (Chapman, 1968) in which he reaffirmed his belief in Thomism and the historic Christian faith, and criticized a number of more radical trends including the teaching of Teilhard de Chardin.

warranted to abandon metaphysical inquiry. In his famous Bampton Lectures on *Finite and Infinite* he argued that 'All finites, in being themselves and expressing their natures in their acts, are expressing also the creativity of God'.[3]

But the Neo-Thomists have not been concerned simply with restating the older arguments for natural theology. They have also become involved in the contemporary debates. Mascall's *Words and Images* is one of the most perceptive contributions to British linguistic philosophy. His *Secularisation of Christianity* is the most substantial critique yet published of *Honest to God* and the work of Paul van Buren.[4] He delivered the Bampton Lectures for 1956 on *Christian Theology and Natural Science: Some Questions in their Relations*.[5] Maritain has entered into debate with the Existentialists, and in *Existence and the Existent*[6] he has argued that a genuine Existentialism must be grounded in a philosophy of being such as is presented by Thomism.

Neo-Thomism has found distinguished advocates of considerable learning. But perhaps its real strength lies in the willingness of its representatives to look at new ideas, but to look at them critically. Unlike some of the new radicals, they are not swept away by the latest philosophical fad or fashion. Their attempts to restate natural theology must each be judged on its own merits. I, for one, have not found them particularly helpful or convincing. The weakness of the movement lies in the fact that it is so wedded to Catholic theology. Perhaps this is a matter of attitude and tradition. Perhaps (as in the original Thomist synthesis of philosophy and faith) it is due to the intrusion in theology of alien philosophical ideas. But even though the Neo-Thomist synthesis as a whole is questionable, there can be no question that Neo-Thomists as individual thinkers have made important contributions to the modern debates about philosophy and faith.

---

[3] Dacre Press, 1943, p. 299.   [4] See above, pp. 208ff., 218f.
[5] Longmans, 1956.
[6] Eng. tr. by Lewis Galantiere and Gerald B. Phelan (1948; Image Books, 1957).

V PHILOSOPHY AND REFORMED THEOLOGY

If Catholics have sometimes been guilty of allowing philosophical ideas to distort Christian truth, it could be said that Evangelicals have been guilty of allowing the case to go by default. As we saw when we were looking at theological trends in the nineteenth century, Evangelicals made great contributions to evangelism and even to biblical scholarship; but they contributed little or nothing to the philosophical defence of their faith.[7] For many, scholarship had a largely negative value. It was useful to defend the faith against hostile criticism. Few Evangelicals seem to have considered the philosophical implications of a faith based upon God's revelation of himself and their significance for apologetics. It is not surprising, therefore, that friends and foes alike tended to think that Reformed, evangelical theology had nothing to contribute to the intellectual debates of our time. For long enough it has been assumed that the only live option in apologetics was some form of natural theology based upon permutations and combinations of Thomism and Idealism. When this crumbled before hostile criticism it was inevitable that people started talking about the death of God and believing that Christianity had no valid philosophical basis.

But this is not quite the whole story. Although British Evangelicals gave philosophy a wide berth, a number of independent thinkers on the Continent and in the United States were alive to the situation. We shall conclude this survey of philosophy and faith in the twentieth century by taking a look at three of them: Cornelius Van Til, Karl Barth and Francis Schaeffer. All are agreed that natural theology is a blind alley. It is wrong in both its conclusions and methods. They agree that the proper starting-point for thinking about God is God himself and his revelation. They differ, however, in the way that they work this out.

Cornelius Van Til

Cornelius Van Til stands in the conservative tradition of Dutch Reformed theology. He has become a focal point of this stream of thought in the new world in the same way that

[7] See above, pp. 8of., 164ff.

Herman Dooyeweerd[8] has in the old. Like Dooyeweerd, Van Til was born in the Netherlands, but he has spent most of his academic life in the United States. He did research at Princeton University and was awarded a doctorate there. For a time he was on the staff of the Princeton Theological Seminary. When the Westminster Theological Seminary was founded, he was appointed Professor of Apologetics and has spent the remainder of his academic career in that post. His writings include his Tyndale Lecture on *The Intellectual Challenge of the Gospel*,[9] two critiques of Barth, *The New Modernism* and *Christianity and Barthianism*[1] and an essay on *Christianity and Idealism*.[2] He is the author of a lengthy philosophical introduction to B. B. Warfield's *The Inspiration and Authority of the Bible*.[3] But the most comprehensive statement of his position appears in *The Defence of the Faith*.[4]

Even at its best, Van Til argues, natural theology leads to the idea of an impersonal first cause which falls far short of the living God of the Bible and experience.[5] The reason is not so much the faulty logic of the different steps in the argument as its false starting-point. In thinking about God we must either begin with God or man. From Aristotle onwards secular philosophers (and Christians adopting their arguments) have begun with the latter. The result is that, whether they are for or against God, they have been debating a figment of the

[8] Dooyeweerd became Professor of the Philosophy of Law at the Free University of Amsterdam in 1926. He is a Fellow of the Royal Dutch Academy of Sciences. His chief contribution to philosophy is contained in his monumental treatise, *A New Critique of Theoretical Thought* (1935–36, Eng. tr. in 4 vols. by David H. Freeman and others, H. J. Paris, Amsterdam, and Presbyterian and Reformed Publishing Company, 1953–58). His school of thought is known as the Philosophy of the Cosmonomic Law-Idea. It is expounded by J. M. Spier in *An Introduction to Christian Philosophy* (PRPC, 1954), and by E. L. H. Taylor in *The Christian Philosophy of Law, Politics and the State* (Craig Press, Nutley, N.J., 1966). Perhaps the best short appraisal is the article by William Young in P. E. Hughes (ed.), *Creative Minds in Contemporary Theology* (Eerdmans, Grand Rapids, 1966), pp. 270–305.

[9] Tyndale Press, 1950.

[1] James Clarke, 1946; and PRPC, Philadelphia, 1962.

[2] PRPC, Philadelphia, 1955.   [3] Marshall, Morgan and Scott, 1951.

[4] PRPC, Philadelphia, 1955.

[5] *The Intellectual Challenge of the Gospel*, p. 8; *The Defence of the Faith*, pp. 175–180, 302–356.

human imagination. Christian thought must begin with the living, triune God who is perfect and self-contained.

Van Til sees the history of secular philosophy as a massive commentary on the apostle Paul's observations to the Corinthian Christians: 'Where is the wise? where is the scribe? where is the disputer of this world? hath not God made foolish the wisdom of this world? For after that in the wisdom of God the world by wisdom knew not God, it pleased God by the foolishness of preaching to save them that believe.'[6] In other words, men have been looking for God in the wrong place and in the wrong way. On the other hand, Van Til argues that 'The eternal power and Godhead of Paul's gospel are clearly visible to all men everywhere.[7] . . . It is not as though the evidence shows that *a* god exists or that God *probably* exists. If such were the case then there would be some excuse for man if he did not bow before his Maker. Paul makes bold to claim that all men know deep down in their hearts that they are creatures of God and have sinned against God their Creator and their Judge.'[8]

For Van Til, therefore, the point of contact between the Christian message and the non-Christian world is a 'head-on collision'.[9] There can be no position of neutrality. Not only does the gospel reveal God but every single fact in existence does so too. For all things are created and controlled by God. As such they are part of his purpose for the universe, and as such they reveal him.[1] When confronted by the gospel, men 'cannot react neutrally towards it; they must accept it or suppress it because they do not want to believe it. Paul knows that those who cling to the "wisdom" of the world do so against their better judgment and with an evil conscience. Every fact of "theism" and every fact of "Christianity" points with accusing finger at the sinner, saying: "You are a covenant breaker; repent and be saved!" '[2]

[6] i Corinthians 1:20f.; *cf. The Intellectual Challenge of the Gospel*, p. 3.
[7] Romans 1:19.
[8] *The Intellectual Challenge of the Gospel*, p. 5; *cf. The Defence of the Faith*, pp. 115, 172.
[9] *The Defence of the Faith*, p. 116.
[1] *Ibid.*, pp. 116, 132ff., 164, 191ff., 232ff.
[2] *The Intellectual Challenge of the Gospel*, p. 5.

The task of Christian apologetics is not to try to discover some neutral, common ground on which the believer and the unbeliever may both stand. For this fails to appreciate that the unbeliever is already aware of God's existence and his own responsibility before God. The task is to force him to face up to this and to show that there are no legitimate escape-routes. In other words, it is to lay bare the presuppositions of our thinking. Van Til does not believe in the old proofs of the existence of God. The existence of the God of Christian Theism is presupposed by all rational thought and behaviour.

The man who denies God and yet who tries to think rationally about the world is like a man made of water, trying to climb out of an ocean by means of a ladder made of water! 'On his assumption his own rationality is a product of chance. On his assumption even the laws of logic which he employs are products of chance. The rationality and purpose that he may be searching for are still bound to be products of chance. So then the Christian apologist, whose position requires him to hold that Christian theism is really true and as such must be taken as the presupposition which alone makes the acquisition of knowledge in any field intelligible, must join his "friend" in his hopeless gyrations so as to point out to him that his efforts are always in vain.'[3]

Van Til sums up his position by saying that 'the existence of the God of Christian theism and the conception of his counsel as controlling all things in the universe is the only presupposition which can account for the uniformity of nature which the scientist needs. But the best and only possible proof for the existence of such a God is that his existence is required for the uniformity of nature and for the coherence of all things in the world. We cannot *prove* the existence of beams underneath a floor if by proof we mean that they must be ascertainable in the way that we can see the chairs and tables of the room. But the very idea of a floor as the support of tables and chairs requires the idea of beams that are underneath. But there would be no floor if no beams were underneath. Thus there is absolutely certain proof for the existence of God and

---

[3] *The Defence of the Faith*, p. 119.

the truth of Christian theism. Even non-Christians presuppose its truth while they verbally reject it. They need to presuppose the truth of Christian theism in order to account for their own accomplishments.'[4]

Van Til does not imagine that a demonstration of the irrationality of secular philosophy is sufficient to win all and sundry over to Christian belief. The non-Christian will accept the gospel, 'if God pleases by his Spirit to take the scales from his eyes and the mask from his face. It is upon the power of the Holy Spirit that the Reformed preacher relies when he tells men that they are lost in sin and in need of a Savior'.[5] Nevertheless, the Reformed apologist must adopt this course in the interests of truth.

When we look at Van Til's work as a whole, even a sympathetic critic is bound to admit that some things are obscure. So much of it is given over to crossing swords with various commentators whose names are of little interest to the general reader and whose views could with profit be relegated to appendices. An even greater difficulty is that all too often Van Til assumes the defence of a biblical position without showing that it really is a biblical position.

A good deal of time is spent reiterating points without really explaining them. This is true, for example, when he says that every fact reveals God. What does he mean? The existence of God is not immediately apparent to all when we tell them to look at a stone, or a tree, or a date in a history book. Van Til does not mean to say that the existence of God can be inferred from them in the manner of the cosmological arguments.[6] It has been suggested that with Van Til *fact* and *meaning* are virtually synonymous.[7] In this case it would seem that the meaning of everything derives from God, and that each individual fact is an indication of the kind of God that God really is. It does not reveal God by itself. It reveals God only in the context of the belief-system which, Van Til says, we must presuppose. It reveals him in so far as we pre-

---

[4] *Ibid.*, p. 120.   [5] *Ibid.*, p. 121.
[6] For discussion of their weaknesses, see above, pp. 26ff., 98.
[7] B. Ramm, *Types of Apologetic Systems* (Van Kampen Press, Wheaton, Illinois, 1953), p. 188.

suppose that the fact derives from God and that God does indeed exist.

From Aquinas to Van Til many writers have made much of Paul's assertion that 'what can be known about God is plain to them, because God has shown it to them. Ever since the creation of the world his invisible nature, namely, his eternal power and deity, has been clearly perceived in the things that have been made'.[8] But few have attempted to explain what this revelation is and how it works. Van Til is no exception. Aquinas attempted an explanation, but the answer that he gave can hardly be right. What Paul seems to have meant is that nature and history show us the *kind* of God that God is, in particular, his power and his sovereignty. But the existence of God is not a matter of rational deduction. Rather it is a profound inner intuition that makes us aware of God and of the relation of the created order to him.

In this case, God is not a mere hypothesis invoked to provide a feasible explanation of the evidences of rationality in the universe. He is one whom we know as a person and the author of existence.

There are gaps and obscurities in Van Til's thought. Nevertheless, Van Til has taken some real steps towards a philosophical appreciation of biblical religion. His discussion of presuppositions and reminder that men do not need to have God proved to them, for they are aware of him already, are of the utmost importance.

Karl Barth

The present writer has already discussed in some detail elsewhere Barth's teaching.[9] But no survey of philosophy and faith today would be complete without mention of him. Like Van Til, Karl Barth was born on the Continent (at Basel in 1886; died 1968), and grew up in the Reformed church. But whereas Van Til belonged to the conservative Dutch Calvinistic wing, Barth grew up in the liberal Protestant wing.

Barth studied at several universities, sitting at the feet of many of the foremost liberal teachers of the day. But in his

[8] Romans 1:19f.
[9] C. Brown, *Karl Barth and the Christian Message* (Tyndale Press, 1967).

first pastorate at Safenwil, he became increasingly discontented with liberalism. Its great advocates wrote much about man, his gifts and religious capacities; very little was said about the living God. Matters came to a head during the first World War. Barth came to see the Bible not merely as a collection of ancient documents to be examined critically, but as a witness to God. His changed outlook bore tangible fruit in a commentary he wrote on *The Epistle to the Romans*.[2] The book was hardly a commentary at all in the normal sense of the term. Anyone who turns to it for a careful explanation of the apostle's letter will come away disappointed. The work is really a string of excited discoveries and observations about God and man.

It glosses over nothing. Man is shown as a sinner who has turned his back on God and who is blind to him. It is not in man's power to know God as and when he pleases. Knowledge of God is a gift of God that comes through Christ. Man can do nothing to deserve it. He can only receive it in simple faith. These insights were not new. They have been shared by Christians all down the ages, especially those in the Reformed, evangelical traditions. But it was new to generations who had been steeped in liberal theology. Moreover, it was presented by Barth in quasi-philosophical terms borrowed from thinkers ranging from Plato to Kant and Kierkegaard. The resultant mixture was known as Dialectical Theology.

Barth's big point was that there was what Kierkegaard called an 'infinite qualitative distinction' between eternity and time, heaven and earth, and God and man.[3] God was *Wholly Other*. In a sense Barth's position was the exact opposite from John Robinson's in *Honest to God*. Whereas the latter rejects the idea of God 'out there' and wants to find him in the processes of nature and human life, Barth sees God as utterly transcendent. He is not to be identified directly with anything in the world, not even the words of Scripture. Revelation comes to men in the same way as a vertical line intersects a horizontal plane, or as a tangent touches a circle. Because it is contact

[2] Eng. tr. by Sir Edwyn Hoskyns (OUP, 1933) based upon the 6th German edition which largely follows the 2nd radically revised version of 1921. The book first appeared in 1919.
[3] *The Epistle to the Romans*, p. 10.

with the *Wholly Other* we cannot even describe it. All we can do (and all that the biblical writers can do) is to describe what they felt like after it.

Dialectical Theology certainly had something. It brought with it a vivid awareness of God and of man's inadequacy. But in the 1920s and 1930s Barth came to realize that it was not the whole story. In 1921 Barth accepted a call to teach theology at Göttingen (from where he eventually moved to Münster, Bonn, and Basel after his ejection by the Nazis). From now on the rest of his life was to be spent in academic work. Over the years he has considerably modified his position as he has studied the Bible and the classical writers of Protestant and Catholic theology. Barth has written over 500 books, papers and articles. But the great work of his life is his *Church Dogmatics.*[4] The work itself falls into four main volumes, each subdivided into part volumes. They deal with the Word of God, God, Creation and Reconciliation. A fifth volume was planned on Redemption (*i.e.* eschatology) but this has now been abandoned. For all its faults, the *Church Dogmatics* is the most impressive work of modern times to be written by a single author. We shall not here attempt to discuss all of Barth's teaching even in outline. Instead, we shall confine attention to what can be learnt from Barth about revelation as a starting-point for theology and its significance for philosophy.

It cannot be stressed too strongly that for Barth the knowledge of God is not something separate from the gospel of Jesus Christ. It is not something that man can arrive at just as he wishes by following certain subtle philosophical arguments. Knowledge of God is the result of encounter with God which in turn is the result of encounter with Christ. For Christ is the revealing Word of God to man. From first to last it is a gift of God. Barth himself sums it up like this:

> The knowledge of God occurs in the fulfilment of the revelation of His Word by the Holy Spirit, and therefore in the reality and with the necessity of faith and its obedience. Its content is the existence of Him whom we must fear above

[4] Eng. tr. by a team of scholars working under the general editorship of G. W. Bromiley and T. F. Torrance (T. and T. Clark, Edinburgh, 1936–   ).

all things because we may love Him above all things; who remains a mystery to us because He Himself has made Himself so clear and certain to us.[5]

In making this point Barth is repeating the testimony of the Bible. The only way to real, personal knowledge of God is through encounter with Christ. According to Matthew 11:27, Jesus said: 'All things have been delivered to me by my Father; and no one knows the Son except the Father, and no one knows the Father except the Son and any one to whom the Son chooses to reveal him.' According to John 14:6, Jesus said: 'I am the way, the truth and the life; no one comes to the Father, but by me.' Statements like this could easily be multiplied.[6]

Knowledge of God arises out of encounter with God. It is mediated by the Son. But according to the New Testament, there can be no knowledge of God without the illuminating work of the Holy Spirit.[7] Moreover, to make progress in the knowledge of God, it is not a matter of intellectual acuteness. The knowledge of God operates, as it were, on a different plane. What matters more is faith, love, humility and prayer.[8]

Moreover, this knowledge of God, as Barth rightly points out, does not lay claim to be an absolute knowledge. It is not a claim to know God as he is in himself. It is a mystery in the sense that it sheds light on experience, although there is much about it which remains obscure. It does not enable us to see the whole landscape of reality. But the Word of God sheds sufficient light to enable those who will to find their way.

In saying all this, Barth is going back to the position of the Reformers in the sixteenth century. As he expounds his teaching he has kept an eye on the philosophical debates of the intervening centuries. Nevertheless, he insists that God's

---

[5] *Church Dogmatics*, II, 1, p. 3.

[6] *Cf.* (*e.g.*) Matthew 13:10–23; John 3:3ff.; 5:20ff.; 8:12; 12:39ff.; 17:3, 6ff.; 1 Corinthians 1:30.

[7] *Cf.* (*e.g.*) John 16:13ff.; 1 Corinthians 1:18 – 2:5; 2 Corinthians 3:14 – 4:6.

[8] *Cf.* (*e.g.*) Matthew 5:8; 6:1ff.; 7:7ff., 21–27; John 7:17; 1 Corinthians 13; Ephesians 3:14–19. For Barth's treatment of this aspect of theology see especially his *Evangelical Theology*, Eng. tr. by Grover Foley (Weidenfeld and Nicolson, 1963, and now a Fontana paperback).

revelation of himself is the only possible starting-point for thought about God.

There has been no shortage of those who have protested that this is irrationalism and obscurantism. How do we know God? What objective proof have we? Barth replies that in the very nature of the case there can be no 'objective' proof in the sense of external evidence from outside our encounter with the Word of God. The old-fashioned proofs of God's existence do not really lead to the living God. Natural theology is a futile enterprise. It is like trying to 'cook' a theorem in geometry by digging up proofs that do not really work. Encounter with God brings its own proof. The argument may be circular, but it is not viciously so.[9] As we said in discussing the Reformers,[1] there is a sense in which the ultimate truth of the Word of God is self-evident. It cannot be reduced to something other than itself. When we see it, we know it.

Barth's teaching has brought him into sharpest conflict with Van Til and others of his school when he discusses the actual content of revelation. In his dialectical phase Barth had compared the Word with a tangent touching a circle and a line intersecting a plane. But just as a line may be defined as length without breadth, so Barth's doctrine of the Word seemed to be encounter without content. For the God who revealed himself is not an object of time and space. He is one who is *Wholly Other*, and therefore, strictly speaking, indescribable. And if this is really the case, there is nothing more to be said. But in the *Church Dogmatics* Barth has clarified his position (though not, it must be said, to everyone's complete satisfaction). Here he speaks of the threefold form of the Word of God: Christ, Scripture and proclamation.[2]

In the primary sense of the term Christ is the Word of God. But he is witnessed to by the Scriptures (and also Christian testimony) which become the vehicle of the Word of God. For the authors of Scripture are commissioned witnesses in the same sense that the disciples were witnesses. 'He who receives you receives me, and he who receives me receives him

---

[9] *Church Dogmatics*, I, 2, p. 535.
[1] See the discussion above on pp. 47f.
[2] *Church Dogmatics*, I, 1, pp. 98–140.

who sent me.'[3] As we receive their testimony, so we receive Christ. The converse is also true. To reject the God-given witness is to reject the way of knowledge that God has provided. There is thus an indirect relationship between God and the Scriptures. 'The Bible is God's Word so far as God lets it be His Word, so far as God speaks through it ... The Bible therefore *becomes* God's Word in this event, and it is to its *being* in this *becoming* that the tiny word "is" relates, in the statement that the Bible *is* God's Word.'[4] The Word of God is never a static thing. 'What God utters is never in any way known and true in abstraction from God Himself. It is known and true for no other reason than that He Himself says it, that He in person is in and accompanies what is said by Him.'[5] It is in this context that Barth discusses the whole question of the inspiration and authority of the Bible today.[6]

The relationship between the divine and the human in revelation might be described as sacramental.[7] Just as bread and wine remain what they are but become the vehicle of communion, so the words of the authors of Scripture remain human words but become the means of God's encounter with man. 'Thus God reveals Himself in propositions by means of language, and human language at that, to the effect that from time to time such and such a word, spoken by the prophets and apostles and proclaimed in the Church, becomes His Word.'[8] Having said this, two further observations must be made. On the one hand, 'the personality of the Word of God is not to be played off against its verbal character and spirituality'.[9] Thus there is a real identity of God with the words of Scripture. But on the other hand, this identity is an indirect one. For Scripture uses the language of time and space to speak of God who is beyond time and space. Its language is therefore metaphorical and analogical. 'Thus we can, indeed, say what the Word of God is; but we must say it indirectly. We must recall

[3] *Cf.* Matthew 10:40; Luke 10:16; John 5:39; 13:20; *Church Dogmatics*, I, 2, pp. 487ff.

[4] *Ibid.*, I, 1, pp. 123f.   [5] *Ibid.*, I, 1, p. 155.

[6] For fuller discussion of this see C. Brown, *Karl Barth and the Christian Message*, pp. 54–62.

[7] *Church Dogmatics*, I, 1, p. 98.   [8] *Ibid.*, I, 1, p. 156.

[9] *Ibid.*, I, 1, p. 156.

the forms in which it is real for us and from these three forms which it takes infer *how* it is. That "how" is the reflected image, attainable by man, of the unattainable nature of God.'[1]

In this way Barth brings us back to the debates of modern philosophical theology. He sees God as transcendent, not in a crude physical way as a grandfatherly figure hovering somewhere above the stars, but as one who is *other* than man and the processes of nature. At the same time God is deeply concerned with human affairs. He is the creator of the world. He sustains the universe. He even sent his Son to redeem the world.[2] Moreover, God takes the initiative in making himself known to man. Barth sees revelation as a dynamic event in which God himself is personally involved. He recognizes that it involves human and material elements as well as the spiritual. His way of relating the two makes a suggestive contribution to the debates on religious language. For on the one hand, it is a reminder that our language and thought about God has to be analogical if it is meaningful at all.[3] And on the other hand, it points out that the vindication of Christianity in general and of its language about God in particular is not to be sought outside itself. It rests in its capacity to illuminate our lives and to reveal God to us.

Nevertheless, Barth's position raises numerous important questions. His stress on revelation through Christ has seemed to some to present an easy way out of the dilemma posed by radical, biblical criticism. There have been those who wanted to have revelation in Christ without having to bother about defending the integrity of Scripture, trying to ignore the fact that the only Christ we know of is the Christ who is witnessed to by Scripture and who endorsed the integrity of Scripture.[4] And there have been those who have treated the Bible as re-

[1] *Ibid.*, I, 1, pp. 149f.
[2] For discussion of Barth's teaching on God, creation and redemption see C. Brown, *op. cit.*, pp. 99–139.
[3] On the question of analogy and religious language see above, pp. 30ff. and 176. On Barth's teaching see further C. Brown, *op. cit.*, pp. 47–54.
[4] On this last point *cf.* Matthew 4:4ff.; 5:17ff.; 19:4ff.; Mark 7:8, 13; 12:26; Luke 4:21; 24:25ff.; John 5:39–47; 10:35, *etc.*, and see further J. W. Wenham, *Our Lord's View of the Old Testament* (Tyndale Press, 1953).

velation in the pulpit, but in their studies and lecture rooms as a collection of ancient stories which may or may not be true. But such a position cannot be adopted without having a split mind. Here Barth himself is far from satisfactory.[5] For on the one hand, he says that the whole of Scripture is inspired, and that we must treat all its words 'with the same measure of respect'.[6] But on the other hand, he is willing to concede that the biblical writers were mistaken.[7] Such a position can be accepted only if we are prepared to commit double-think. It treats the Bible as true and false at the same time – true in so far as it is the revealing Word of God, and false in so far as it is the erring word of man. (It is not a case of some parts being inspired and reliable, whereas others are not, but of the same passage being both.) In practice Barth seems simply to ignore the difficulty.

This indifference to history and the physical world[8] is the Achilles' heel of Barthianism. The early Barth stressed the supernatural character of revelation to the point of denying any factual content. And the later Barth is more interested in theological interpretation than in the historicity of the events he interprets. But Christianity is no mere esoteric, other-worldly religion. It claims to be grounded in history and experience. In principle, its pronouncements on matters of fact are open to the same verification and falsification as any other such pronouncements. The resurrection of Jesus is put forward in the New Testament as an event in time and space.[9] Its credibility depends in no small measure upon the credibility of the witnesses that attest it. The same applies to the life and

[5] Klaas Runia, *Karl Barth's Doctrine of Holy Scripture* (Eerdmans, Grand Rapids, 1962) gives a detailed exposure of Barth's weaknesses.
[6] *Church Dogmatics*, I, 2, pp. 517f.
[7] *Ibid.*, I, 2, pp. 528ff. On this point see further C. Brown, *op. cit.*, pp. 54–62.
[8] Barth not only rejects all natural theology, but has next to no room in his thinking for any revelation through nature. On this see C. Brown, *op. cit.*, pp. 77–98. The later Barth's interest in the physical world consists largely in reading into it his own particular brand of covenant theology (*cf. ibid.*, pp. 110–123, 149ff.).
[9] *Cf.* Matthew 12:39ff.; 16:4; 28; Mark 8:31; 16; Luke 24; John 20; 21; Acts 1:3; 2:22ff.; 4:10; 5:30f.; 9:5ff.; 10:40; 13:30ff.; 17:31; 22:8; 26:15, 23; Romans 1:4; 8:11; 1 Corinthians 15; Galatians 1:1; Ephesians 1:20; 1 John 1:1ff.

I

teaching of Jesus and to biblical pronouncements in general. The agnostic is entitled to be sceptical about the latter, if their historical basis is dubious. This is the view of the New Testament writers themselves. 'If Christ has not been raised, then our preaching is in vain and your faith is in vain.'[1] The whole fabric of the Christian faith collapses, if the central events of the life, death and resurrection of Jesus presented by the New Testament are unhistorical.

In short, Barthianism is no short cut which enables us to side-step historical questions. We cannot have revelation and biblical theology without being prepared to defend their historical basis. Barth himself appears indifferent to this, and consequently his teaching seems to be left hanging in mid air.[2] The radicals abandon it altogether, but in so doing they abandon Christianity in all but name, and present the world with a collection of ideas so attenuated, that the non-Christian concludes that it is not worth bothering his head about. The alternative is to ask ourselves whether this flight from history has not been over-hasty, and to set about the long, arduous but vital task of examining afresh the historical basis of the Christian faith.[3]

Having said this, the question has also to be asked whether it is legitimate to appeal to revelation at all in answering philosophical questions. Is not Barth, or indeed anyone who appeals to revelation, guilty of irrationalism? To answer this charge, one has to decide first what it means. If the opposite of irrationalism means a determination to accept only what is comprehensible to reason or verifiable in a scientific laboratory, then Barth is guilty of the charge. But so too is every other theologian, philosopher and scientist who accepts that there are areas of experience which are above this type of inquiry. Or again, if by a rational approach we mean proving everything first conclusively by rational arguments, then Barth is

[1] 1 Corinthians 15:12ff.; cf. Romans 6:5; 7:4; 1 Corinthians 6:14; 2 Corinthians 4:14; Galatians 2:20ff.; Ephesians 2:6; Philippians 2:9; 3:10f.; Colossians 2:12; 3:1; 1 Thessalonians 1:10; 2 Timothy 2:8, 18; Hebrews 9:28; 10:12; 13:20f.; 1 Peter 1:3; 3:21.
[2] On Barth and the resurrection of Jesus see C. Brown, op. cit., pp. 64ff.
[3] For works on historical method in general and on the historicity of the New Testament in particular see below, pp. 276–285, 307.

obviously guilty. But then so, too, are most other people, including scientists. For valid scientific statements depend not on what can be argued beforehand but upon the results of empirical observation.

However, there is a different approach to the question of what is rational. An idea may be said to be rational if it is warranted by experience. A conclusion might not be rationally demonstrable purely by logical argument, but it might still be demanded by observation of events. This is, in fact, the method of the natural sciences to draw conclusions from observable phenomena. In this sense Barth's approach is not irrational, for it is grounded upon experience of the Word of God. In this process reason is not disparaged. But its use and place are decided by the object in question – in apprehending the Word of God.

In the case of theology, encounter with God through revelation of the Word is primary. And in this sense, Barth argues, theology is a science. '1. Like all other so-called sciences, it is a human effort after a definite object of knowledge. 2. Like all other sciences, it follows a definite, self-consistent path of knowledge. 3. Like all other sciences, it is in the position of being accountable for this path to itself and to every one – every one who is capable of effort after this object and therefore of following this path.'[4]

If this is so, it is completely beside the point to argue that an appeal to revelation is irrelevant to modern man and modern philosophy. It would be just as sensible to argue that physics and chemistry are irrelevant, because we do not happen to like the methods they employ. To say that they are irrelevant is not to pronounce a factual judgment at all, but simply to announce to the world our private prejudices. For reality is not shaped by our private likes and dislikes. Any philosophy worthy of the name must take into account things as they in fact are, and not things as the private individual might like them to be.

How, then, does philosophy relate to Barth's approach? In Van Til's case we saw him arguing that there is no genuine common ground between the believer and the unbeliever.

[4] *Church Dogmatics*, I, 1, p. 7.

What has to be done is to show the inadequacies of all world
views and that the only view which really makes sense is that of
Christian Theism. Barth's approach is more modest. He
recognizes that, for good or ill, we all have our preconceived
philosophies.[5] They may be sophisticated or naïve. They may
give valuable insights into the nature of things, or they may
not. But because we are men and not God, no philosophy can
ever be exhaustive. Moreover, every philosophy requires
modification in the light of experience, not least in the light
of the Word of God. Those philosophies are most sterile
which approach experience with a rigid system and try to
force everything into a pattern shaped by their preconceived
ideas. At best, therefore, each philosophy is no more than a
working hypothesis. 'It cannot in any way become an end in
itself.'[6] The Christian must remember Paul's warning: 'See
to it that no one makes a prey of you by philosophy and empty
deceit, according to human tradition, according to the elemental spirits of the universe, and not according to Christ.'[7]

In the very nature of the case, when it comes to the question
of the knowledge of God, we must begin with the primary
datum of the Christian faith – God's revelation of himself in
his Word. It is in the light of the Word of God that we must
judge our preconceived ideas, and not *vice versa*.

Francis Schaeffer

The last thinker that we shall mention in our survey is Francis
Schaeffer. Before the War he studied for his doctorate in the
United States, where he was a pastor from 1938 to 1948.
Since then he has lived and worked in Europe where he runs
L'Abri Fellowship, based in Switzerland. Dr. Schaeffer is one
of the few contemporary evangelical thinkers who have tried
to get to grips with secular culture. In a recent essay, *Escape
from Reason*,[8] he has sought to analyse the broad trends not
only of philosophy and theology but of art and literature from
the Middle Ages to the present.

[5] *Ibid.*, I, 2, p. 728.   [6] *Ibid.*, I, 2, p. 731.   [7] Colossians 2:8.
[8] Inter-Varsity Fellowship, 1968. Schaeffer's larger study, *The God Who
is There* (Hodder), was also published in 1968, but appeared too late to be
taken into account here.

Modern man's despair and sense of meaninglessness stem from his autonomous rationalism, his desire to make himself and his own reason the sole judge of everything. This is rooted in his divorce of God and nature, of the supernatural and the natural. Schaeffer traces this back to the distinction, drawn by Thomas Aquinas in the Middle Ages, between nature and grace.[9] Whenever the two are divorced, the natural tends to push out the supernatural, or (to use Schaeffer's phrase) nature 'eats up' grace.[1] In the realm of art this showed itself in the increasingly naturalistic representations of Renaissance religious painting which superseded Byzantine art with its symbolic attempt to depict divinity.[2]

The trend towards secularization has continued with increasing momentum down to the present day. In the Middle Ages Aquinas's scheme of thought left room for revelation, but by the Age of Enlightenment the supernatural was banished from rational thought. 'Rationalism was now well developed and entrenched; and there was no concept of revelation in any area. Consequently the problem was now defined, not in terms of "nature and grace", but of "nature and freedom".'[3] In Kant's deterministic universe freedom is not a rational concept, but an idea posited by ethics. Rousseau sought freedom in the irrational. Already in their mechanistic world 'freedom makes no sense, and thus autonomous freedom and the autonomous machine stand facing each other'.[4]

Schaeffer sees the intellectual and cultural history of the next two hundred years as the outworking of this dilemma. The divorce between the rational and the irrational is complete. But, however much he tries to, man cannot do without the 'irrational'. His rationalism may condemn it, but it cannot suppress it. It finds expression in the formlessness of so much modern art,[5] and the increase of drug taking.[6] It manifests itself in the curious, but not uncommon, phenomenon of a secular philosopher adopting a strong rationalistic line on something, only to leap to an utterly unwarranted conclusion at the end.[7] The same thing is true of a good deal of modern,

[9] *Escape from Reason*, p. 9.   [1] *Ibid.*, p. 13.   [2] *Ibid.*, p. 12.
[3] *Ibid.*, p. 33.   [4] *Ibid.*, p. 34.   [5] *Ibid.*, p. 58.   [6] *Ibid.*, p. 53.
[7] As an instance of this Schaeffer cites the case of Anthony Flew who in a

critical theology. It looks down patronizingly on orthodox theology which, it proclaims, modern, rational man can no longer accept, only to present him with something even more irrational.[8] The optimism of the secular humanist is no different. It has no rational foundation. Ironically, Schaeffer concludes that, 'The significant thing is that rationalistic, humanistic man began by saying that Christianity was not rational enough. Now he has come around in a wide circle and ended as a mystic – though a mystic of a special kind. He is a mystic with nobody there.'[9]

In philosophy an argument may be invalid if one of the links in its chain of reasoning will not hold, or if its premises are wrong. What Schaeffer is doing (like Van Til and Barth in their different ways) is to challenge the premises of modern, secular thought. Modern despair is warranted, if we start in the same place as modern secular man. By making himself autonomous, 'Modern man has not only thrown away Christian theology, he has thrown away the possibility of what our forefathers had as

BBC Third Programme broadcast 'addressed himself to the question "Must Morality Pay?". He used the broadcast to show that, on the basis of his own presuppositions, morality does not pay. And yet he cannot stand this. At the very end he brings in out of thin air the concept that, in spite of the fact that morality does not pay, a man is not a fool to be scrupulous. This is a titanic leap without a basis as to why a man is not a fool to be scrupulous' (*ibid.*, p. 55; *cf. The Listener*, 13 October 1966).

[8] 'The New Theology seems to have an advantage over secular existentialism because it uses words that have strong connotations as they are rooted in the memory of the race; words like "resurrection", "crucifixion", "Christ", "Jesus". These words give an illusion of communication. The importance of these words to the new theologians lies in the illusion of communication, plus the highly motivated reaction men have on the basis of the connotation of the words. That is the advantage of the New Theology over secular existentialism and the modern secular mysticisms. One hears the word "Jesus", one acts upon it, but it is never defined. The use of such words is always in the area of the irrational, the non-logical. Being separated from history and the cosmos, they are divorced from possible verification by reason downstairs, and there is no certainty that there is anything upstairs. We need to understand, therefore, that it is an act of desperation to make this separation, in which all hope is removed from the realm of rationality. It is a real act of despair, which is not changed merely by using religious words' (*ibid.*, pp. 52f.).

[9] *Ibid.*, p. 56.

a basis for morality and law.'[1] It is not surprising that he frantically tries one philosophy after another, only to discard it, because it proves unsatisfactory. It is the same with the fads and fashions of theology. Man still holds out hope, but on the basis of his rationalism all hope of a cogent philosophy of life is doomed to failure.

In this situation Schaeffer contends that, 'Christianity has the opportunity . . . to speak clearly of the fact that its answer has the very thing that modern man has despaired of – the unity of thought. It provides a unified answer for the whole of life. It is true that man will have to renounce his rationalism, but then, on the basis of what can be discussed, he has the possibility of recovering his rationality.'[2] By Christianity Schaeffer means the Christianity that is based upon the Bible. With the Reformers he insists that we must not play off the authority of Christ against that of Scripture.[3] Moreover, Christ must be Lord of all. He must be Lord not only over our spiritual life, but over our whole intellectual life.[4]

The Bible thus presents Schaeffer with his frame of reference. He describes the landscape within the frame like this. 'The Bible says, first of all, that in the beginning all things were created by a personal-infinite God, who had always existed. So what is, therefore, is intrinsically personal rather than impersonal. Then the Bible says that He created all things outside of Himself. The term "outside of Himself" is, I think, the best way to express creation to twentieth-century people. We do not mean to use the phrase in a spatial sense, but to deny that creation is any kind of pantheistic extension of God's essence. God exists – a personal God who has always existed – and He has created all other things outside of Him-

[1] *Ibid.*, p. 81.   [2] *Ibid.*, p. 82.
[3] 'But you cannot have this answer unless you hold to the Reformation view of the Scriptures. It is not a question of God revealing Himself in Jesus Christ only, because there is not enough content in this if it is separated from the Scriptures. It then becomes only another contentless banner, for all we know of what that revelation of Christ was comes from the Scriptures. Jesus Himself did not make a distinction between His authority and the authority of the written Scriptures. He acted upon the unity of His authority and the content of the Scriptures' (*ibid.*, p. 83; *cf.* above, pp. 43–49, 254ff.).
[4] *Ibid.*, p. 83.

self. Thus, because the universe begins with a truly personal beginning, love and communication (which are a burden of twentieth-century men's hearts) are not contrary to that which intrinsically is. . . . In this setting of a significant history, the Bible says that God made man in a special way, in His own image. If I do not understand that man's basic relationship is upward, I must try to find it downward. In relating it downward, a person is very old-fashioned today if he finally relates himself to the animals. Today, modern man seeks to relate himself to the machine.'[5]

The alternative is 'that man is a product of the impersonal, plus time, plus chance'.[6] But the Bible has still more to say about man. It diagnoses man's misery as the result of his sin. But, for all that, man does not cease to be man. 'The fact that man has fallen does not mean that he has ceased to bear God's image. He has not ceased to be man because he is fallen. He can love, though he is fallen. It would be a mistake to say that only a Christian can love. Moreover, a non-Christian painter can still paint beauty. . . . The marks of mannishness are still upon him – love, rationality, longing for significance, fear of non-being, and so on. This is the case even when his non-Christian system leads him to say these things do not exist. . . The Bible teaches that, though man is hopelessly lost, he is not nothing. Man is lost because he is separated from God, his true reference point, by true moral guilt. But he never will be nothing. Therein lies the horror of his lostness.'[7] But the Bible also points man to the way out of his predicament by proclaiming redemption in Christ, reconciliation with God and with his fellow man, which alone enables him to realize his true being.

Escape from Reason must be read and judged for what it is – not a definitive history of thought, but a suggestive and provocative essay. With his American and continental background Schaeffer is apt to pass rather too lightly over some aspects of British thought. His style is swashbuckling. The whole thing is like a speeded-up lantern lecture in which pictures, names and ideas follow each other in breath-taking succession. Points are often suggested rather than proved. But then many seminal

[5] *Ibid.*, pp. 86f.   [6] *Ibid.*, p. 87.   [7] *Ibid.*, pp. 83ff.

works in the history of thought have done the same. What we are concerned with here is not the details of the argument but the main thesis.

The strength of Schaeffer's position lies in two things. On the one hand, it seeks to present an integrated view of the whole of life. It is not interested merely in what critics are pleased to call *post-mortem* salvation, although it recognizes that salvation is an essential part of Christianity. Nor does it restrict the Christian's interest and activity to the cultivation of personal piety and devotion. It seeks to relate the Christian faith to the whole of life. On the other hand, it takes the Bible seriously. Unlike some versions of Christianity, especially the more radical ones of the past two hundred years, it is not a case of working out a preconceived philosophy, and then dressing it up in theological language. It is an attempt to work out a philosophy of life which integrates the natural and the supernatural on the basis of the primary – and indeed unique – source of Christian origins, the Bible.

But for some, this is precisely the difficulty. Schaeffer's system may be more or less well worked out, but how do we know that it is a valid system? Schaeffer does not prove God in the same way as the old-fashioned proofs which, in any case, he rejects. He seems to take God's existence for granted. In reply, the present writer would make the following comments. Schaeffer presents his philosophy as a belief-system. He does not demonstrate every single part of it, *e.g.* that there is a life after death. Such items of belief are unverified (and in this life unverifiable). Although clues to their meaningfulness may be picked up in this life, in the last analysis they are accepted on the authority of other parts of the belief-system. But on what grounds do we accept these other parts?

Schaeffer's approach may be compared with a set of hypotheses in science. In the first instance, a hypothesis presents an unproved theory designed to account for something hitherto not understood. A good hypothesis is one which makes sense of the observed facts and takes into account the maximum number of other observed facts. Schaeffer makes a twofold claim. On the one hand, secular philosophy utterly fails to make sense of man, the world, history and personal experience as a whole by refusing to accept anything but what its rational-istic premises will allow. And on the other hand, the belief-system presented by the Bible does make good sense.

But does not this reduce Christianity to the status of a hypo-thetical system? The answer is that it need not. The word 'system' has become a kind of bogey-word among some Christians who have a horror of precise thinking. But in itself the term simply denotes a set of beliefs which hang together. Of course, it is perfectly possible for someone to become more wrapped up in his system than in life itself. But the New Testa-ment presents Jesus as having a co-ordinated set of beliefs. Yet this did not strangle his life. Rather, it gave it direction and purpose. Nor need we be afraid of the term 'hypothesis'. For the kind of hypothesis that the Bible presents is not a re-mote, static, abstract one, but an interpretation of life which makes sense as we go along living it. It applies to doctrines, such as the Christian view of God, creation and reconciliation. It also applies to moral precepts such as the two great com-mandments of the Christian faith: 'You shall love the Lord your God with all your heart, and with all your soul, and with all your mind, and with all your strength' and 'You shall love your neighbour as yourself'.[8] The rightness of these command-ments is not proved beforehand. It is perceived in the act of apprehending them, and it is confirmed in life in situations where the commands are applicable. Moreover, it is as he listens to Scripture, and seeks to act upon it, that the believer becomes aware of God dealing with him personally.[9]

But does not all this suppose that we should take a high view of the authority of Scripture? The answer is, of course, that it does. If the belief-system leads us to accept Christ's Lordship, it means that we must accept his Lordship over our minds. And this in turn means accepting his view of authority and truth. But for the Christian this is not a fetter to scientific inquiry, but a spur. It gives him a sense of direc-tion. It gives him a basis from which to operate. This does not preclude historical investigation into the books of the

[8] Mark 12:30f.; cf. Matthew 22:34-40; Luke 10:25-28; Deuteronomy 6:4; Leviticus 19:18.
[9] Cf. above, pp. 43-48, 80, 252-256.

Bible. Indeed, it requires it. For to understand them, they have to be seen in the context in which they were written. In principle the events of the Bible are open to the same verification and falsification as any other events. The language of the Bible must be studied in the light of the same hermeneutical techniques that are applicable to other literature. For the Bible claims to be speaking about real events through the medium of human language. This is not the same as saying that every and any fashionable theory about the Bible is true. Rather, it is a declaration that those who accept the authority of the Bible have everything to gain from genuine, scientific investigation of its contents. But this brings us to the borderland between philosophy and history. And as such it must be the theme for other books.[1]

[1] On the question of history see below, pp. 276–285, 307.

5 POSTSCRIPT: THE CHRISTIAN AND PHILOSOPHY

The foregoing chapters have taken us on a conducted tour of many of the curiosities of western philosophy. It is high time to sum up. We could do this by embarking upon an even quicker tour, retracing our steps over the same ground, only at a gallop, and seeing even less of the landscape. But instead of this it will be much more useful to concentrate attention on some of the questions raised by what we have already seen. We shall do this, first by looking at some of the lessons that are to be learnt from the past, and then by asking what is the value of philosophy for the Christian today.

I LESSONS FROM THE PAST
a. *The incompleteness of philosophical systems*
If there is one thing that stands out from our survey of over a thousand years of debates between philosophers and Christians in the western world, it is that no system of philosophy has ever turned out to be complete and perfect. In fact, it could be said that those systems which, like Absolute Idealism, have laid the greatest claims to comprehensiveness and completeness are precisely those which are the most defective. At almost regular intervals down the centuries someone will hit upon an idea which has some claim to truth. It is then blown up into a system which is thought to be capable of explaining everything. It is hailed as a key to unlock every door. But sooner or later its advocates find themselves obliged to deny the existence of anything that their key fails to unlock, or to admit that it was not quite what they thought it was. For a time the

system may carry all before it. In the end, however, people become disillusioned and they try something new.

What often happens in philosophy is that someone stumbles across something that has long been ignored or feels a need to account for some aspect of experience or relate it to 'modern' thought. The Rationalists of the seventeenth century felt the need for clear thinking and rational demonstration. The Idealists of the nineteenth century felt the need to relate the whole of experience to an ultimate spiritual cause. Kierkegaard in the same century felt that the explanation given by the Idealists left the individual and real life out of account. In each case the thinkers concerned were so impressed with their particular insight that they built it into a more or less rigid system which virtually destroyed its original usefulness.

This is not to say that no belief is ever valid, and that nothing can truly be known. Rather it is that, if anything is to be learnt from the history of philosophy, we should be cautious in embracing one set of philosophical ideas to the exclusion of others, and critical in our evaluation of all of them. Just as no single human being has exhaustive knowledge of the whole of reality, but may have partial and valid insights into this or that field of experience, so no philosophy is all-embracing. Its insights and methods are often tentative and provisional. It may have a valid apprehension of this or that. Its methods may be fruitful in exploring certain particular fields. But if we are wise, we shall be on our guard against definitive systems and allegedly omnicompetent methods of approach.

b. The dangers of allying the Christian faith too closely with any single philosophical system

This first observation should put us all the more on our guard against aligning Christianity too closely with any one particular philosophy. This is one of the perennial pitfalls of the philosophically minded. The procedure works in two ways. On the one hand, there are some who feel obliged to capitulate to the most fashionable ideas of the moment, and reinterpret Christianity accordingly. And on the other hand, there are those who feel that this or that system is *the* answer to the

needs of the hour. In our own day Paul van Buren seems to
have swallowed, hook, line and sinker, the most radical and
short-sighted form of linguistic analysis. He, therefore, feels
obliged to dismember Christianity according to its dictates.
On the Continent Rudolf Bultmann sees Heidegger's Existentialism as *the* philosophical basis of Christianity. But a century
ago it was some form of Idealism that was seen to be the only
possible philosophical basis for the Christian faith. Further
back still Christianity has been wedded to Aristotelianism and
Platonism. But, as we have seen, in each case Christianity has
been forced to lie upon a Procrustean bed of alien ideas, and
sooner or later the philosophy which seemed so full of promise
turned out to be wanting. When the next generation came
along, they wondered how stupid their predecessors could
have been to have taken so seriously that particular brand of
Rationalism or Empiricism, Idealism or Positivism.

Sometimes it happens that a theologian takes over a philosophy almost lock, stock and barrel. But sometimes it also
happens that a theologian becomes dazzled by a particular
idea which he then proceeds to make into a key to everything.
A case in point here is Schleiermacher's notion of the essence
of religion as *the sense of absolute dependence*. Few people would
dream of denying that this is an element in religious experience.
But in Schleiermacher's hands it became a yardstick for measuring all religious truth. And with disastrous results. It
prevented Schleiermacher from recognizing much that was
essential in Christianity and left him with an emasculated creed.
As we saw, the grounds on which he arrived at his criterion were
inadequate. It could hardly be otherwise when we try to
reduce religion to a single idea.

The dangers of aligning Christianity too closely with a
particular philosophical system or idea are at least twofold.
On the one hand, the Christian faith has to be manipulated
to make it fit. Some things have to be stretched, while others
have to be lopped off or at least discreetly ignored. And
on the other hand, when some flaw is detected in the system,
the impression is given that the Christian faith must collapse
together with the system it has been wedded to. It is not
surprising that in many philosophical circles today it is

assumed that because the old Aristotelian, rationalistic arguments for the existence of God have fallen, all grounds for rational belief in God have collapsed with them.

All this is not to say that there is no value in philosophy whatsoever. One of the great values of secular philosophy – in this it is not unlike heresy – is the stimulus it gives to Christian thinkers to rethink their position. The assaults on the old proofs of the existence of God have forced some at least to ask on what valid grounds do we believe in God. The attacks of Logical Positivism and sceptical linguistic analysis have led some Christian thinkers to examine further and in a new way the nature of revelation and the part which language and communication play in Christian faith.

The moral of all this is that we should neither fall over ourselves in the naïve way of some sophisticated intellectuals to embrace the latest philosophical fashion, nor run away in panic like some unsophisticated pietists. Rather we should take a cool, hard look at every new trend and evaluate it in the light of our experience and faith.

c. Natural theology

Natural theology has something of the irrepressible quality of a yo-yo. However much it is repulsed, there has always been someone or other who has tried to bring it back. A few years ago it was called 'the sick man of Europe'.[1] Certainly it has taken quite a battering from the philosophers on the one hand and the Barthians on the other. But more recently, in *Soundings*, Howard Root has entered a wistful plea for its revival.[2] His essay combines something of the tone of don't-shoot-the-pianist-he's-doing-his-best and the claim that theology inevitably involves metaphysical theology. And by implication this means natural theology. Admittedly, the matter is not so naïvely straightforward as philosophers such as Descartes imagined it was. Nor does Professor Root say what form he envisages that it will take (apart from dropping a hint that in

[1] Ninian Smart in *Prospect for Metaphysics*, ed. I. T. Ramsey (Allen and Unwin, 1961), p. 80.
[2] 'Beginning All Over Again', in *Soundings*, pp. 3-19.

future natural theology should look more to the arts and creative imagination).

What are we to say to all this? On the basis of our survey the following points may be suggested as guidelines for future thought. (1) The traditional rationalistic arguments for the existence of God will not hold water. Their logic is suspect and they fail to bring us to the God of Christian faith and experience. We saw this right at the outset when we discussed Anselm and Aquinas. The point was underlined when we looked at the classical debates of thinkers such as Descartes and Kant. In our own day the ventures of John Robinson and Paul Tillich into the realms of natural theology have proved equally fruitless. (2) But this, in the opinion of the present writer, is no great loss. It brings no honour to God to resort to dubious arguments in his defence! Nor does it help the faith of the believer to be propped up by such proofs which are drawn from outside the Christian revelation. Moreover, as we saw in looking at the influence of medieval philosophy, natural theology opened the door to all kinds of speculation which had the effect of obscuring the Christian gospel. Instead of opening up man's mind to the challenge of the Christian revelation, it has proved a perennial temptation to fashion God in the image of man.

(3) On the other hand, writers like the early Barth fall into the opposite error when they insist that man has no knowledge at all of God apart from the gospel. It would seem to be both the common experience of men and also the testimony of several important strands of Scripture,[3] that men have an awareness of God regardless of whether they have heard the gospel and regardless of whether they respond or not. This awareness may be dim. It is certainly not that intimate, personal knowledge of God in Christ through the Holy Spirit to which the apostle Paul testified and claimed to be unique to Christian experience.[4] Christians all down the ages have endorsed Paul's claim at this point. On the other hand, it is precisely this awareness of God as one to whom we are ulti-

---

[3] Cf. Psalm 19:1f.; Acts 14:17; 17:22–31; Romans 1:19ff., 32; 2:12–16.
[4] Cf. Romans 8:15ff.; 1 Corinthians 2:6–16; Galatians 2:20; Ephesians 2:1; 3:17ff.

mately responsible which provides a point of contact for the Christian message and which clinches man's guilt in his persistent turning away from God.

This general awareness of God gains added point when we reflect on the question whether we really believe that the universe that we live in with all its apparent evidence of design is purely the product of accidental chance or whether it points to some sort of connection with a rational mind. To my mind the former alternative is incredible, however incomplete and puzzling the universe may be. I think that Professor Root has something when he directs attention to men's awareness of God in art, literature and experience. But this does not seem to add up to anything capable of being called a theology except in the most rudimentary sense. Natural theology (in the sense of a coherent knowledge of God and his relationship with the world without recourse to the Christian revelation) is a blind alley. On the other hand, it seems legitimate on the basis of both common experience and the witness of the biblical writers to speak of a revelation in nature and a natural awareness of God. And these deserve due attention in preaching, apologetics and the philosophy of religion.

(4) It would be interesting to investigate in more detail Howard Root's plea for a new type of natural theology in the light of Van Til's and Schaeffer's views on the importance of presuppositions. In discussing the latter it was suggested that the Christian faith could be seen as a hypothesis.[5] It suggests explanations for phenomena which are otherwise inexplicable. It makes sense of what at first seemed senseless. It gives a wholeness to life which is missing in other views. This is so whether we look at the universe in general or at personal experience of life. On atheistic, humanistic premises the whole universe is the product of blind chance. All human values are accidental and arbitrary. If this is so, life is what Macbeth said it was, 'a tale told by an idiot, full of sound and fury, signifying nothing'.[6] On these premises, it would be right simply to live for oneself. Pleasure, profit, drugs[7] – whatever gave the individual

---

[5] See above, pp. 265ff.   [6] *Macbeth*, Act V, Scene 5.
[7] In *The Humanist Frame* (Carson, 1961) Aldous Huxley pleads for the use

the maximum of pleasure and the minimum of discomfort –
would be the obvious options. But there is something in man
which cries out against this. Is it merely wishful thinking?
Does it make best sense of this highly complicated universe to
say that it just happened, that it is a purely fortuitous collection
of atoms?[8]

Van Til and Schaeffer say that the universe in general and
human life in particular make real sense only on Christian
premises. What they are saying is not natural theology in the
accepted sense of the term. The key to meaning is not derived
simply from reflecting on phenomena. The latter is more
like a jig-saw puzzle with vital pieces missing, or perhaps one
so complex that the pieces just do not make sense without the
aid of a picture from outside. By beginning with himself and
his rationalism man just cannot make sense of it as a whole.

To say this is not to claim that the Bible explains everything.
Clearly it does not. It does not pretend to do the job of the
scientist for him. It does not say everything there is to know
about God himself. But it does provide a key which gives
coherence and meaning to life as a whole. To argue in this way
is not to relapse into the discredited God-of-the-gaps arguments of old-fashioned apologetics. It is not a case of saying
that we have a gap here in scientific explanation, therefore,
God must have done it, only to find later on that there was a
natural explanation. The argument here is on a different
plane. It concerns the presuppositions of naturalistic explanation. By itself scientific explanation gives an account of particular phenomena. The question then arises whether we are to
say that these rational accounts are, in the last analysis, about
the irrational and absurd.

To adopt this line of thought is not to say that Christian
theology is merely a presupposition or hypothesis. (In any case,
presuppositions are not just arbitrary ideas picked out of the
air. Their validity is tested by whatever is built upon them.
If they are incapable of bearing the weight, they must be

---

of drugs by 'healthy people' for the 'First-order experience' (*cf.* Schaeffer,
op. cit., pp. 53f.).
[8] On this see above, pp. 29f., 248f., 262ff.

scrapped, and others sought.) The Christian belief that God created all things outside of himself is a presupposition of Christian thought about life generally. But the Christian interpretation of life does not remain in the realm of the theoretical. What the Bible says about forgiveness, faith, being born again, about love and the whole range of human activity is validated by the Christian as he tries it out in life. It gives meaning to experience. It is precisely at the conjunction of experience and interpretation through the gospel that there takes place that encounter with God which in Christian theology is termed revelation.

(5) All too often in the past it has been assumed that the philosophy of the Christian religion was synonymous with natural theology. No doubt this was partly due to the fact that those Christians who were interested in philosophy tended to be devotees of some established brand of secular philosophy or advocates of the methods of natural theology. But in fact this is not the only option. There remains the possibility that the philosophy of the Christian religion should be worked out on the basis of the Christian revelation and the practising Christian's experience of God.

This is not an attempt to turn the Christian message into an esoteric philosophy. Men encounter God in their total personalities through the gospel presented by the church, and not through abstruse arguments. Philosophy is not everybody's cup of tea. A man can be a perfectly good Christian without any great grasp of the subject. Nevertheless, because the Christian faith lays claims to a type of knowledge and asserts that certain events in the past are decisive for humanity, Christianity inevitably raises philosophical questions. In so far as the phenomenon of the gospel raises philosophical issues, it is this which should provide the subject-matter for the philosophy of the Christian religion. This is, in fact, what has happened to some extent in recent years in those philosophical circles which have been interested in examining the nature and function of religious language. To that extent the analytic movement in philosophy is something to be welcomed by the Christian, as is the renewed interest of the past couple of decades in the philosophy of history.

The point can be put another way round. The Christian
gospel must henceforth stand or fall – from the philosophical
point of view – by itself. Christianity must be capable of vindicating itself by itself. Our proof of the existence of God must
derive from our experience of God *through the whole gospel* and
not be made dependent upon hypothetical abstract arguments
borrowed from outside. All too often in the past the Christian
apologist has put himself in the position of the schoolboy who
knows how the theorem should come out, but, through not
following the proper proof, has found himself obliged to
'cook' it. Just as the shrewd eye of the maths. master soon
spots the cooking, so the modern secular philosopher refuses
to be taken in by the lame arguments of natural theology.
In future Christian philosophers must be prepared to vindicate
Christianity by a more thorough investigation of the Christian
revelation, or quit the field altogether.

d. Revelation and history

We shall not attempt to work out here a comprehensive
account of revelation and history. But these themes have
cropped up repeatedly in our survey, and some comment here
is justified.

We have suggested that revelation is the significant self-
disclosure of God. Although we have spoken of a revelation
in nature,[9] the chief locus is personal experience of God in
Christ interpreted by the Word of God in Scripture.[1] This
is a complex phenomenon which, though basic to Christian
faith, requires even more careful investigation than has
hitherto been given it. It is no less complex than the involved
questions of Christology in the early church, where some parties said that Jesus was a mere man, others that he was not
human at all, and others that he was some kind of hybrid.
It is tempting to pursue the point that modern radicalism,
with its stress on some things at the expense of others, is falling
into all the old pitfalls all over again, but we must content
ourselves by saying that in revelation there is both a human

[9] *Cf.* above, pp. 29f., 45, 74, 247f., 257.
[1] *Cf.* above, pp. 246–250, 257, 272ff. On the question of the validity of
taking revelation into account see pp. 253ff., 258ff.

element and a divine element. If we are to understand it, we must be careful not to play off one against the other.

Modern thinkers are in danger of falling into opposite extremes. The existentialist radical says that the Bible is a collection of largely unhistorical stories about human self-understanding. They are of value today because they still help us to understand human existence better. In reply the Evangelical is apt to say that there is no truth in this at all, and that the Bible is the means of communicating a number of divinely-revealed truths which could not otherwise be known.

As a matter of fact, there is some truth in both positions. It is almost, though not quite, a case of men being right in what they affirm and wrong in what they deny. The Evangelical is apt to overlook in theory (though not altogether in practice in his preaching and devotions) that there is a very large existential element in Scripture. A great deal of it is devoted not to the communication of new facts but to getting us to see the old facts in a new light. We might instance the Psalms, where the writer meditates upon his plight and then upon God, and ends by seeing things differently, having been brought into the presence of God through his reflections. The main purpose of a parable, such as that of the Good Samaritan,[2] is not so much to pass on facts, as to confront the hearer with himself and his motives, so that he will 'go and do likewise'.

The Existentialist goes wrong when he says that there is no more to it than this. On his premises it is difficult to see why we should make such a fuss about Christianity and have all the bother of going to church and keeping an organization going which most people do not seem to want. In fact, this is precisely what the outsider thinks, and naturally he does not bother, especially when the radical tells us that we can know very little of what Jesus really said and did. He can enlarge his understanding of human existence simply by sitting at home, reading a novel or watching television (even if the latter is showing only a Donald Duck cartoon).

The radical, existentialist account of Scripture falls short

[2] Luke 10:25–37.

on three counts. First, it fails to do justice to the claim of the biblical writers, that they are not just recounting any parabolic story, but that they are speaking in their own human words the Word of God. What they utter is, in the first instance, directed to a particular human situation. Nevertheless, they claim that what they say is God-given and is of decisive importance. We cannot disentangle the existential element without distorting the rest. Secondly, in Scripture the existential element is inextricably bound up with the communication of information. This ranges from statements about the character of God, the requirements he makes of man, and what he does for man, to the interpretation of particular events such as the Exodus and the life, death and resurrection of Christ. Again we cannot have the one without the other. Thirdly, the biblical understanding of life is bound up with historical events – acts of God in history. If the latter did not happen, then the Christian faith is groundless. Such events, plus the interpretation given them in Scripture, are all part and parcel of the Christian revelation. As such, they are relevant not only to the presentation of the Christian message to the modern world, but to any philosophy of the Christian religion.

The Christian faith claims to bear witness to what God has done and will do in time and space. The record of such past events is in principle open to the same verification and falsification as any other historical record. Otherwise, they would forfeit the claim to be historical events. Today the objection is sometimes raised that the supernatural cannot be entertained by the modern, critical historian. Everything must be interpreted in terms of a closed system of finite causes. Otherwise, the door is open to every superstition and fable. The supernatural and the miraculous are discounted from the start. Clearly, the historian needs criteria which will help him to sift fact from fiction. But to adopt this over-strict line seems to the present writer to misconceive the task of the historian. It decides beforehand to a large extent what may or may not have happened without even looking at the evidence.

The phenomenon of history is the sum total of events in the past. But the academic discipline that we call history is no such catalogue of events. It is not even, to use Ranke's celebrated phrase, the record of an event 'as it actually happened'.[3] For one thing, the historian cannot get back into the past and see things for himself (unless he happened to be an eyewitness). For another thing, he does not write down everything that he unearths. He selects. He has to, in order to get it into a book. He discriminates. He tries to trace causes and assess influence. In doing this he is not reconstructing the past, for the past cannot literally be reconstructed. What he is doing is more like building a model. A model is a representation of something else which enables us to see what that something else is or was like. Some of the material for the model may be taken from documents which the historian believes contain original utterances or eyewitness accounts (though sometimes they may not be available to him). But other parts of the model will be of his own making. It is these latter parts which not only hold the original fragments together, but which determine how such fragments are to be fitted together.

To describe history in this way might suggest that it is a highly arbitrary affair, depending a great deal upon the fads and fancies of individual historians. My answer to such a query would be that it sometimes is, but need not be so. The quality of a historian depends both upon his use of material and upon his interpretations. But the latter need not be something foisted upon the former. Although the historian will draw upon his own experience to help him envisage a personality or an event, his own background should not prejudge the issue.

In fact, it is the very data which suggest the interpretation. This point has been stressed recently in Germany by Wolfhart Pannenberg who says that, 'An historical faith is not limited in that it cannot get through to the meaning of events, but can only see them as brute facts. . . . Rather, events always bring along their original meaning out of the context in which they are reported as happening.'[4] In connection with the resurrec-

---

[3] The phrase appears in the preface to an early work by Leopold von Ranke, *Geschichte der romanischen und germanischen Völker, 1494-1535* (1824).
[4] 'Einsicht und Glaube' in *Theologische Literaturzeitung*, 88 (1963), cols. 86ff.; quoted by Daniel Fuller, *Easter Faith and History* (Tyndale Press, 1968), p. 183.

tion of Jesus this means that, 'It is the close examination of the reports of the resurrection that determine its historicity, and not the prior judgment that all events in history must be more or less the same.'[5]

The American philosopher of history J. W. Montgomery has suggested that facts and interpretations are like feet and shoes. The interpretation that the historian brings to his data should be neither too tight nor too loose. The point could be pressed even further. The critical historian is like a shoe sales-man. He has at his disposal numerous pairs of shoes. His job is to look at the data before him and try on various interpreta-tions until he finds one which is neither too big nor too small and which suits. This is especially important in trying to trace connections and assess significance. When he is confronted by the question of whether a particular event happened or not, he has to judge the most probable explanation in the light of the data before him, paying attention to the credibility of the data and its consistency with his model as a whole.

It may happen that the data before him may require the historian to revise his whole general scheme. He may, for example, start out from the premise that miracles do not happen today. This is the basic position of many radical New Testament scholars. They are then confronted by the alleged miracles of the Bible, not least the resurrection of Jesus. Some of them reject this as myth without more ado. But the present writer would submit that the proper course of action is to examine the data in detail, together with all possible alterna-tive explanations, such as that Jesus did not really die, or that the disciples stole the body, or simply invented the story, or suffered from hallucinations. None of these theories actually tallies with the data. They all mean that the whole thing was a gigantic fraud. They all equally fail to explain the change that came over the disciples and their motivation and charac-ters, if what they claimed had not in fact happened. It may sound naïve to some thinkers today, but if God is God, and the giver of life in the first place, there is nothing inherently incredible in the belief that he can restore life. To the present

[5] 'Heilsgeschehen und Geschichte' in *Kerygma und Dogma*, 5 (1959), pp. 266f.; *cf.* D. Fuller, *op. cit.*, pp. 178, 181.

writer the most satisfactory explanation is that Jesus was actually raised from the dead.

We have cited the case of the resurrection of Jesus as an event by which Christianity stands or falls, and as an illustration of the way in which the very data help to decide the interpretation and not *vice versa*.[6] All too often in the past hundred and fifty years the historical study of the Bible has been vitiated by arbitrary criteria. Interpretations which were either too slack or too tight have been hastily preferred to painstaking examination of the text itself. The present writer would submit that a great deal of contemporary scepticism among radical theologians is not due to their superior knowledge and techniques but to their lack of them. A recent case in point is R. H. Fuller's *The Foundations of New Testament Christology*.[7] Fuller's work is a large-scale study of considerable learning, devoted to the very foundations of Christianity. In order to ascertain these Fuller employs the form-critical techniques developed by the Bultmann school in Germany.

Basic to Fuller's position is the belief that the Gospel stories 'reflect the christological beliefs of the post-resurrection church'.[8] In his hands this is no mere truism. It does not simply mean that when the Gospels came to be written the authors knew the end of the story from the beginning and arranged their material accordingly. Rather it is used like a Procrustean bed. Anything that does not quite fit in with the way Professor Fuller wants to use this as a historical criterion is automatically lopped off.

With this in mind, Professor Fuller coolly lays down the following historical maxim: 'As regards the sayings of Jesus, traditio-historical criticism eliminates from the authentic sayings of Jesus those which are paralleled in the Jewish

[6] Obviously, the whole question requires much more thorough examination than is given here. Recent sceptical explanations are given by Joel Carmichael, *The Death of Jesus* (Pelican, 1966) and Hugh J. Schonfield, *The Passover Plot* (Hutchinson, 1965). For a moderate reappraisal of the question in the light of modern historical methods see Alan Richardson, *History: Sacred and Profane* (SCM Press, 1964), pp. 184–212. For more detailed discussions see pp. 73, 307.

[7] Lutterworth Press, 1965.

[8] *The Foundations of New Testament Christology*, p. 103.

tradition on the one hand (apocalyptic and Rabbinic) and those which reflect the faith, practice and situations of the post-Easter church as we know them from outside the gospels.'[9] In other words, we are to assume, on the one hand, that Jesus could have had nothing at all in common with his contemporaries. And on the other hand, we are to rule out any possibility that Jesus foresaw either the church or his own resurrection. What we have here is a categorical denial of the traditional understanding of Jesus' mission – that he came to die and rise for, and found, the church. It is, moreover, an *a priori* denial! When these twin tests are applied, an enormous amount of teaching attributed to Jesus in the Gospels is *automatically* denied to him before we even start to examine the evidence of the texts themselves. But if the traditional understanding of his mission is at all valid – and surely this possibility ought not to be ruled out *a priori* – the very thing that we should expect to find is that Jesus would have tried to convey to his followers something of the meaning of his death and resurrection and also something about the nature, meaning and conduct of the church. It is right to seek sound historical criteria to help distinguish fact from hearsay and credulity. But these are criteria which could not stand up in any court of law or be used by any sane, secular historian. The whole undertaking is like trying to avoid swallowing germs by drinking carbolic acid.

But in addition to these two criteria, Professor Fuller lists a third. 'When this is done, it is still necessary that authentic sayings of Jesus should be conceivable as developments within Palestinian Judaism. They should use its categories, and if possible reflect the language and style of Aramaic.'[1] The first part of this canon seems to be at variance with what has gone before. For it insists that Jesus *must* have taught things in common with his background. It even denies to Jesus what Fuller is only too anxious to grant to the early church – liberty to teach something *new*. The second part means that Professor Fuller is prepared to entertain as genuine only those passages where the Gospel writers (or their sources) made a *bad* job of translating the original Aramaic into Greek. If a good, idio-

[9] *Ibid.*, p. 18.   [1] *Ibid.*, p. 18.

matic translation has been made, the writer has defeated his own object. The authenticity of his work is automatically suspect. (One wonders what Professor Fuller's students feel when they read this. Do they get better marks when their translations do not read like good English and still retain awkward Greek idioms?) But conversely, for a saying to retain an Aramaic flavour is no guarantee of authenticity. It still could have been devised by *anyone* who spoke Aramaic, on Professor Fuller's premises.

This discussion of R. H. Fuller may seem to have taken us some way off the course of our main discussion. But Fuller is not untypical of the fashionable radical scholar. Our point is to draw attention to the immense importance of criteria and to what in fact lies behind the sceptical pronouncements of a number of modern writers. It could be said of historians – no less than theologians and philosophers – that by their criteria ye shall know them. Of course, we are bound to be sceptical about the foundations of the Christian faith, if we adopt Fuller's criteria. And if we are sceptical, we are bound to abandon it altogether or look around for some substitute philosophy like existentialism to fill the void. But the present writer would submit that, despite the learning and industry that have gone into Fuller's book, the results are useless. It could not be otherwise on his basis. For the tests that he applies can neither prove nor disprove that a single saying of Jesus is authentic.

It has become fashionable today to talk about the 'live options' open to us in theology. The phrase is notoriously question-begging. It relieves its user of the solid slog of thinking out his approach from first principles, and helps to salve his conscience when he ignores the unwelcome opinions of others. We live in an age of mini-commentaries and popular paperbacks of pre-digested theology, when what is needed is scrupulous examination of primary sources. All too often, even in larger books, critical scholars begin by taking for granted certain theories of date and literary dependence, when what is needed is to start with the original text with a truly open mind, ready to examine all possible interpretations. It is not a case of ignoring critical theories, but of looking really critically at everything. It is the belief of the present writer that when this is done, scepticism is unwarranted; but when it is not done, scepticism is very much a 'live option'.

The American liberal theologian John Knox has claimed that historical scholarship could not impair faith.[2] There is, I think, a fallacy here. A faith which goes on believing regardless of the evidence is not a faith worth having. The biblical idea of faith is trust in God because of what God has done and said. If it could be shown that there were no good reasons for believing that God had said or done these things, the faith would be empty and vain. In saying this, we are not tying faith to the latest book of the scholar who happens to be most fashionable at the time. But we are saying that scholarship has a real place. Its job is to strengthen faith by its demonstration of truth (or, if it cannot do this, it should say so plainly and throw faith overboard). In saying this we are only carrying on what the biblical writers themselves were doing. The Bible is not a promise-box full of blessed thoughts. So much of it is devoted to arguments, demonstrations and appeals to history. To get the point, we need think no further than the Epistles of the New Testament or of the opening words of Luke's Gospel which stress the historicity of the story of Jesus as the basis of faith.[3] It is on the truth of such arguments that Christian devotion depends. The ordinary believer is not required to work out all the arguments. But someone has got to do it somewhere for the sake of the faith.

What in fact Luke is doing here – in common with the other Evangelists and historical writers of the Bible – is to do what all good historians attempt to do. He is constructing a model to enable his readers to see what his subject was like.[4] He does

[2] *Criticism and Faith* (Hodder, 1953), p. 9.
[3] 'Inasmuch as many have undertaken to compile a narrative of the things which have been accomplished among us, just as they were delivered to us by those who from the beginning were eyewitnesses and ministers of the word, it seemed good to me also, having followed all things closely for some time past, to write an orderly account for you, most excellent Theophilus, that you may know the truth concerning the things of which you have been informed' (Luke 1:1–4).
[4] There is a sense in which all our mental impressions are like a model of the things they represent. It is only by such means that we are able to think at all about things outside us.

not say everything that there is to be said. The question is immaterial whether he is writing a biography in the modern sense of the term. What matters is his criteria and materials. The finished product is a model, made out of words, through which we may perceive the reality which it represents. If the materials are inaccurate and unreliable, then faith must be shaken. But if investigation shows otherwise, then faith is so much the more well founded. It does not pretend to bring us face to face with God. That is something which is reserved for what Christians call heaven. But without it there can be no knowledge of God. For the historical model, made up of the utterances and pronouncements of Scripture, is the very stuff of revelation. It is through this medium of words, images, ideas and symbols that we come into living contact with God in Christ through the Holy Spirit.

II. THE VALUE AND TASK OF THE PHILOSOPHY MEBER
OF THE CHRISTIAN RELIGION

a. The value of philosophy

What then is the value of philosophy? It seems to be threefold. (1) On the lowest level, philosophy is a form of intellectual P.T. It helps to loosen up the mind. This in itself is no bad thing. Some students make the complaint that philosophy gets you nowhere. The charge is not entirely without justification. So many of the great movements of philosophy have ended up in blind alleys. But at least a study of them shows where the blind alleys are, and in the process anyone who has tried to follow them is bound to have acquired an increased mental agility. He will have become more aware of what counts as a valid argument and what does not. The study of the form of certain arguments and the acquisition of the ability to follow them and evaluate them is a very worth-while pursuit. But just as there are some people who devote their whole lives to P.T., there are also philosophers whose minds never seem to rise above exercises in logic. For most people physical training can never become an end in itself, but it is very useful as a means to greater proficiency in this or that. It is the same with philosophy.

(2) But the value of philosophy does not end there. The study of the history of philosophy is like an exercise in navigation. It helps you to see where you are. By studying the various movements in philosophy and comparing them with the Christian faith we can plot our position on the intellectual map. This does not, of course, apply only to the Christian but to everyone else. If we know something of the history of ideas and the numerous debates surrounding them, we are in a much better position to appreciate and evaluate the ideas and movements of our own day. A striking example of this is presented by the new radicalism. The chance reader who picks up a book like *Honest to God* might think that its ideas are strikingly new. Anyone who is acquainted with the development of European thought in the past two hundred years will know that what is new in the new radicalism is not self-evidently true, and what is true is not particularly new. The point is not that a knowledge of the antiquity of a particular idea will automatically settle its truth for us. But at least it will help us to appreciate it in the context of the history of thought. And knowledge of the debates surrounding it will often help us to weigh up its pros and cons.

A knowledge of the history of ideas will often help us in showing us where they lead. We see this, for example, in the case of Locke's theory of perception. What at first seemed a corrective against the views of the continental rationalists was pushed by Hume to its logical and barren conclusion. We see it in the case of the traditional proofs of the existence of God. What at first sight seemed so clear and convincing leads to an intellectual impasse. The individualistic Existentialism of Kierkegaard was originally designed to salvage Christianity from the ravages of Idealism. But it, too, led to an impoverishment of the faith. Examples could be cited from every chapter and section of our survey.

But for the Christian perhaps the greatest value of a study of the history of philosophy is the way it should help him to see Christianity in perspective. The Christian faith is not a religious form of Platonism, Aristotelianism, Idealism, Existentialism, or any other -ism. And consequently it is neither to be defended nor attacked as such. In the last analysis its validity

depends upon the validity of Christian belief in Christ, the
biblical revelation and all that they entail.

(3) It is with this question of validity that the philosophy of
the Christian religion is concerned, and which gives the subject its importance. Perhaps the unique significance of the
philosophy of the Christian religion could be brought out by
drawing a distinction between *form* and *content*. Disciplines like
biblical theology and systematic theology are concerned with
the *content* of Christian faith. The former investigates the
teaching of the Bible in the light of its historical origins; the
latter seeks to draw together the different strands of biblical
teaching to help us decide what is the biblical view of this or
that question as a whole. Philosophical theology, on the other
hand, is concerned with the *form* of Christian faith. The distinction must not be overpressed and the terms taken in a
way not originally intended. It is not like a tin of Heinz beans,
where the tin is the form in which they come and which, when
opened, may be thrown away. In the case of religious belief
form and *content* go together. You cannot have one without the
other. When we talk about the *form* of Christian faith, we have
in mind its structure and shape: what is involved in faith, revelation and religious language, the relationship of the natural
to the supernatural, as they are found in the Christian religion.
The contention of this essay is that the philosophy of the Christian religion is concerned with the *form* of Christian belief,
that this form is given its essential shape by the content of
Christian belief. It investigates the character, inner logic and
validity of the Christian faith in contrast with other forms of
knowledge.

A good case could be made out for saying that there is no
such subject today as philosophy. It is not a subject in its own
right, such as chemistry, English history, or modern languages.
In the nature of the case it has no autonomous subject-matter.
Philosophy is really always the philosophy of something else,
whether it be the philosophy of science, the philosophy of history or the philosophy of knowledge and communication.
It has no private realm of its own. But it is none the worse for
this. Indeed, it is precisely this which makes it a discipline of
the first importance. For in each case it is concerned with the

validity of the methods and the status of the results of the discipline in question. It is the same with the philosophy of the Christian religion. Its subject-matter is identical with that of biblical and systematic theology. The two are really different ways of looking at the same thing. And this brings us to our last main point: the task of the philosophy of the Christian religion.

b. The task of the philosophy of religion

In the Middle Ages Anselm of Canterbury coined what has become a kind of motto for the Christian approach: *Credo ut intelligam*, 'I believe so that I may understand.' In the thousand years that have elapsed since then there have been many who have parted company with Anselm. It has often looked as if those who have followed in his footsteps have been out on a limb. At various points (such as our discussions of medieval philosophy and the approach of the Reformers) we have tried to weigh up the pros and cons. We shall not repeat the arguments here. But in retrospect Anselm's basic approach seems to be right. It is not a case of proving first and then believing. It is only on the basis of examining the Christian faith itself that we can see its truth. It is precisely the act of belief which puts us in a position to understand what is involved. Admittedly the outsider can see certain things, but he sees them at a distance. He may well be able to evaluate such things as differences of historical method. But in the last analysis, the subject-matter of the philosophy of the Christian religion is our relationship with God. And only those who enjoy a conscious, filial relationship with God in Christ are in a position to know at first-hand what that relationship involves. It is precisely because so many debates in the past and present have tried to talk about God in the abstract that they have become futile and lost all sense of reality. The sceptical philosopher who pontificates about the meaninglessness of religious language in the light of his preconceived, artificial criteria is bound to talk through his hat. He has not put himself in the position of those who use religious language. The task of the philosophy of religion is the descriptive and critical analysis of the act, content and presuppositions of belief.

Because Christians lay claim to a knowledge of God, philosophy of religion will ask what that knowledge claims to consist of, what are its forms, what are its grounds and criteria. It will ask how it compares with other forms of knowledge, such as scientific knowledge. Because Christianity claims to bear witness to the action of God in time and space, philosophy of religion will study the significance and methods of historical research. It will ask in what sense the events of the past can be significant for us today. It will study the techniques and presuppositions of the secular historian and examine their relevance for the study of sacred history. Because Christianity involves communication, the philosophy of religion will pay special attention to the structure and function of language and the part it plays in religious experience. It will seek to analyse the phenomenon of prayer, and the validity of claims that are made that God answers prayer. It will be interested in the credentials of alleged miracles (both biblical and otherwise). The question of the existence of evil is one which each generation has to face. It will be specially interested in the Christian claim that God is the creator of the world and its sustainer in the light of the widespread assumption that the world is to be explained entirely in terms of natural causes.

The study of philosophy is no task for those who have opted out of life. It is a fallacy to think that the only quality needed is impassive detachment. Much more than this is needed by those who would see through the clichés, half-truths, slogans and unquestioned assumptions which confront all of us every day. There are many unsolved problems. Courage, patience, insight and ruthless integrity are required of those who would set about them. But because the Christian is convinced that God is the God of all truth, he will not lose heart.

K

A NOTE ON BOOKS

The purpose of this brief survey of literature available is to provide a guide to some of the more important reference works and specialized studies which anyone wishing to study the subject further may need to consult. Mention of a work obviously does not imply agreement with the author's interpretations and conclusions. Many of them are written from a standpoint very different from that of this book. What follows, therefore, is not a reading list for the Christian approach to philosophy but simply a guide to books where useful information can be found and where systems and views criticized in this volume can be studied at first hand. Details of primary sources and recent editions will be found, of course, in the main body of the text and are not repeated here.

General

There are two basic ways of looking at the philosophy of religion. One is to attempt a historical survey of the main movements, debates and personalities (as here) and to look in passing at whatever problems they throw up. The other is to draw up a list of key problems and discuss them with reference to the relevant movements, debates and thinkers. Among recent works which do the latter are John Hick, *Philosophy of Religion* (Prentice-Hall, Englewood Cliffs, N.J., 1963), Geddes MacGregor, *Introduction to Religious Philosophy* (Macmillan, 1959, and now a paperback) and H. D. Lewis, *Philosophy of Religion* (Teach Yourself Books, EUP, 1965) and *Our Experience of God* (Allen and Unwin, 1959). All have their strong points, though none of them grapples particularly with biblical religion and evangelical belief. Hick is probably the clearest and most concise introduction for the beginner. To this list may be added

Alan Richardson's *Christian Apologetics* (SCM Press, 1947, and numerous reprints), though its title indicates its more specialized interests.

A. Caldecott and H. R. Mackintosh, *Selections from the Literature of Theism* (T. and T. Clark, 1904) was for long the standard anthology of extracts from classical philosophers from Anselm to Ritschl. Although it has been revised to include more recent thinkers, it has now been largely superseded by Ninian Smart, *Historical Selections in the Philosophy of Religion* (SCM Press, 1962, and now a paperback) and John Hick, *Classical and Contemporary Readings in the Philosophy of Religion* (Prentice-Hall, 1964). Both are supplied with clear and helpful notes and comments, though Smart is rather fuller. Whereas Hick arranges his material topic-wise, Smart follows a chronological order. Smart confines himself to writers who are now dead, but Hick includes contemporary thinkers. Obviously, anyone may pick a quarrel with their choice; but their works enable the beginner and general reader to study at first hand the thoughts of the famous. Hick has also edited *The Existence of God* (Macmillan paperback, 1964), which contains many of the great debates from ancient times to the present.

Among the books dealing with philosophy of religion from a historical angle is James Richmond's paperback *Faith and Philosophy* (Hodder and Stoughton, 1966) which begins with Kant and Hume and goes up to the present (though with certain deliberate, conspicuous omissions such as Hegel, Kierkegaard and Tillich). An older but still valuable general survey is J. V. Langmead Casserley, *The Christian in Philosophy* (Faber, 1949, and reprints). His strong point is his interesting discussion of salient points rather than exhaustive classification of minutiae. *God in Modern Philosophy* (Routledge and Kegan Paul, 1960) is a lengthy work by an American professor, James Collins. It should be noted that for all practical purposes his title denotes the period from the Renaissance to the nineteenth century with a few glances into the twentieth. Ninian Smart's *Philosophers and Religious Truth* (SCM Press, 1964) is a brief paperback which singles out for discussion five classical philosophers.

The reader who wants more detailed treatment will often be obliged to turn to the more general studies and reference works. The standard history in English is the work of the Jesuit scholar Frederick Copleston, *A History of Philosophy* (Burns and Oates, 1946–   ). It is a monumental model of painstaking erudition. The first eight volumes cover both secular and religious philosophy from Greece and Rome to the nineteenth century. The work is also being published in smaller paperbacks. It is not Fr. Copleston's intention to extend far into the twentieth century, but he has touched upon aspects of Existentialism and linguistic philosophy in *Contemporary Philosophy* (Burns and Oates, 1956; also in paperback). The standard one-volume history is D. J. O'Connor (ed.), *A Critical History of Western Philosophy* (Free Press, New York, and Collier-Macmillan, 1964). It is the work of an international team of eminent scholars, and combines clarity with detail. Although religious issues crop up, its main interest is more general. Bertrand Russell's mordant *History of Western Philosophy* (Macmillan, 1946, and numerous reprints including paperback) is perhaps the only history of the subject that can be read in bed with pleasure, though his complete lack of sympathy with anything Christian is undisguised.

An interesting work from a Christian standpoint is Bernard Ramm's *Types of Apologetic Systems* (Van Kampen, Wheaton, Ill., 1953), which reviews eight sample types from Aquinas to Van Til. It has reappeared in revised form under the title of *Varieties of Christian Apologetics* (Baker Book House, Grand Rapids, 1961) with certain team changes: Van Til and Carnell are replaced by Calvin and Kuyper.

An important work of reference is *The Encyclopaedia of Philosophy*, edited by Paul Edwards in eight volumes (Macmillan and Free Press, New York and London, 1967). Its high price will make it all but prohibitive for the private reader to buy. But it is certainly worth consulting for philosophy of religion even though its main interest is more general. For the most part the articles are thoroughly up to date and are written in a way which the non-specialist can grasp. On a smaller scale, but very useful, especially on religious matters, are F. L. Cross (ed.), *The Oxford Dictionary of the Christian*

Church (OUP, 1957, and reprints) and Alan Richardson (ed.), *A Dictionary of Christian Theology* (SCM Press, 1969). On an even smaller scale but useful for quick reference are Van A. Harvey, *A Handbook of Theological Terms* (Allen and Unwin, 1966) and Bernard Ramm, *A Handbook of Contemporary Theology* (Eerdmans, Grand Rapids, 1966). The most recent editions of the *Encyclopaedia Britannica* contain some first-class articles on numerous matters relating to philosophy.

Two paperback series deserve mention, although neither is specifically concerned with philosophy of religion. *The Mentor Philosophers* (New American Library, New York) consists of six volumes giving selections from leading thinkers with introductions and comments. The *Pelican Philosophy Series* consists chiefly of essays written by leading contemporary philosophers on famous thinkers of the past. There is no single series which gives a representative selection of Christian thought from the earliest times to the present, but *The Library of Christian Classics* (SCM Press and Westminster Press) gives an excellent selection of writings in modern translation from the early church to the Reformation. A series which starts more or less where the latter stops is *A Library of Protestant Thought* (OUP, New York). A series which so far has concentrated chiefly on philosophical theology is Black's *Library of Modern Religious Thought*. Mention may also be made of the SCM Press's *Library of Philosophy and Theology*, which is devoted largely to contemporary writing. Several of its more outstanding volumes are mentioned in the present work individually under their author and title.

Medieval Philosophy

Our chapter on the Middle Ages began with a backward glance at the early church and classical Greek philosophy. The standard work on the thought of the early church is J. N. D. Kelly, *Early Christian Doctrines* (Black, 1968[4]). For background see Henry Chadwick, *The Early Church* (Pelican, 1968) and B. Altaner, *Patrology* (Herder-Nelson, 1960). For brief discussions of classical thought see W. K. C. Guthrie, *The Greek Philosophers from Thales to Aristotle* (Methuen, 1950) and A. H. Armstrong and R. A. Markus, *Christian Faith and*

Greek Philosophy (Darton, Longman and Todd, 1960). Guthrie is also producing a five-volume *History of Greek Philosophy* (CUP, 1962–). A. H. Armstrong has also edited *The Cambridge History of Later Greek and Early Medieval Thought* (1967). Paul Tillich, *A History of Christian Thought* (SCM Press, 1968) is a series of lectures edited by Carl Braaten on the period up to the Reformation.

The handiest general introduction to medieval history is G. S. M. Walker's *The Growing Storm: Sketches of Church History from A.D. 600 to A.D. 1350* (Paternoster Press, 1961), while the two best introductions to the thinking of the period are Gordon Leff, *Medieval Thought: St. Augustine to Ockham* (Pelican, 1958) and David Knowles, *The Evolution of Medieval Thought* (Longmans, 1962, and reprints including paperback). A standard work is Étienne Gilson, *History of Christian Philosophy in the Middle Ages* (Sheed and Ward, 1955).

For a pocket version of the writers themselves there is Richard McKeon's *Selections from Medieval Philosophers* (Scribner's, 2 vols., 1957² and 1958²). The second volume contains a useful Latin-English glossary of technical terms. In discussing Aquinas mention was made of the new definitive Latin-English version of the *Summa Theologiae*. In all Thomas wrote nearly one hundred works. The most convenient compend for most students will be the two volumes edited by Thomas Gilby, *St. Thomas Aquinas: Philosophical Texts* (OUP, 1951) and *Theological Texts* (1955). H. A. Obermann, *Forerunners of the Reformation: The Shape of Late Medieval Thought, Illustrated by Key Documents* (Lutterworth Press, 1967) gives unusual insight into the ferment before the Reformation. On the outlook of Renaissance thinkers see *The Renaissance Philosophy of Man*, edited by E. Cassirer, P. O. Kristeller and J. H. Randall, Jr. (University of Chicago Press, 1948).

From the Reformation to the Age of Enlightenment
For books on the teaching of the Reformers and their successors see above, pp. 41–45. Fascinating glimpses into their thinking and progress (and that of their adversaries) can be got from Hans J. Hillerbrand, *The Reformation in its Own Words* (SCM Press, 1964). Owen Chadwick's *The Reformation*

(Pelican, 1964) is a useful pocket-size history of the period, though it is not always sympathetic to the theology of the Reformers.

The best sketch of theological trends from the sixteenth century to the present is Alan Richardson's *The Bible in the Age of Science* (SCM Press paperback, 1961). Among the surveys covering part or the whole of the period of the seventeenth and eighteenth centuries are Paul Hazard, *The European Mind, 1680–1715* (Pelican, 1964) and *European Thought in the Eighteenth Century: from Montesquieu to Lessing* (Hollis and Carter, 1954); Ernst Cassirer, *The Philosophy of the Enlightenment* (Beacon Press, Boston, 1955); W. R. Sorley, *A History of British Philosophy to 1900* (CUP, 1920; paperback, 1965); John Tulloch, *Rational Theology and Christian Philosophy in England in the Seventeenth Century*, 2 vols. (1872); Sir Leslie Stephen's *History of English Thought in the Eighteenth Century*, 2 vols. (1876; Hart-Davis paperback, 1962); G. R. Cragg, *Reason and Authority in the Eighteenth Century* (CUP, 1964); R. N. Stromberg's *Religious Liberalism in Eighteenth-Century England* (OUP, 1954); and Basil Willey's *The Seventeenth Century Background* and *The Eighteenth Century Background* (Chatto and Windus, 1934 and 1940; now in Peregrine paperbacks).

For those who would like to sample the writings of the period at first hand, J. M. Creed and J. S. Boys Smith give an interesting selection in *Religious Thought in the Eighteenth Century, Illustrated from Writers of the Period* (CUP, 1934). For American thought see Paul Kurtz (ed.), *American Thought before 1900: A Source Book from Puritanism to Darwinism* (Macmillan, 1966) and Herbert W. Schneider, *A History of American Philosophy* (Columbia University Press, 1963²).

The Nineteenth Century

The religious thought of the nineteenth century may be studied at first hand in two recent anthologies: B. M. G. Reardon, *Religious Thought in the Nineteenth Century* (CUP, 1966) and A. O. J. Cockshut, *Religious Controversies of the Nineteenth Century* (Methuen, 1966). Cockshut has also written a study of secular thinkers, *The Unbelievers* (Collins, 1964), and Reardon has edited an anthology of *Liberal Protestantism*

(Black, 1968). Standard background works are Basil Willey's *Nineteenth Century Studies* and *More Nineteenth Century Studies* (Chatto and Windus, 1949 and 1956). Essential reading on this period is Karl Barth's *From Rousseau to Ritschl: Being the Translation of Eleven Chapters of Die Protestantische Theologie im 19. Jahrhundert* (SCM Press, 1959). As the title indicates, it goes well back into the eighteenth century. The English version covers scarcely half of the German original which gives even fuller coverage to theological issues. By comparison Paul Tillich's posthumous lectures on *Perspectives on Nineteenth and Twentieth Century Protestant Theology*, edited by Carl E. Braaten (SCM Press, 1967) looks rather pale and thin, even though Tillich is much nearer in sympathy to the thought he is describing. An older survey of similar scope which has not entirely been superseded is H. R. Mackintosh's *Types of Modern Theology: Schleiermacher to Barth* (Nisbet, 1937; now a Fontana paperback). John Passmore, *A Hundred Years of Philosophy* (Duckworth, 1957) is a basic introduction to secular thought.

The standard survey of revelation and authority in modern thought is the two volumes of H. D. McDonald, *Ideas of Revelation: An Historical Study, A.D. 1700 to A.D. 1860* (Macmillan, 1959) and *Theories of Revelation: An Historical Study, 1860–1960* (Allen and Unwin, 1963). For trends in theological and critical thought see also V. F. Storr, *The Development of English Theology in the Nineteenth Century: 1800–1860* (Longmans, 1913); Albert Schweitzer, *The Quest of the Historical Jesus: A Critical Study of its Progress from Reimarus to Wrede* (Black, 1910, 1954[3]) and *Paul and his Interpreters* (Black, 1912, 1956); Stephen Neill, *The Interpretation of the New Testament, 1861–1961* (OUP, 1964; now in paperback); Alec R. Vidler, *The Church in An Age of Revolution: 1789 to the Present Day* (Pelican, 1961); Walter Kaufmann (ed.), *Religion from Tolstoy to Camus* (Harper Torchbook, 1964[2]); A. M. Ramsey, *From Gore to Temple: The Development of Anglican Theology between Lux Mundi and the Second World War, 1889–1939* (Longmans, 1960); and J. K. Mozley, *Some Tendencies in British Theology: From Lux Mundi to the Present Day* (SPCK, 1962).

A recent detailed survey of secular thought is Karl Löwith's *From Hegel to Nietzsche: The Revolution in Nineteenth-Century*

Thought (Constable, 1964). There have been many recent studies of individual thinkers, and it is invidious trying to draw up a short list. But mention may be made of the following: R. R. Niebuhr, *Schleiermacher on Christ and Religion* (SCM Press, 1965); Walter Kaufmann, *Hegel: Reinterpretation, Texts and Commentary* (Weidenfeld and Nicolson, 1965); Sir Isaiah Berlin, *Karl Marx: His Life and Environment* (OUP, 1939, and revised editions); R. E. D. Clark, *Darwin: Before and After* (Paternoster Press, 1948; now in paperback); G. E. and G. B. Arbaugh, *Kierkegaard's Authorship: A Guide to the Writings of Kierkegaard* (Allen and Unwin, 1968); and Paul Sponheim, *Kierkegaard on Christ and Christian Conscience* (SCM Press, 1968). In the United States Sponheim's book is published by Harper and Row as part of a series on *Makers of Modern Theology*. Other titles include P. C. Hodgson, *The Formation of Historical Theology: A Study of Ferdinand Christian Baur* (1966); P. Hefner, *Faith and the Vitalities of History: A Theological Study based upon the Work of Albrecht Ritschl* (1966); and G. Wayne Glick, *The Reality of Christianity: A Study of Adolf von Harnack as Historian and Theologian* (1967).

The Twentieth Century

Some of the more important surveys have already been mentioned, since they overlap the nineteenth and twentieth centuries. John Macquarrie's *Twentieth-Century Religious Thought: The Frontiers of Philosophy and Theology, 1900–1960* (SCM Press, 1963) is a kind of mini-encyclopaedia which pigeonholes everybody and everything that has happened within its appointed span. As a companion piece Macquarrie has edited *Contemporary Religious Thinkers: From Idealist Metaphysicians to Existential Theologians* (SCM Press, 1968). For those who prefer more of an essay-type approach Leslie Paul's *Alternatives to Christian Belief: A Critical Survey of the Contemporary Search for Meaning* (Hodder and Stoughton, 1967) covers not only philosophers but psychologists and writers as well.

For a shrewd and amusing assessment of the contemporary scene the writings of the Indian journalist Ved Mehta are strongly recommended. He is of Hindu extraction and has studied at Oxford and Harvard. As a journalist on the staff of the *New Yorker* he was commissioned to write two series of articles, first on philosophers and historians and then on theologians. The result was *Fly and the Fly-Bottle: Encounters with British Intellectuals* (Weidenfeld and Nicolson, 1963; Pelican, 1965) and *The New Theologian* (Weidenfeld and Nicolson, 1966; Pelican, 1968). His work is based on personal interviews and his own reading. Definitely not to be missed.

The best all-round survey of modern theologians is the symposium edited by P. E. Hughes, *Creative Minds in Contemporary Theology* (Eerdmans, Grand Rapids, 1966; enlarged edition, 1968). S. Paul Schilling's *Contemporary Continental Theologians* (SCM Press, 1966) is rather narrower in scope and less incisive, but it introduces the reader to a number of less well-known writers. On a decidedly smaller scale Daniel Day Williams, *Interpreting Theology, 1918–1952* (SCM Press, 1953) and Alec R. Vidler, *20th Century Defenders of the Faith: Some Theological Fashions* (SCM Press, 1965) give more general impressions. *Theologians of our Time*, edited by A. W. and E. Hastings (T. and T. Clark, 1966) contains reprints of articles on twenty-one theologians which first appeared in *The Expository Times*. John Bowden and James Richmond give a handy collection of modern philosophical theology in *A Reader in Contemporary Theology* (SCM Press, 1967). For a cross-section of contemporary American thought see Dean Peerman (ed.), *Frontline Theology* (SCM Press, 1967), in which eleven thinkers (most of whom are various shades of radical) write on 'How I am making up my mind'.

The series of *Makers of Contemporary Theology* (formerly published by the Carey Kingsgate Press and now by Lutterworth Press) is an interesting collection of readable pen-portraits and essays. In about fifty pages the reader is introduced to the life and main ideas of an influential thinker. So far the series includes Ian Henderson, *Rudolf Bultmann* (1965); J. Heywood Thomas, *Paul Tillich* (1965); Sam Keen, *Gabriel Marcel* (1966); Bernard Towers, *Teilhard de Chardin* (1966); E. H. Robertson, *Dietrich Bonhoeffer* (1966); Ronald Gregor Smith, *Martin Buber* (1966); Donald Hudson, *Ludwig Wittgenstein* (1968); and John Macquarrie, *Martin Heidegger* (1968).

A number of series dealing with philosophical theology are

at present mushrooming up. On a fairly technical level *New Frontiers in Theology: Discussion among German and American Theologians*, edited by J. M. Robinson and J. B. Cobb, Jr. (Harper and Row) brings together papers by leading scholars on both sides of the Atlantic. The specialist student will also be interested in the *Journal for Theology and Church*, edited by Robert W. Funk in association with Gerhard Ebeling (Harper and Row, New York, and J. C. B. Mohr, Tübingen) which is virtually a series of paperback books containing reprints from the *Zeitschrift für Theologie und Kirche*. Somewhat more popular are *New Directions in Theology Today*, 7 vols. edited by William Hordern (Lutterworth Press) and the Epworth Press's *New Reformation Series*. The volumes which have appeared so far in such series are at best essays and sketches. The reader who ploughs his way through them will come across many suggestive ideas. But as often as not, he will have to evaluate them for himself, especially when it comes to asking what biblical justification there might be for the writer's position. And if he wants an over-all picture of Christian faith today, he will have to do it himself.

Perhaps the best beginner's guides to secular philosophy today are G. J. Warnock's *English Philosophy since 1900* (Home University Library, OUP, 1958) and Mary Warnock's *Ethics since 1900* (HUL, OUP, 1960). On a larger scale there are several symposia which survey the contemporary scene: C. A. Mace (ed.), *British Philosophy in Mid-Century* (1957); Ian Ramsey (ed.), *Prospect for Metaphysics* (1961); *Contemporary British Philosophy*, Third Series edited by H. D. Lewis (1956) (the first two series being published in the 1920s). All these are published by Allen and Unwin. On American thought Paul Kurtz has provided a sequel to his earlier volume which covered the period up to 1900 in *American Philosophy in the Twentieth Century. A Sourcebook from Pragmatism to Philosophical Analysis* (Macmillan, 1967).

A great deal has been written on religious language. Among the most important books are: Antony Flew and Alasdair MacIntyre (eds.), *New Essays in Philosophical Theology* (SCM Press, 1955; now in paperback); Basil Mitchell (ed.), *Faith and Logic* (Allen and Unwin, 1957); Ian T. Ramsey, *Religious*

Language (SCM Press, 1957); E. L. Mascall, *Words and Images* (Longmans, 1957); Sidney Hook (ed.), *Religious Experience and Truth* (Oliver and Boyd, 1962); Frederick Ferré, *Language, Logic and God* (Eyre and Spottiswoode, 1962); Donald D. Evans, *The Logic of Self-Involvement* (SCM Press, 1963); William Hordern, *Speaking of God* (Epworth Press, 1964); Hugo Meynell, *Sense, Nonsense and Christianity* (Sheed and Ward, 1964); J. A. Martin, *The New Dialogue between Philosophy and Theology* (Black, 1966); and J. Macquarrie, *God-Talk* (SCM Press, 1967). W. P. Alston's *Philosophy of Language* (Prentice-Hall, 1964) is probably the best introduction to language in general.

There are numerous books dealing with Existentialism. Often they begin by probing its nineteenth-century background. A very useful introductory volume containing extracts of key writings is Walter Kaufmann's paperback, *Existentialism from Dostoevsky to Sartre* (World Publishing Company, Cleveland and New York, 1956, and reprints). Other discussions include H. J. Blackham, *Six Existentialist Thinkers* (Routledge, 1952; paperback, 1961); F. H. Heinemann, *Existentialism and the Modern Predicament* (Black, 1954^2); William Barrett, *Irrational Man: A Study in Existential Philosophy* (Heinemann, 1961) and Mary Warnock, *The Philosophy of Sartre* (Hutchinson, 1965). Karl Jaspers has expounded his own approach at some length in *Philosophical Faith and Revelation* (Collins, 1967).

Axel Hägerstrom's *Philosophy and Religion* (Allen and Unwin, 1964) is representative of the anti-metaphysical philosophy which grew up in Sweden at the University of Uppsala in the first half of the century. It is comparable with Logical Positivism. This volume of essays is prefaced by a memoir of their author by C. D. Broad.

With regard to works on individual British philosophers the following are written on a fairly popular level with the accent on biography: Norman Malcolm, *Ludwig Wittgenstein: A Memoir, with a Biographical Sketch by G. H. von Wright* (Oxford paperback, 1958); Alan Wood, *Bertrand Russell: The Passionate Sceptic* (1957) and H. Gottschalk, *Bertrand Russell: A Life* (1965) (both the latter are now Unwin paperbacks). On a larger scale, though not always more critical, is Ralph

Schoenman (ed.), *Bertrand Russell: Philosopher of the Century* (Allen and Unwin, 1967). Russell is also producing his own multi-volume autobiography. Alan R. White's *G. E. Moore: A Critical Exposition* (Blackwell, 1958) and George Pitcher, *The Philosophy of Wittgenstein* (Prentice-Hall, 1964) are fairly technical but readable studies.

Books on contemporary philosophical theologians are legion, and it is often very difficult to say which are the best buys. In some cases there are at least half a dozen books of roughly equal merits each devoted to a particular thinker. To save space, we shall refer the reader back to relevant sections of the text and ration ourselves to mentioning a maximum of four further books on each thinker.

In the inter-war years William Temple was one of the most fashionable philosophical theologians, but since then his influence has sharply dipped. A recent reassessment is Owen C. Thomas, *William Temple's Philosophy of Religion* (SPCK, 1961). The standard life by F. A. Iremonger, *William Temple, Archbishop of Canterbury* (OUP, 1948), contains a chapter on Temple as a philosopher by Dorothy Emmet. The best study of Schweitzer is probably Werner Picht, *Albert Schweitzer: The Man and his Work* (Allen and Unwin, 1964).

Studies of Tillich are best read with his *Systematic Theology* and a volume of his sermons open on the table before you. Bernard Martin's *Paul Tillich's Doctrine of Man* (Nisbet, 1966) is the work of a perceptive Jewish scholar who thinks that Tillich abandons the historic Christian position. The title of the symposium, *Paul Tillich and Catholic Thought*, edited by T. A. O'Meara and C. D. Weisser (Darton, Longman and Todd, 1965) is self-explanatory. It contains an 'afterword' by Tillich himself and a foreword by J. Heywood Thomas, who in addition to the small sketch already mentioned has written a full-scale critique, *Paul Tillich: An Appraisal* (SCM Press, 1963). *The Theology of Paul Tillich*, edited by C. W. Kegley and R. W. Bretall (Macmillan paperback, New York, 1961), is an important symposium to which Tillich himself has contributed an autobiographical reflection and a reply to criticisms.

On Bonhoeffer there is the doctorate thesis by the American J. D. Godsey, *The Theology of Dietrich Bonhoeffer* (SCM Press, 1960), and several symposia. *I Knew Dietrich Bonhoeffer*, edited by W. D. Zimmermann and R. G. Smith (Collins, 1967) contains personal reminiscences and views of friends and colleagues. The paperback edited by Martin E. Marty, *The Place of Bonhoeffer* (SCM Press, 1963) is largely the work of American scholars, while *World Come of Age*, edited by R. G. Smith (Collins, 1967), brings together essays chiefly by British and continental theologians.

An Introduction to the Theology of Rudolf Bultmann (SCM Press, 1968) is based upon lectures given by a disciple and former pupil, Walther Schmithals, in honour of Bultmann's eightieth birthday. More advanced is the symposium edited by C. W. Kegley, *The Theology of Rudolf Bultmann* (SCM Press, 1966) which contains an autobiographical reflection and a reply by the subject himself. Earlier studies include L. Malevez, *The Christian Message and Myth* (SCM Press, 1958), and H. P. Owen, *Revelation and Existence* (University of Wales, 1957). John Macquarrie has written on themes raised by Bultmann and Existentialism generally in *An Existentialist Theology* (SCM Press, 1955), *The Scope of Demythologizing* (SCM Press, 1960) and *Studies in Christian Existentialism* (SCM Press, 1966).

Something new either on or by Teilhard de Chardin seems to appear every other month. Robert Speaight's *Teilhard de Chardin, A Biography* (Collins, 1967) and C. F. Mooney's *Teilhard de Chardin and the Mystery of Christ* (Collins, 1966) are fair-sized, readable, non-technical introductions. Claude Cuénot's *Teilhard de Chardin: A Biographical Study* (Burns and Oates, 1965) and Émile Rideau's *Teilhard de Chardin: A Guide to his Thought* (Collins, 1967) are well-nigh definitive. All four are written by Catholics and all four are very sympathetic. Although there are many who query Teilhard's mixture of theology, philosophy and science, a detailed critique has yet to appear from this quarter.

T. F. Torrance's *Karl Barth: An Introduction to his Early Theology, 1910-1931* (SCM Press, 1962) is important for understanding not only Barth but also Dialectical Theology in the 1920s. Herbert Hartwell, *The Theology of Karl Barth* (Duck-

worth, 1964) gives a concise, sympathetic introduction, while
G. C. Berkouwer's *The Triumph of Grace in the Theology of Karl
Barth* (Paternoster Press, 1956; now in paperback) sees the
leit-motiv of Barth's thought in terms of all-triumphant grace.
Barth himself has rejected this as being too abstract, but has
commended the study. The present writer has attempted to
analyse the main themes of Barth's teaching and their relevance to thought today in *Karl Barth and the Christian Message*
(Tyndale Press, 1967).

Books on other thinkers and theologians include C. W.
Kegley's symposium on *The Theology of Emil Brunner* (Macmillan, New York, 1962) which follows the same pattern as the
other volumes in the *Library of Living Theology* edited by Kegley
and Bretall; P. K. Jewett, *Emil Brunner's Concept of Revelation*
(James Clarke, 1954); C. W. Kegley and R. W. Bretall (eds.),
Reinhold Niebuhr: His Religious, Social and Political Thought
(Macmillan, New York, 1956, paperback, 1961); June Bing-
ham, *Courage to Change: An Introduction to the Life and Thought
of Reinhold Niebuhr* (Scribner's, New York and SCM Press,
1961); Clyde S. Kilby, *The Christian World of C. S. Lewis* (Mar-
cham Manor Press, 1965); Michael de la Bedoyère, *The Life
of Baron von Hügel* (Dent, 1951); James Carpenter, *Gore: A
Study in Liberal Catholic Thought* (Faith Press, 1960); and F. G.
Healey's *Religion and Reality: The Theology of John Oman* (Oliver
and Boyd, 1965). These writers have figured only on the fringe
of the present study, but these books are mentioned for the
sake of the interested reader who would like to know more
about them.

There are several books on the more radical versions of
Christianity. Two of the most important are by E. L. Mascall
who writes with great acumen and learning from an orthodox
Catholic position. *The Secularisation of Christianity: An Analysis
and a Critique* (Darton, Longman and Todd, 1965) deals at
some length with Paul van Buren and *Honest to God*, but includes a positive statement on science, the secular and the
supernatural and on the historicity of the Gospels. His earlier
paperback, *Up and Down in Adria* (Faith Press, 1963) was a
reply to *Soundings*. *The Honest to God Debate*, edited by David
L. Edwards (SCM Press, 1963) is a largish, but by no means

complete, anthology of reviews and reactions to the said book together with a reply by its author. Thomas W. Ogletree gives a brief introduction to the 'death of God school' in America in *The 'Death of God' Controversy* (SCM Press, 1966). Conservative replies to the school have come from Kenneth Hamilton, *God is Dead: The Anatomy of a Slogan* (Eerdmans, Grand Rapids, 1966) and J. W. Montgomery, *The 'Is God Dead?' Controversy* (Zondervan, Grand Rapids, 1966). Thomas J. J. Altizer and William Hamilton have restated their case in *Radical Theology and the Death of God* (Pelican, 1968). *God in Process* by Norman Pittenger (SCM Press, 1967) is a brief non-technical introduction to Process Philosophy by a leading member of that school.

Books on Special Topics

Antony Flew's *God and Philosophy* (Hutchinson, paperback, 1966) is devoted to attacking arguments based upon both philosophy and revelation. H. P. Owen restates a philosophical approach in *The Moral Argument for Christian Theism* (Allen and Unwin, 1965), while Helmut Gollwitzer surveys recent thought on *The Existence of God, as Confessed by Faith* (SCM Press, 1965). R. W. Hepburn's *Christianity and Paradox* (Watts, 1958) is sympathetic but finds difficulties in the Christian case. Edward Farley, *The Transcendence of God* (Epworth Press, 1962) gives an introduction to modern debates. Victor White's *God the Unknown* (Harvill Press, 1966) restates the Roman Catholic position making use of natural theology. His earlier book, *God and the Unconscious* (1952; now in Fontana paperback) contains an appreciative foreword by C. G. Jung. A pre-war review of different viewpoints which has gone through numerous editions and is still helpful though somewhat dated is John Baillie's *Our Knowledge of God* (OUP, 1939). David Jenkins's *Guide to the Debate about God* (Lutterworth Press, 1966) is a chatty conducted tour from Bishop Butler to Bonhoeffer.

F. H. Cleobury has made a lucid plea for *A Return to Natural Theology* (James Clarke, 1967). In *Theological Explanation* (Nisbet, 1958) G. F. Woods compares the types of explanation used in science, history and theology. John Hick's *Faith and*

Knowledge (Macmillan, 1967²) reviews different approaches and attempts his own restatement, while his symposium *Faith and the Philosophers* (Macmillan, 1964) brings together the papers and discussions of a conference at Princeton. Other modern discussions of belief and philosophy include J. V. Langmead Casserley, *Graceful Reason* (Longmans, 1955); Nels F. S. Ferré, *Reason in Religion* (Nelson, 1963); Carl Michalson, *The Rationality of Faith* (SCM Press, 1964); Dom Illtyd Trethowan, *An Essay in Christian Philosophy* (Longmans, 1954); Dorothy M. Emmet, *The Nature of Metaphysical Thinking* (Macmillan, 1945); and D. Z. Phillips's anthology *Religion and Understanding* (Blackwell, 1967). An evangelical approach to faith, reason and authority is outlined by J. I. Packer in *'Fundamentalism' and the Word of God. Some Evangelical Principles* (IVF, 1958).

There is no single exhaustive treatment on miracles, but several books give suggestive leads. They include C. S. Lewis's *Miracles* (1947, now in Fontana paperback); B. B. Warfield's *Miracles: Yesterday and Today, True and False* (Eerdmans, Grand Rapids, 1954; formerly published as *Counterfeit Miracles*); Alan Richardson's *The Miracle Stories of the Gospels* (SCM Press, 1941, and paperback reprints); C. F. D. Moule (ed.), *Miracles: Cambridge Studies in their Philosophy and History* (Mowbray, 1965); D. J. West's *Eleven Lourdes Miracles* (Duckworth, 1957); V. Edmunds and C. G. Scorer, *Some Thoughts on Faith-Healing* (Tyndale Press, 1966²); and J. S. Lawton's valuable historical survey of different attitudes to the miraculous since the rise of modern science, *Miracles and Revelation* (Lutterworth Press, 1959).

The body-mind relationship has received a good deal of philosophical attention in recent years. Gilbert Ryle subjected naïve ideas to sharp scrutiny in *The Concept of Mind* (1949; Peregrine paperback, 1963). Another important study of the post-Positivist era is P. F. Strawson's *Individuals* (Methuen, 1959). *On Selfhood and Godhood* was the subject of C. A. Campbell's Gifford Lectures (Allen and Unwin, 1957). H. D. McDonald has surveyed the field from an evangelical standpoint in *I and He* (Epworth Press, 1966). Austin Farrer devoted his Gifford Lectures to a philosophical examination of

The Freedom of the Will (Black, 1958). More recently D. M. MacKay gave his Eddington Memorial Lecture on *Freedom of Action in a Mechanistic Universe* (CUP, 1967). But alongside these philosophical treatments the student of religion should read Martin Luther's theological exposition of *The Bondage of the Will*, translated with an introduction by J. I. Packer and O. R. Johnston (James Clarke, 1957).

John Hick has given a massive survey of different approaches in *Evil and the God of Love* (Macmillan, 1966). Although the view he finally adopts seems less satisfactory than some of the others that he mentions, his book is likely to remain for many years the standard work. A recent important study of prayer from a philosophical standpoint is D. Z. Phillips, *The Concept of Prayer* (Routledge, 1965).

A subject which is receiving increasing attention is that of history. The most important British work on the subject is Alan Richardson's Bampton Lectures on *History: Sacred and Profane* (SCM Press, 1964). Richardson's approach is itself the subject of a doctorate thesis by a Catholic scholar, John Navone, *History and Faith in the Thought of Alan Richardson* (SCM Press, 1966). Secular approaches to the science of history include E. H. Carr's racy Pelican paperback, *What is History?* (1964[2]); R. G. Collingwood's *The Idea of History* (Oxford paperback, 1961); William H. Dray's introductory textbook *Philosophy of History* (Prentice-Hall, 1964) and his symposium *Philosophical Analysis and History* (Harper and Row, 1966). Radical Christian approaches include R. R. Niebuhr's *Resurrection and Historical Reason* (Scribner's, 1957) and Van A. Harvey, *The Historian and the Believer* (SCM Press, 1967). H. D. Lewis's *Freedom and History* (Allen and Unwin, 1962) is a collection of papers on more or less related subjects. T. A. Roberts, *History and Christian Apologetics* (SPCK, 1960) adopts a positivistic approach. J. W. Montgomery's *The Shape of the Past* (Edwards Brothers, Ann Arbor, Michigan, 1962) and Daniel Fuller's *Easter Faith and History* (Tyndale Press, 1968) are works by American evangelical scholars.

The borderland between science and religion has been a well-trodden battleground in the last hundred years. A useful book for putting the debates in perspective is Charles Singer,

A Short History of Scientific Ideas to 1900 (OUP, 1959; paperback, 1961). On the battle itself see John Dillenberger, *Protestant Thought and Natural Science* (Collins, 1961); D. L. Dye, *Faith and the Physical World* (Paternoster Press, 1968); E. L. Mascall, *Christian Faith and Natural Science* (Longmans, 1956); J. S. Habgood, *Religion and Science* (Mills and Boon, 1964); A. F. Smethurst, *Modern Science and Christian Beliefs* (Nisbet, 1955); and Ian G. Barbour, *Issues in Science and Religion* (SCM Press, 1968²). A radical view of religion is taken by T. R. Miles in *Religion and the Scientific Outlook* (Allen and Unwin, 1959) and a downright hostile one by Alan Isaacs in *The Survival of God in the Scientific Age* (Pelican, 1966). A book which throws light on passages in the Bible where difficulties have been found in the past is Bernard Ramm's *The Christian View of Science and Scripture* (Paternoster Press, 1955; now in paperback). More briefly *Christianity in a Mechanistic Universe and Other Essays*, D. M. MacKay (ed.) (IVF, 1965) contains four studies by Christians holding scientific chairs in British universities. Also of interest are R. E. D. Clark's *The Universe: Plan or Accident?* (Paternoster Press, 1949; revised as a paperback) and *The Christian Stake in Science* (Paternoster Press, 1968).

Ethics is also a borderland subject between philosophy and religion. Historical surveys include Jacques Maritain, *Moral Philosophy: A Historical and Critical Survey of the Great Systems* (Bles, 1964) and the paperback by Alasdair MacIntyre, *A Short History of Ethics* (Routledge, 1967). Standard textbooks on the general problems of ethics include A. C. Ewing, *Ethics* (Teach Yourself Books, EUP, 1953); P. Nowell-Smith, *Ethics* (Pelican, 1954); and W. Frankena, *Ethics* (Prentice-Hall, 1963). An up-to-date handbook covering a wide range of moral and religious questions with articles on important thinkers is *A Dictionary of Christian Ethics*, edited by John Macquarrie (SCM Press, 1967).

R. M. Hare, *The Language of Morals* (1952; Oxford paperback, 1964) applies linguistic philosophy to moral problems. Brand Blanshard's *Reason and Goodness* (Allen and Unwin, 1961) restates the older Idealist position. The anthology edited by Ian T. Ramsey, *Christian Ethics and Contemporary*

Philosophy (SCM Press, 1966), is perhaps the best all-round introduction to the ethical debates of modern philosophy on a technical level. The full-blown radical position is argued by the American Joseph Fletcher in *Situation Ethics: The New Morality* (SCM Press, 1966) and *Moral Responsibility: Situation Ethics at Work* (SCM Press, 1967). A shrewd if somewhat earlier reply to the radical position appears in Arnold Lunn and Garth Lean, *The New Morality* (Blandford Press, 1964). Other recent studies include Paul L. Lehmann, *Ethics in a Christian Context* (SCM Press, 1962); G. F. Woods, *A Defence of Theological Ethics* (CUP, 1966); G. F. Thomas, *Christian Ethics and Moral Philosophy* (Scribner's, 1965); W. G. Maclagan, *The Theological Frontier of Ethics* (Allen and Unwin, 1961) and H. D. Lewis, *Morals and Revelation* (1951) and *Freedom and History* (1962) (both Allen and Unwin). The paperback edited by A. W. and E. Hastings, *Important Moral Issues* (T. and T. Clark, 1966) contains reprints of articles which first appeared in *The Expository Times*. A series which aims to provide adequate introductions to various subjects at a non-technical level in a fairly short space is Macmillan's *New Studies in Ethics*.

Surveys of biblical teaching include L. H. Marshall, *The Challenge of New Testament Ethics* (Macmillan, 1947; paperback reprint); William Lillie, *Studies in New Testament Ethics* (Oliver and Boyd, 1961); and Rudolf Schnackenburg, *The Moral Teaching of the New Testament* (Herder and Burns and Oates, 1965). Approaches to modern problems from a biblical standpoint include John Murray, *Principles of Conduct* (Tyndale Press, 1957); Carl Henry's massive *Christian Personal Ethics* (1957) and much briefer *Aspects of Christian Social Ethics* (1964) (both Eerdmans, Grand Rapids); William Lillie, *The Law of Christ: The Christian Ethic and Modern Problems* (Saint Andrew Press, 1966²); and Helmut Thielicke, *Theological Ethics*, Vol. I, *Foundations* (Black, 1967).

Addenda

Since the first edition of this book a number of important works have appeared. Antony Flew's *An Introduction to Western Philosophy: Ideas and Argument from Plato to Sartre* (Thames and

Hudson, 1971) will doubtless establish itself as a standard, general introduction. Studies of particular questions and thinkers include: H. P. Owen, *The Christian Knowledge of God* (University of London, 1969); H. D. Lewis, *The Elusive Mind* (Allen and Unwin, 1969); H. H. Price, *Belief* (Allen and Unwin, 1969); I. Trethowan, *Absolute Value: A Study in Christian Theism* (Allen and Unwin, 1970); J. N. Findlay, *Ascent to the Absolute* (Allen and Unwin, 1970); Stuart C. Brown, *Do Religious Claims Make Sense?* (SCM, 1969); K. T. Fann, ed., *Symposium on J. L. Austin* (Routledge, 1969); Peter Winch, ed., *Studies in the Philosophy of Wittgenstein* (Routledge, 1969); C. A. van Peursen, *Ludwig Wittgenstein: An Introduction to his Philosophy* (Faber, 1969); D. F. Pears, *Bertrand Russell and the British Tradition in Philosophy* (Fontana, 1967); the *Royal Institute of Philosophy Lectures* (Macmillan) on *The Human Agent* (1968) and *Talk of God* (1969); C. W. K. Mundle, *A Critique of Linguistic Philosophy* (OUP, 1970); S. Körner, *What is Philosophy?* (Penguin, 1969); A. Boyce Gibson, *Theism and Empiricism* (SCM, 1970); Charles Hartshorne, *Creative Synthesis and Philosophic Method* (SCM, 1970); and Malcolm Jeeves, *The Scientific Enterprise and Christian Faith* (Tyndale Press, 1969). Bernard Jones's *Earnest Enquiries after Truth* (Allen and Unwin, 1971) is an anthology of excerpts from past Gifford Lectures on natural theology. Ian T. Ramsey's *Words about God: The Philosophy of Religion* (SCM, 1971) gives extracts on religious language from the early centuries to the present day.

Several new series have been launched in recent years. Macmillan's *New Studies in the Philosophy of Religion,* under the general editorship of W. D. Hudson, provide brief introductions to particular questions, such as *Death and Immortality* by D. Z. Phillips. The somewhat larger volumes on *Philosophy of Religion,* edited by John Hick (also Macmillan) include Hick's *Arguments for the Existence of God* and H. P. Owen's *Concepts of Deity.* Macmillans also publish two further series of more general interest. Their *Controversies in Philosophy* (general editor A. G. N. Flew) include *The Is–Ought Question,* edited by W. D. Hudson (1969). The slightly earlier *Modern Studies in Philosophy* are symposia on individual philosophers. They include *Descartes* (W. Doney, ed., 1967); *Hume* (V. C. Chappell, ed., 1968); *Kant* (R. P. Wolff, ed., 1968); and *Wittgenstein* (G. Pitcher, ed., 1968). Routledge's *Studies in Ethics and the Philosophy of Religion,* edited by D. Z. Phillips, include Peter Geach, *God and the Soul*; Anthony Kenny, *The Five Ways*; Nelson Pike, *God and Timelessness*; and Rush Rhees, *Without Answers*. The *Oxford Readings in Philosophy* (general editor, G. J. Warnock) include *Knowledge and Belief*, edited by A. P. Griffiths (1967).

On the more theological front the *Pelican Guide to Modern Theology* (1969–70) consists of W. Nicholls, *Systematic and Philosophical Theology*; J. Daniélou, A. H. Couratin and J. Kent, *Historical Theology*; and R. Davidson and A. R. C. Leaney, *Biblical Criticism*. *Twentieth Century Theology in the Making*, edited by J. Pelikan (3 volumes, Fontana, 1969–70) consists of extracts from the pre-war edition of *Die Religion in Geschichte und Gegenwart*. These often represent concise statements on crucial questions by the big names in German theology.

Studies of contemporary theologians include Mary Bosanquet, *The Life and Death of Dietrich Bonhoeffer* (Hodder, 1968); E. Bethge, *Dietrich Bonhoeffer: Theologian, Christian, Contemporary* (Collins, 1970); A. Malet, *The Thought of Rudolf Bultmann* (Irish University Press, 1969); D. Gareth Jones, *Teilhard de Chardin: an analysis and assessment* (Tyndale Press, 1969); and R. P. Scharlemann, *Reflection and Doubt in the Thought of Paul Tillich* (Yale, 1969). In *Religion and Change* (Hodder, 1970[2]) David L. Edwards surveys the general scene and prophesies that the wind is blowing in a radical direction. John Macquarrie's *Principles of Christian Theology* (SCM, 1970[2]) might be described as the first textbook designed to restate Christian teaching from the standpoint of an existential ontology.

Wolfhart Pannenberg's understanding of the importance of history which was touched upon in the final chapter may be studied more fully in *Revelation as History*, edited by Pannenberg (Sheed and Ward, 1969), and Pannenberg's *Jesus—God and Man* (SCM, 1970[2]) and *Basic Questions in Theology* (SCM, 1970). T. F. Torrance has developed his own post-Barthian position in *Theological Science* (OUP, 1969); *Space, Time and Incarnation* (OUP, 1969); and *God and Rationality* (OUP, 1971).

INDEX